Atmosphere
Anatomies

Atmosphere Anatomies

On Design, Weather, and Sensation

Silvia Benedito

Photographs by Iwan Baan

Lars Müller Publishers

Foreword

Breathing Shades of Design

In an age exacerbated by environmental change, to what extent has our thermal comfort been modified by the landscapes and urban environments that we have created? Is the grid city the ideal pattern for facilitating air flow through a city, or is it a hindrance to ambient terrain and meteorological conditions? Recent research at MIT shows that cities that have grown organically in congruence with their surroundings tend to cope with urban heat island effects much better than those laid out as geometric grids.[1] This makes sense; convective air streams tend to follow natural relief in a given territory, rather than geometric planning patterns. Between the conflicting urban dogmas of CIAM and the Garden City movement, which model has proven to be best adapted and most valid in term of thermal comfort? Does this mean that we should reconceptualize our modern cities entirely, or can remedial measures taken at a more local scale help improve living conditions?

It may provide solace to hear that numerous architects have preceded us in this inquiry and have given thought to thermal comfort at the scale of a landscape, a site, or a building. In times preceding the modern high-rise grid city, thermal comfort was attained by seeking inspiration from practices deeply embedded in local customs and experience. In *Garden and Climate,* Chip Sullivan demonstrates how ancient wisdom concerning basic cooling principles was applied to some of the most celebrated Italian Renaissance gardens.[2] Climate is, first and foremost, the product of a deeper cultural bond with the land. Until recently this principle resulted from countless trails and errors on ways of living, working, and relaxing in extreme climatic conditions. For our current needs, it makes little sense to rely on mechanical means to solve all our heating and cooling problems. Rather, we should trust our senses as we adapt to rapidly changing climes. We have learned from desert people how to provide exquisite shade in the most torrid places. The shaded patio in dappled light, bearing the heady scents of roses and the delightful trickle of water, is one of the oldest archetypes of pleasure and luxury that we know. Forest people, too, seek to escape the dark and damp forest floor, replete with the moldy smells of moss and ferns, by bursting an artificial clearing through the tree canopy into the sky. Here too, local climate is manipulated and accommodated to fit the needs of a society in quest of blazing light and thermal comfort.

There is a definite need for a more elementary approach to landscape and architecture, one that would combine the elements of earth, air, water, and fire, and awaken our senses. This would mean, for instance, that we learn to sense the sounds of the earth, the touch of the air, the taste of water, the smell of fire, and the glimpses of light and shade. Our senses, if listened to, could positively help us discern, refine, and play with the thermal variations that surround us. There is little place for the virtual when it comes to the human sensory apparatus, because our body connects immediately to the atmosphere through shivers and sweat, in response to fragrance and stench, to cold, moisture, or dryness. The achievement of sensory balance is always a delicate construct, where the composite understanding of distinct elements is not necessarily the sum of the parts. These elements are diverse yet clearly discernable and complementary, each apprehensible and alive in its own way. In combination they qualify the thermal comfort of a place as unique.

Bernard Rudofsky's *Architecture Without Architects,* a 1964 Museum of Modern Art (MoMA) exhibition and book on non-pedigreed architecture, is an explicit manifesto against Modernism.[3] It postulates a compelling plea for a return to the roots of existence, for regaining consciousness of our senses and our most basic needs. Through black and white photographs of various forms of vernacular architecture and landscape, Rudofsky shows people dwelling happily in contact with rustic nature. This openness to the world reminds me of a tenet Henry David Thoreau derived from his experiment in simple living close to nature: "Live in each season as it passes; breathe the air, drink the drink, taste the fruit, and resign yourself to the influence of the earth."[4] There is theoretically nothing standing in the way of a building that breathes in unison with its landscape. Walden's hut at Walden Pond is a good example of such a quest for proximity to nature. In order to realize this objective, Thoreau took a step away from the consumerist delights of his age to spent two years, two months, and two days meditating on the overwhelming distance between the world and ourselves. His primitive hut operated as an organic shell or membrane between himself and the external world. Thoreau was a transcendentalist thinker who expressed precise notions about sensing and feeling the external world from within the confines of his hut. His book *Walden* is probably one of the best examples of a mindful approach to nature in Western culture.[5] There he addressed the urge for an environmental symbiosis in which all living things might merge unconditionally. Why should modern buildings breathe in the manner of the hut at Walden Pond, when all modern conveniences are readily available at the flick of a switch? Since the time of Vitruvius and Jean-Jacques Rousseau, the humble construct of the

Luis Barragán
Public park Luis Barragán
Gardens of El Pedregal, Mexico City

Germán del Sol
Geometric Hot Springs, Pucón

primitive hut has taken a special place in the minds of architects as a reflection of the mediation between humankind and the world.

The French philosopher Michel Serres has observed that the characteristic quality of contemporary architecture is "the square," or the closed-in cube. In this very "square" day and age, it is refreshing to catch a glimpse of other cultural positions describing possible ambient atmospheres. Such positions have primarily been confined to theoretical books. *In Praise of Shadows,* first published in 1933 and only translated into English in 1977, was written by the Japanese polemicist Jun'ishiro Tanizaki.[6] In opposition to the precepts of Modernism, Tanizaki revealed the exquisite aesthetics of a cooler and darker, "non visible" world in which smell, cold, touch, and sound are commingled. In describing the delight of experiencing a traditional Japanese outhouse in the heat of a summer night, Tanizaki was evoking the primitive hut. As Tanizaki suggests, could it be that we have been blinded by our dazzling faith in an always brighter view of things: a view that has become so precise and narrow that it has caged in most of our senses in "square" and coded built environments, set behind air tight windows that no longer breathe or even open to the world? The same could be said of sound, where double glazing and normative silence have replaced what once was the very voice, soul, and signature of a place. Despite the prevailing discourse on "skin" in contemporary architectural circles, we have tended to enclose ourselves more and more within some sort of

Alexandre Chemetoff
Circular chamber
("Le Cylindre Sonore")
Bamboo Garden, Paris

Pirro Ligorio
Cardinal's Walk
Villa d'Este, Tivoli

technoïdal, chrysalid membrane that has brought about a general sensory numbness. This explains, in part, the vertiginous distance between us and the outside world, where nature is, more often than not, listened to through headsets. It is about time that design schools and practices open up to the outside world again.

A year before Rudofsky launched his show at the MoMA, Victor Olgyay published *Design with Climate*.[7] Probing the ways people have adapted to regional climatic conditions, Olgyay pursued a single principle: the functional interaction between the human body, the immediate physical context of a building, and the broader urban and landscape environments. The book presents a problem-based, functionalist approach to questions of microclimatology that could be applied directly to the mainstream modernist trends of the time. Although it remains a useful reference in matters of climate comfort and energy management, Olgyay's book is notably absent from current architectural and landscape architectural curricula, owing largely to its identification with late Modernism. It is indeed surprising how little of this precious material is taught in schools of design today, as if we were meant to invent the wheels of modern HVAC techniques all over again! In the meantime, architects have tended more and more to seal their buildings hermetically from the outside for the sake of energy efficiency. Aren't we missing the point when it comes to a building's so-called efficiency? Olgyay's book borrows respectfully from architectural traditions across four regions of the world, carefully examining the beneficial effects of meteorological events on architecture, while theorizing about the active exchange that could take place between architectural form and natural processes. It is a pity to miss this open invitation to rethink our deeply flawed relationship to the environment. By feeling, breathing, and touching architecture and its landscape, by opening our buildings more to the wind and sounds, a new topology of architecture could be born into something never before conceived of, in which landscape could regain a central role. The world of sound, space, smell, and touch is part of a spatial continuum that has only recently been interrupted by contemporary planning, engineering. and architectural practices. This realization should be an open invitation to rethink architecture as something no longer divorced from our bodily experience.

In her compelling research, Silvia Benedito grasps the underlying force and principle of intelligent climatic design for architects and landscape architects. Marginalized in our own scientific age, the voices of our senses have become muted and overrun by the dominant rational scientific language of the information age. This lacuna affects contemporary architectural and landscape architectural practice tremendously. *Atmospheres Anatomies* comes as a welcome blessing in this age of systematic doubt. The title itself plays on the intermingled scales of the human body and a much broader universe. By drawing on climatic examples from various regions of the world, Benedito leads us through projects by various protagonists who have operated at different moments in history and at different scales. From Paley Park in New York City to Chandigarh in India, the grid is examined critically as a potential tool of thermal comfort in design; from the river Cherwell at Rousham, England, to the hot springs resort of the Cajon Negro in Chile, the natural world is captured in highly contrasting environments where each example is aptly adapted to its geological and atmospheric context. The juxtaposition of different styles of projects operates together with the juxtaposition of texts, sometimes scholarly and at other times more like reports or interviews. In juxtaposing multiple facets of a complex subject, this book should be taken as a provocation to reflect more deeply upon our present landscape and architectural condition. It brings to mind Michel Serres's polemic against the Cartesian tradition in *The Five Senses.* In praising what he calls "empiricism" by retracing the genealogy of human perception, Serres demonstrates, repeatedly and lyrically, the sterility of systems of knowledge that are divorced from bodily experience and location. Yet, as Serres defines it, the empirical world has become fragile. It has long resisted attempts to contain and catalog it, but we must beware that it might disappear beneath the relentless heap of late capitalist consumerism and information technology. Silvia Benedito's book is both refreshing and heart-warming: each project she analyzes can almost be smelled and tasted; every page is alive and rich in descriptions of feelings and senses. We have reached an age where data has almost come to replace true sensory pleasure. We are now less interested in the actual taste of a thing than its brand. What can we really know about the world that we design, when we have completely forgotten how to apprehend, engage, and live in what our senses best describe?

Atmospheres Anatomies is an open invitation to reflect upon ourselves and our relationship as architects and landscape designers to a rapidly changing world. In lieu of a conclusion I leave you with this quote from Michel Serres: "The skin is a variety of contingency: in it, through it, with it, the world and my body touch each other, the feeling and the felt, it defines their common edge. Contingency means common tangency: in it the world and the body intersect and caress each other. I do not wish to call the place in which I live a medium, I prefer to say that things mingle with each other and that I am no exception to that."[8]

Christophe Girot
ETH Zurich, July 2019

1 J. M. Sobstyl, T. Emig, M. J. Abdolhosseini Qomi, F.-J. Ulm, and R. J.-M. Pellenq, "The Role of City Texture in Urban Heat Islands at Night Time," CSHub @MIT, January 31, 2018.
2 See Chip Sullivan, *Garden and Climate* (New York: McGraw-Hill, 2002).
3 See Bernard Rudofsky, *Architecture without architects, an introduction to nonpedigreed architecture* (New York; Museum of Modern Art and Garden City, NY: Doubleday, 1964).
4 Henry David Thoreau, *Journal*, vol. 7 (August 23, 1853), in *The Quotable Thoreau*, J. S. Cramer, ed. (Princeton: Princeton University Press, 2011), 15.
5 See Henry David Thoreau, *Walden; or, Life in the Woods* (Boston, MA: Ticknor and Fields, 1854).
6 See Jun'ichiro Tanizaki, *In Praise of Shadows* (New Haven: Leete's Island Books, 1977).
7 See Victor Olgyay, *Design with Climate: Bioclimatic Approach to Architectural Regionalism* (Princeton, N.J.: Princeton University Press, 1963).
8 Michel Serres, *The Five Senses, A Philosophy of Mingled Bodies* (London: Bloomsbury Academic, 2016), 12.

Dissecting Atmosphere in Five Spatial Propositions

Atmosphere Anatomies: On Design, Weather, and Sensation emerges from a single question: Should we reconceptualize spatial practices to consider space as atmosphere, as weather? If so, how might we understand "atmosphere" relative to spatial affordances? While the term has been mostly framed in phenomenological domains relative to the affective properties of space, this book probes atmosphere and its climatic phenomena as a design medium in its capacity to stir sensations associated with well-being. Sensations, as deceptively simple as cooling or warming, for instance, are nonetheless the corporeal registration of bio-climatic conditions "crafted" by precise spatial techniques, material behaviors, and associated thermodynamic processes occurring in a specific time and space. To consider atmosphere as weather is to acknowledge the human body as a homeostatic sensor framed in its psychophysiological and biological domains. To sense *space* is, therefore, to sense *weather:* the atmospheric conditions produced by the meteorological parameters of wind, heat, sunlight, humidity, and rain as registered through one's sensory apparatus. If space is reconceptualized in terms of thermal performances, for instance, how can this alignment be constructed or designed in the realms of urban design and landscape architecture, as the disciplines of the "outdoors" where weather is mostly manifested and sensed? Although weather is of vital importance to the formation of the built environment, scholars have largely overlooked its potentials and processes: its thermodynamic exchanges and affective implications. A hazy comprehension of weather may reside in its ubiquitous but nonetheless paradoxical nature; weather is not only subjectively sensed and invisibly felt but also analytically registered and scientifically categorized in a complex manner. This apparent antagonism makes the task of *designing with weather* a puzzling enterprise. Despite such challenges, the act of building for humankind is indisputably a project of acclimatization for the sustenance of life. One could maintain that the Garden of Eden is, de facto, the primordial manifestation of such acclimatization. There, among the basic elements of thick walls, shady trees, water, and sources of nourishment, life allegorically takes its own path. This rudimentary repertoire of elements forms foundational bio-climatic

Robert Zion & Harold Breen
Paley Park, New York City

Lina Bo Bardi
"Indian Solarium"
("beach of São Paulo")
SESC Pompéia Community
Center, São Paulo

conditions: spatial premises for a paradise to flourish and nurture life, like an oasis in a desert.

In pursuit of this reconceptualization of space as weather, this book examines selected examples of landscape architecture, architecture, and urban design, based on the premise that in each case space was constructed utilizing atmosphere and its meteorological elements as design "matter" at its inception. Rather than encompassing an extensive survey accounting for all the climatic zones or cultural contexts for each example, this ensemble of cases reflects key moments in which a spatial sensibility is centered on the "crafting" of atmospheres with bio-climatic effects. By integrating weather as design substance, these projects not only foreground the psycho-physiological well-being of the individual human body but also bring associated benefits to the public domain and the civic life for which they were constructed.

When atmosphere and weather are considered as space, a question remains as to how they have been *conceived* of as design matter in the construction of space? *Atmosphere Anatomies* probes a set of examples based on particular spatial propositions: atmosphere as IMMERSIVE JOURNEY, as THERMAL THRESHOLD, as PROGRAM, as SHARED SITUATION, and as THERMAL CONTRAST. While each proposition is unique, bringing attention to a particular spatial interpretation, it is not exclusive. Each is probed through two or more projects that share a certain atmospheric

Le Corbusier
Lake Sukhna, Chandigarh

sensibility. Atmosphere as IMMERSIVE JOURNEY alludes to the construction of space through movement, bringing attention to the body's episodic psychophysiological entanglement with its surrounding environment. This way of conceiving of space prioritizes climatic variety in an intermittent manner, prompting tactical "on-and-off" engagement with the designed milieu. Atmosphere as THERMAL THRESHOLD addresses the boundaries between indoors and outdoors, liquid and vapor, private and public, architecture and landscape. Each boundary, interdisciplinary at its core, expands to address energetic, health, and civic priorities, as varied thermal thresholds offer possibilities for climatic amelioration and improved civic inhabitation. Atmosphere as PROGRAM focuses on the constructed microclimatic condition as a principal source of delight. Rather than conventional programs to "activate" the commons, this proposition involves ideas of silence, rest, or induced contemplation, according to an individual's physiological metabolism, activities, or desires. Atmosphere as SHARED SITUATION foregrounds the civic nature of the induced meteorological events in their capacity to elicit, invite, and stimulate collective delight as a community. The political dimension of both the individual and the collective body is foregrounded in their mutual capacity to recognize weather as a shared domain in a manner reminiscent of ancestral practices and biological dependencies on the larger cosmos. Atmosphere as SPATIAL CONTRAST positions the body in more radical and unexpected environments, considering discomfort as an integral aspect of spatial experience. Here, the amelioration or amplification of particular thermodynamic conditions and microclimatic behaviors depends upon the body's deliberate exposure to their dramatically contrasting effects, foregrounding the realization of bodily limits and vulnerabilities relative to climatic thresholds. *Atmosphere Anatomies* "dissects" the atmospheric and bio-climatic moments of these projects through watercolor drawings and photographs that comprise an atlas of the associated thermodynamic processes and technical nomenclature. The notion of dissection provided an important conceptual foothold for the book. On the one hand, each project was scrutinized by directly sensing and physiologically registering its site; on the other hand, archival and historical examination and, whenever possible, conversations with the designers led to other possible interpretations of a project's ethos. To dissect is to analyze, compare, and discern hidden relationships in the designed space: from the designer's aims to the disciplinary resolution; from the spatial materialization to the effects on the users' individual and collective bodies.

If "dissection" is the *modus operandi* for the analysis of the projects and their corresponding effects, then the idea of human anatomy consolidates the essays as a whole "body" composed of different formats: essays, photographs, and drawings. *Atmosphere Anatomies: On Design, Weather, and Sensation* focuses on the human body in both its psychophysiological and biological domains. Furthermore, it reveals each project in its bio-climatic moments as formed by specific acclimatizing affordances that result from curating the meteorological parameters of wind, heat, sunlight, humidity, and rain through built form and materiality. Setting up the argument that space is an accumulation of physical and invisible (albeit sensed) properties, the book is both analytic and descriptive. Historical and archival examination frames each project in its cultural context and spatial aims; the atlas of watercolor drawings captures bio-climatic moments derived from embodied scrutiny on site—experienced on particular days, under particular weather conditions and seasons. Iwan Baan's photographic essays, both evocative and revelatory, take us on a spatial journey. His work showcases glimpses of a larger story about everyday living in each project: people loving, smiling, resting, playing, walking, or, simply, rejoicing in their curated entanglement with the surrounding world, with atmosphere, with weather.

The Necessary Paradigm Shift: Space as Atmosphere

Somos todos escravos de circunstâncias externas: um dia de sol abre-nos campos largos no meio de um café de viela; uma sombra no campo encolhe-nos para dentro, e abrigamo-nos mal na casa sem portas de nós mesmos; um chegar da noite, até entre coisas do dia, alarga, como um leque [que] se abra lento, a consciência íntima de dever-se repousar.
Fernando Pessoa, *O Livro do Desassossego* [1913]

Whether we like it or not, we are slaves to the hour in all its forms and colors, we are the subjects of heaven and earth. The part of us that despises its surroundings and punches deepest into the forest within us does not take the same path when it rains as when the sky is clear. Simply because it's raining or has stopped raining, obscure transmutations take place, felt only perhaps in the very heart of our most abstract feelings; we feel these transmutations without knowing it because we feel the weather even when we are unaware that we do.
Fernando Pessoa, *The Book of Disquiet*[1]

This study begins with two assumptions. The first is that the atmosphere and its meteorological processes are integral to the disciplines of architecture, landscape architecture, and urbanism as spatial practices. The second, closely tied to the first, is that the interdependency of atmospheric processes and their meteorological elements—wind, temperature, sunlight, cloud cover, precipitation, humidity, and atmospheric pressure—is primary to the anatomico-physiological mechanisms and the affiliated sensations for both individual and collective well-being. If one assumes that these assumptions are legitimate and that the *making* of urban space for the well-being of humankind is central to these design practices, then it is important to strengthen their interdependency in the challenging context of anthropogenic climates.

While these assumptions may be met with approval, their critical examination and potential application in the design of our cities and urban spaces have been overlooked in recent years. This disciplinary deferral seems consistent with the contemporary ocular-centric dependency in mediating the world: one that ontologically dismisses the body's capacity to be affected by the intangible and invisible exchanges occurring in inhabited space. Landscape architecture, for example, has taken on a larger disciplinary responsibility toward the solid, the vegetative, and the aqueous, rather than toward the aerial or *things of a meteorological kind*.[2] This disciplinary emphasis on the visual and physical echoes the French philosopher Luce Irigaray's remarks on the challenging ontology of air and its apparent absence in Western thought: that air has been unnoticed because it "does not show itself. As such, it escapes appearing as [a] being. It allows itself to be forgotten due to its ubiquity."[3]

This obliviousness to air, although justified by its ubiquity, is nonetheless paradoxical, as inherent to being outdoors is the *de facto* condition of living with and within the meteorological elements and their constant variability. How, then, can one design with meteorological elements that escape "appearing," when design is, conversely, about making apparent—about building and constructing? How does one design for the collective milieu while accounting for sensation, so personal and particular? Lastly, how can architecture, landscape architecture, and urbanism address the body's anatomico-physiological vulnerability in the context of increased atmospheric vigilance? To address these questions, a paradigm shift must be considered: one that realigns design's disciplinary inquiry toward the recognition of air and atmosphere as spatial media and the body as an anatomico-physiological sensor in the all-enveloping environment.

I. The body: An anatomico-physiological cosmonaut

The construction and definition of the public realm are inherently associated with the disciplinary scopes of architecture, landscape architecture, and urbanism. Often considered through economic, ecological, and civic lenses, public space is also an aerological volume in the city. It is a place for human inhabitation with associated atmospheric perils or pleasures, often stirred by multisensorial interactions with atmospheric elements and forces, namely the weather. Frequently used synonyms for this space and volume are, nonetheless, the "in-between," or the "void." But what is this "void"? From the perspective of meteorologists, the void is where the natural processes reside; from the perspective of microbiologists, it is where organic particles live and are transported; from the perspective of immunologists, it is where spores and pollen travel and affect millions of people; from the perspective of public agencies, it is where people come together to exercise their right to protest, to act, and to live their everyday lives as a community. In design practices, the void has been dissociated from ontological premises, possibilities, or perils. Nothing is more antagonistic than to designate the in-between environment that is inhabited by organic life as "void." In ontological terms, the term suggests hollowness and emptiness; in organic and biological terms, human life cannot exist in a void without respiratory support. In complex modes of highly specialized analysis, moreover, the concepts of void and emptiness are considered to be abstract and non-sensual. The French philosopher Hubert Damisch, in his book *A Theory of /Cloud/: Toward a History of Painting,* adds that the acceptance of "emptiness" alludes to a neutralization or annihilation produced "by the institution of the perspective space in the guise of an objective setting."[4] In other words, as a fundamental form of portraying space, perspectival representation may have led to the disappearance of the un-representable and the palpable: the atmosphere. This failure to recognize the ontology of air and of atmospheric phenomena defies not only their objective representation and legibility but also their visible and palpable qualities, which are stable and quantifiable means to communicate a sense of spatiality. In contrast to diagrams or other analytical forms of representation, photography, film, and literature have often been more effective for capturing the embodied and sensed affordances, or even the challenges, that inhabited space offers to human life.

In design practices, the concept of "the void" has been used to reflect two interchangeable possibilities: first, as a condition of "emptiness," and second, as an opportunity for design action within transient economic scenarios. The urban theorist Ignasi de Solà-Morales characterizes the void as a metonym for design potentials: "void, absence, yet also promise, the space of the possible, of expectation."[5] Similarly, the urban designer Marcel Smets argues for recognizing the void as a landscape figure in the "production of the contemporary city, in the underlying uncertainty of what is to come and our incapacity to shape it in a definitive form, capable of coping with future development." While such positions have been productive in expanding landscape architecture's role in influencing urban growth, it is important to augment the void's ontological constitution, particularly relative to its meteorological possibilities, which are invisible and often unquantifiable. The de-materialized use of the void in design *nomenclature,* although evocative and stimulating, limits design *actions* relative to other reciprocal relationships, such as between weather and human activities, energy and resource conservation, or plant life and public health. If "the void" signifies opportunity due to its uncertainty, then how can design construct presence and stability in the face of meteorological matter? Smets alerts us that "uncertainty should not be confused with lack of clarity," and that urban form should require "a clear spatial configuration."[6] His observations return us to the issue of the void's ontological nature. If we assume that "the void is what does the vessel's holding," as Martin Heidegger elaborated in his 1971 essay "The Thing," then what is the nature of that void?[7] Which of its aspects can be considered as potential determinants for clear spatial configurations? And, to what end? Could light or heat, wind or humidity, shadow or sound, for example, be substances in the void? Critical to the ontology of the invisible, Irigaray alludes to the void as a hollow filled with air and matter. Therefore, the idea of *nothingness* is ontologically unsuitable and does not exist in the realm of earthly design practice.

The connections between the ontological potentials of the void as inducive to urban form, human well-being, and economic development are well represented in the German city of Stuttgart. In coping with its necessary economic development and topographical challenges in the aftermath of World War II, Stuttgart began to plan urban growth by conducting a pioneering study of localized climatic phenomena. The city, which sits within the steep basin-like valley of the Nesenbach, was experiencing frequent temperature inversions that were harmful to the health of its residents. Sustainable urban growth thus depended on the continual ventilation of an urban fabric that was subject to the city's retention of heat and air pollution. The resulting study, *Klimaatlas* [Climate Atlas], created and managed by the department of urban climatology in the Office of Environmental Protection, provided the necessary material to support informed planning and design decisions in the context of economic pressures and climate degradation. In this document, the void is a microclimatic engine, ontologically determined by surface temperature, katabatic and anabatic winds from the adjacent mountains, volume and velocity of cold air, and flow directions. These aeration corridors are regulated pulmonary infrastructures, enabling the city to breathe and to cool down. Here "the void" is synonymous with natural climate control at the urban scale and a necessary ally in sustaining well-being and economic growth. Without this critical understanding of the void and its meteorological affordances as matters of design, Stuttgart would not stand as one of the world's healthiest cities and a planning blueprint for many others, including New York City, Berlin, Tokyo, and Kobe.

From the standpoint of human nurturing in the bio-meteorological and economic domains, the void is the space of both the flexuous atmosphere where weather manifests. From an ontologico-philosophical perspective, the German philosopher Peter Sloterdijk, in his book *Terror from the Air,* alludes to the aerological medium as "human-ambient"—the volume that supports "ecologically-dependent vital functions: respiration, central nervous regulations, and sustainable temperature and radiation conditions." He notes that, "economic conditions excepted, critical attention today is focused on the essential environmental conditions for human survival."[8] Despite the deceptive invisibility and ineffable nature of these atmospheric elements and forces, all humans experience meteorological dynamics—particularly in the out of doors.

The study of the atmosphere, or meteorology, is an ancient empirical field but a fairly recent branch of scientific study.[9] Although access to remote sensing and forecasting technologies has enabled a greater understanding of atmospheric processes, the integration of these subjects in design continues to present challenges. This is due partly to the complex techniques of atmospheric modeling and simulation at a local scale and, more significantly, to the elusive nature of these atmospheric phenomena, which are utterly invisible to the observer.[10] Although these phenomena elude the visual register, they directly affect the skin—the largest sense organ of the human body—in its continual mediation with the enveloping environment. Stephen Rosen, director of the Weather Sensitivity Research Center in New York City and author of *Weathering: How the Atmosphere Conditions Your Body, Your Mind, Your Moods—and Your Health,* writes that "98 percent of our skin is in intimate contact with the ocean of air that engulfs us, at once our ancestral blanket, home, and master, the atmosphere conditions humanity."[11]

Alternately imperceptible, pleasant, or irritating, skin sensations are the gatekeepers of human existence, registering intricate anatomico-physiological relationships with the enveloping atmosphere. While attesting to the atmospheric affordances for survival, nourishment, delight, or, conversely, threat, these sensations make the IMPLICIT conditions of the hosting environment EXPLICIT to the individual and, essentially, to the collective. Sensations accordingly constitute the *sensus communis*—the sense of the commons. Evaluating "what makes sense and what can be sensed," the political scientist Davide Panagia strengthens the role of the anatomico-physiological domains by positioning sensation as a radical manifestation of democratic life in public space.[12] The multiple sensorial registrations, while in homeostatic balance with the atmospheric milieu—cold or hot, bright or dark, humid or dry, pleasant or stressful—generate a form of reciprocity between subjects and their enveloping space. Reinforcing the political dimension of sensation, the philosopher Jacques Rancière expands on the body-public space as the "community of sense," the fabric of collective life, with its shared sensible knowledge woven by art or design practices. As the frame of the new sensorium, shared space is also experienced emotionally. This study accordingly presumes that we come to terms with the notion of sensation and the body—both individual and collective—in the realm of the design disciplines.

The shared and sensed public space in a city is central to the scopes of architecture, landscape architecture, and urbanism as the professional domains that *spatialize* the hollowness of the void. In both his practice and his writing, the French architect Philippe Rahm emphasizes the thickness of the void and the necessary shift in architecture toward the microscopic and the atmospheric, the biological or physiological and the meteorological. Nevertheless, while the sciences have revealed the unseen properties and behaviors of the void—mechanical, chemical, bacteriological, electromagnetic, and toxic—the design disciplines continue to find closer affinities to the solid and the visual. In dialogue with Massimiliano Scuderi, Rahm declares: "climate change is forcing us… to shift our focus away from a purely visual and functional approach toward one that is more sensitive, more attentive to the invisible, climate-related aspects of space."[13] The void contains all the meteorological forces and processes that sustain human comfort, delight, and well-being. It is the space of resonance where light bounces and wind curls; where sound reverberates, and colors expand; and where raindrops manifest and clouds cast their shadows. This "weather-world" is the public domain. And, inversely to delight, it is also the space where extreme heat or pollution endure to threaten human life.[14]

In their book *The Charged Void: Urbanism* (2005), architects Alison and Peter Smithson articulate an alternative terminology for the void by alluding to an idea of "charged" space where meteorological phenomena occur, and humans exert influence. As they elaborate: "The space-between speaks to the sky… the space-between puts a charge into that sky."[15] As agents, humans activate the sky by assigning it with meaning and mythological significance, imbuing it with economic value while harvesting meteorological activity for energy production, embracing it with ideas of pleasure, delight, and wonder, or, conversely, aligning it with anthropogenic matter and dread. We affect this aerological volume just as we are affected by it—as the cosmonauts of our own anatomico-physiologies and related life-regulatory mechanisms.

II. Is Landscape Also Weather?

Whereas the void has become increasingly charged in today's rising awareness of anthropogenic atmosphere, landscape practice still operates closer to the solid, aqueous, planar, and familiar features of the perceptible earth, rather than the aerological and atmospheric. On the one hand, the transformation of LAND lies at the core of landscape architecture; on the other hand, the suffix -SCAPE is commonly associated with scopic regimes, as it derives from the Greek verb *skopein:* "to look." Why has landscape architecture not embraced air and the atmosphere? We may recall Irigaray's remark, cited earlier, on the invisibility of air "due to its ubiquity" and its extreme familiarity; after all, we live surrounded by it. Air and the meteorological elements, neither arbitrated nor acclimatized, are simply "there." What if we question this ubiquitous condition and focus on our *immersion* within it? This would involve readdressing the *substantive* nature of landscape as a total environment and recognizing the body as a sensate being within the thermodynamic exchanges of the meteorological medium. Engaging both atmosphere and the body (functioning as an anatomico-physiological sensor) in the disciplinary domains of public space raises fundamental questions about disciplinary scope and ontological affiliations—the latter based on the discordant etymologies of the term "landscape" as used in geographical inquiry. Although landscape has been significantly examined through the lens of human geography—focused on cultural, political, social, and economic interpretations of the world—landscape as a bio-meteorological phenomenon associated with physiological well-being has captured far less critical attention. In the context of contemporary climatic disintegration, a reformulation of landscape's scope and definition must be devised to include the role and effects of the atmosphere as mediums of design.

In his recent essay "All that is landscape is melted into air," the landscape geographer Kenneth R. Olwig questions landscape's geocentric dependency by inquiring "how unexamined contemporary disciplinary assumptions would change if geography were less ostensibly *geo*centric and more focused on the aerosphere?"[16] What is the pre-history of the presence of the atmosphere in landscape? Moreover, are there any pivotal moments in the genealogy of landscape as a spatial practice in which the atmosphere and the meteorological elements are critically embraced as design mediums?

In 1939, the American geographer Richard Hartshorne examined the conflated meanings, scopes, and etymologies of the term "landscape" in his book *The Nature of Geography*. Explaining the consistent omission of atmospheric conditions in any discussion about landscape, he noted: "By assuming, as geographers commonly do, that we see the areas from above, we eliminate the sky; the atmosphere of the earth is then simply the medium through which we see the solid and liquid forms of the earth's surface."[17] Atmosphere, Hartshorne assumed, is the unperceived medium that one looks through: a medium without presence—like standing in front of large glass window and looking outward. Hartshorne's observation also anticipates the tensions that animate the disciplinary polarities in considering the subject's relation with the landscape—of outside (world) versus inside (body), detached versus immersed, objective versus subjective, observing versus sensual, and planar versus vertical and thick.

Concerning the unresolved polarity in the term "landscape," the cultural geographer Denis Cosgrove reasons that "*landscape* privileges the sense of sight, and what started as a representation of space rapidly became a designation of material spaces themselves, which were... viewed with the same distanciated and aesthetically discriminating eye that had been trained in the appreciation of pictures and maps."[18] The production of maps and pictures—flat surfaces that serve as representations of the various forces and latent potentials associated with land ownership and possession—was of particular relevance amid the maritime enterprises and the rise of mercantile capitalism of sixteenth-century Europe. The world of expanded territories and capital possibilities, Cosgrove notes, required a clear "graphic expression" that could fit the "fluid social and urban context." Land surveying, cartography, and the newly invented linear perspective were pressed into service to represent the land and its visible features. When the perimeters and economic potential of a territory expanded, it came to be viewed as flat, as Cosgrove elaborates: "The Italian Renaissance humanists had encouraged the substitution of a more planar, mathematically proportioned cosmos for the vertically-ascending orders of the medieval conception."[19] If the register of the "planar" cosmos through linear perspective and cartographic representation provided capitalist markets with a wider sense of control and quantification, these representational methods also comprised flattened and compressed images of the vertical world. The firmament and its elementary verticality ceased to exist in the space of landscape, as did the sky and its fluctuating matter. Whereas the term "landscape" has accordingly been primarily understood as a "way-of-seeing," it would also come to reflect an alternative sensibility to the flattened and planar way-of-describing the world, built and natural.

Just as the Renaissance techniques of cartographic representation and linear perspective fit into the fluxes of capital and ownership domains, so another form of territorial portrayal set the foundations for this emerging sensibility: the novel descriptive genre of "landscape." This new sensibility focused on the qualities of the *locus* under scrutiny. Closer to a chorographical description of the built and natural worlds, this genre reflects an interest in capturing phenomena of instability or variability inherent to sites and their potential effects on local populations or audiences. Landscape was understood not only as the world in transformation but also as the *transformation* itself: the subjects in motion that escape static perspectival regimes and the *geometrization* of space. As a means of reflecting a perception of the world, the term "landscape" indicates a resistance to merely capturing the earth's quantifiable aspects. As Hubert Damisch notes, it is a form of description that emphasizes the "system of the firmament… no longer in astronomical terms but in meteorological ones, and in which cloud was presented to the sight of men in the same way as air is presented to their lungs."[20] What triggered the emergence of this new artistic and public interest in "landscape" and in the phenomena associated with its meteorological elements?

There are disparate, but interrelated explanations for this increased sensibility to the natural and built worlds. Recent access to climatological records suggests the occurrence of severe meteorological anomalies—extreme cold temperatures and weather events early in the fifteenth century—"apparently in response to the development of a 'Little Ice Age.'"[21] At the same time maritime enterprises were revealing new worlds associated with increased agricultural potentials and yields through land acquisition and capital exchange. If much has been written about the relationship between landscape and land ownership, far less attention has been devoted to the assumption that climatological phenomena may explain the emergence of the term "landscape" as linked to the rising awareness of a site's local characteristics, including its meteorological qualities and human vulnerability when confronted with the vagaries of erratic weather.

In 1939, the year in which geographer Richard Hartshorne highlighted the exclusion of atmospheric conditions from discussions of landscape, meteorologist L. C. W. Bonacina proposed the phrase "landscape meteorology" to refer to "those scenic influences of sky, atmospheres, weather and climate which form part of our natural environment." Claiming that weather is a function integral to landscape, Bonacina stressed the significance of the various meteorological phenomena for identifying the characteristics of sites as well as their bearing on public good. "Landscape meteorology," Bonacina elaborated, "develops the powers of observation and perception, stimulating the various faculties of body, mind, and soul." Given the effects of landscape on the subject's anatomico-physiological mechanisms, he presented the genre as a complete envelope understood in terms of its meteorological formations. "Medical men," he elaborated, "realize that the imponderable scenic influences of weather and climate must be considered in therapeutics in addition to those cruder elements which we measure with instruments and record in registers."[22]

Whereas landscape appears without sky in Hartshorne's geographical account, in Bonacina's meteorological domain the concept is synonymous with sky, weather, and atmosphere and understood in relation to bodily sensations and the meteorological influences on human health and well-being. Bonacina's "landscape meteorology" thus aligns with the genealogy of "landscape" as a term reflecting the new artistic and societal interest in *things of a meteorological* kind during the sixteenth century.

In his book *Sixteenth-Century Germany: Its Topography and Topographers* the historian Gerald Strauss summarizes the multiple events of a world in flux: "The great voyages of discovery and exploration, the political and military struggles centered about Italy, the constitutional reform movement in the Germany of Maximilian I, the devastating plagues, the religious disputes, the peasant uprisings… It must have been a world that compelled attention, a world that called the active and the thoughtful to participation."[23] As the world as described in cartographic projects became bigger and more complex, humanistic inquiry grew increasingly precise and localized, closer to the particularities of specific sites. For example, the hinterlands of the Veneto region in Italy witnessed an enormous territorial transformation due to economic pressures, while the German empire, as an agglomeration of different lands, sought to find suitable techniques to construct the Germanic identity.[24] Landscape, in all its manifestations—social, cultural, physical, and, now, meteorological—emerged as a medium through which to define, recognize, and comprehend these new worlds.

Art historians Ernst Gombrich and Christopher Wood have situated the origins of the term "landscape" in the artistic production of the Veneto and the Danube valley regions respectively. For Gombrich this occurred in the context of a new trend in Italy that was both artistic and societal, in which art and design, territorial description, and world reception were exercised interchangeably. Artists depicted novel themes in paintings and etchings of subjects engaged in humanistic pursuits, and a new group of wealthy consumers supported their work. "Landscape" thus appeared as a new mode of sensing the world. Rather than capturing allegorical scenes or heroic moments, this new artistic genre engaged topics and events that were less symbolic than previous examples and more representative of meteorological qualities. In paintings that depict a natural world made of shifting appearances, "landscape" became an autonomous subject through scenes that lacked heroic figures or overt symbolic associations.

"It is in Venice," Gombrich noted, "that the term 'a landscape' is first applied to any individual painting." Among the most often cited examples of this new sensibility is Giorgione's *The Tempest* (1508), which the Venetian nobleman Marcantonio Michiel described as a "small landscape [*paesetto*] on canvas, with a thunderstorm, a gipsy, and a soldier."[25] The large meteorological event that gives the painting its name occupies a central position in the composition. Positioned to either side, the gypsy and the soldier frame the storm that fills the space in the distance. The gypsy looks directly out to the viewer, whose attention is drawn to the storm—a juxtaposition that heightens the sense of spatial depth, as the meteorological happenstance in the background appears as both impending and dense. The world is suspended, as the audience imagines the thunder that will follow the lightning bolt that hangs in the air. While the stormy sky fills the background, the foreground at the bottom of the painting looks wet; its dark green shade of ground suggests that the rain has already started to fall. Michiel's term *paesetto,* therefore, refers to the overall scene and to the spatial condition that immerses both the figures and the viewer within its atmospheric events—the impending tempest, the wet ground, the convective clouds, the distinct airstream, the imminent thunder. "Landscape" accordingly aligns with the recognition of the aerological volume as space, matter, and phenomena: space that engulfs the figures and the audience; matter that imbues space with haptic properties; and phenomena that imply time and change. In this new sensibility, "landscape" is a metonym for meteorological phenomena occurring in a particular moment of time and space. The world becomes alive and subject to *time,* a word that in many Romance languages also means "weather."[26]

In sixteenth-century Germany, many artists and literary humanists were debating the historical origins of Germanic culture and its entanglements with nature. Strauss noted that while the global discoveries by the

Portuguese and the Spanish stimulated an awakening to a new world, a "new-found zeal to depict their own country" arose among the reforming impulses of the German humanists. He wrote: "the study of history and descriptive geography was thus not only a response to public interest in these arts but also an expression of the urge to portray country and people."[27] This humanist interest in emphasizing the qualitative characteristics of the *locus* emerged not only as an urge to describe localized characteristics but also as a means to instruct and settle ideas about cultural history—folklore, institutions, politics, soils, population, zoology, botany, physical boundaries, character, and, importantly, the weather and its atmosphere.

In this context, the work of the German painter and architect Albrecht Altdorfer (c. 1480–1538) marks another significant step in the recognition of atmosphere and its associated meteorological phenomena in the definition of space. Altdorfer practiced these disciplines in Regensburg, along the Danube River. Although more research is needed about his work as an architect, Altdorfer's paintings, with their elliptical forms of foliage and atmosphere, are the "first independent landscapes in the history of European art," according to Christopher Wood.[28] Altdorfer's *Danube Landscape near Regensberg* (1522–1525) depicts a characteristic setting of the Danube valley with its vaporous atmosphere, revolving weather, and contrasting light. Rather than repeating the typical horizontal format that many of his contemporaries used for landscape paintings, the painter introduced a vertical format to emphasize the juxtaposition of atmosphere versus land, meteorological versus solid phenomena. This shift allowed for the increased presence of sky, with its convective processes and energy transfers. Compressing the land against the bottom of the frame, Altdorfer represented the atmosphere as transient and muscular in appearance, alluding to its pressure upon both the earth's surface and the human body. Through its forceful verticality, in which each element points to the sky, the painting foregrounds the meteorological dynamics that animate this particular valley. "Landscape" in the painting's title could equally refer to "weather." Rather than producing a quantifiable account of the scene under scrutiny, Altdorfer conveyed qualities that could not (yet) be measured but instead could be sensed as representative of the place.[29] In lieu of creating a scenic or pictorial image, he expressed the spectacle of the essential elements of the cosmos and elicited the overall *Stimmung* of a place that is anatomico-physiologically sensed. The result is a form of chorographic description that is, nonetheless, affiliated with the hierarchies of the cosmographical representation of heavens and the four elements—air, earth, water, and fire—as described by Ptolemy in his influential *Geography* of circa 150 AD.

If the etymology of the term "landscape" in the realm of artistic production arose from the increasing sensory awareness of a changing world in the sixteenth century, has such atmospheric knowledge also been applied in forming space for human accommodation?

III. When does (inhabited) space become atmosphere?

In many ways, the history of cities and public landscapes is not one of passive adaptation to existing climatic conditions. Inherent to designing space for human habitation—whether in the domain of architecture, landscape architecture, or urbanism—is the question of acclimatization. At the core of this issue is the creation of microclimates that can sustain comfort and well-being but are often distinct from their surroundings: hotter or cooler, drier or wetter, sheltered or exposed. Whereas architecture often encompasses countering meteorological conditions, landscape architecture and urbanism are more often concerned with engagement with and mediation of these atmospheric forces. Considering today's climatic disintegration and the associated bio-climatic challenges relative to health and comfort, the recognition of meteorological elements as a focus of design is of critical relevance. This is particularly important for the fields of landscape architecture and urbanism: spatial practices that are inherently related to resource conservation, public health, and human activities.

Although the relationship between landscape and atmosphere, including its meteorological elements, remains relatively overlooked, the origin of the concept of landscape in the artistic realm is founded on the awareness of atmospheric phenomena in association with human perception, as elaborated above. The associated concern for human well-being can be traced to the pioneering urban principles elaborated by the ancient Roman architect and engineer Marcus Vitruvius Pollio in his treatise *De Architectura,* written about 15 BCE and published in numerous translations beginning in 1486. The design of cities should be carried out, Vitruvius argued, so as to avoid unhealthy cold, hot, and moist winds. In this scenario, the architect, as the authority responsible for determining the "healthiest" result, should "be equipped with knowledge of many branches of study and varied kinds of learning... [including] some knowledge of medicine... and be acquainted with astronomy and the theory of the heavens."[30]
Prior to Vitruvius's treatise, the assumption of anatomico-physiological well-being achieved through acclimatization to atmospheric conditions is associated with the idea of a primordial garden, which encompasses concepts of sustainable enclosure, nurturance, and climatic tempering to sustain human life. One of the central elements in the history of landscape design, the quintessential *locus amoenus* or paradise garden is a typology dedicated to providing pleasure through thermal stress reduction in the inhospitable climate of the Persian desert, with its severe blizzards, burning summers, and blinding dust storms. As garden historian Christopher Thacker notes: "In reaction to the open and barren wilderness, the garden

is enclosed, fertile, and rich with fruit and flowers; in reaction to the hostile vastness of the near-desert, it has order and tranquility, and is a place where one may sit in the shade, rather than walk in the fierce light of the sun."[31] In the Persian paradise garden, sensorial delight is paired with climatic amelioration and relief through evaporation and convection on the skin's surface, as the body sweats in homeostatic regulation with the surrounding environment. In this physiological entanglement, the body shivers as it thermo-regulates, and, as with strong emotions, goose bumps emerge on the skin, reflecting the cooling sensations activated by the nurturing microclimatic moment arising from the combination of shade, humidity, and breezes. After an intake of water, the muscles relax, contributing to a sense of emotional and physical respite.

The "life-sustaining oasis" of the paradise garden was contained within walls that maintained moister air and cooler temperatures in relation to the outer, inhospitable conditions.[32] This contrast between inside and outside not only sustained human survival but also promoted spiritual nourishment. These Persian gardens are often depicted as a microcosm of varied sensorial affordances: sheltered by imagined hemispherical clouds of humidity against the desert's dryness and replete with shade trees, flowers, animals, varied watercourses, and people. After traveling throughout Asia, Socrates identified these milieus as "paradise" gardens, elaborating: "Everywhere, the Persian king is zealously cared for, so that he may find gardens wherever he goes; their name is 'Paradise,' and they are full of all things fair and good that the earth can bring forth. It is here that he spends the greatest part of his time."[33] As a synchronized response to constructing a life-sustaining environment, these poetic, anatomico-physiological sites for thermal relief and other pleasant sensations are spatial blueprints for concepts of beauty as well as survival—concepts that are linked in recent scientific studies of beauty and neuropsychology.[34]

Furthering the project of acclimatization for increased human well-being relative to landscape, weather, and the affiliated sensations encountered in the Persian paradise garden, Vitruvius directed his attention to the emerging realm of the polis, or city-state, where the notion of a democratic community emerged through the common recognition of mutually beneficial conditions, such as warmth and light. Elaborating on the origins of society, Vitruvius reasoned that men, previously dispersed in the forest, gathered in a clearing, prompted by the warmth of a fire, which they sought to maintain as a benefit to be shared and accessible to all. As he elaborated: "Observing that they were comfortable standing before the warm fire, they put on logs and, while thus keeping it alive brought other people to it, showing them by signs how much comfort they got from it... then, from indicating by name things in common use, the result was that in this chance way they began to talk, and thus originated conversation with one another. Therefore, it was the discovery of fire that originally gave rise to the coming together of men, to the deliberate assembly, and to social intercourse." The democratic community was accordingly established through a social contract based on the desire to maintain shared atmospherics, mutually sensed and delightfully acknowledged by the individual and the collective human body.

Expanding upon this formulation of the democratic community with respect to the *locus* of the city, Vitruvius cited healthfulness as a prerequisite for choosing an appropriate site. Whereas the clearing comprised an abstract setting with a constructed climate, the siting of a city should be circumstantial, that is, dependent on a particular set of climatic conditions: "high, neither musty nor frosty, and in a climate neither hot nor cold, but temperate."[35] Here Vitruvius was drawing upon Hippocrates's recommendations in his medical treatise *Airs, Waters, and Places* of circa 400 BCE concerning health and physiological equilibrium: "The climate in such a district may be compared with the Spring in that there are no extremes of heat and cold. As a consequence, diseases in such a district are few and not severe."[36]

In the Hippocratic tradition, the human body is considered to be healthy when the four elements of the hosting sites—air, earth, water, and fire—and the conditions resulting from their interactions—warm, dry, moist, and cold—are in balance. Following these principles, Vitruvius cautioned, "if one of these elements, heat, becomes predominant in any body whatsoever, it destroys and dissolves all the others with its violence."[37] Suggesting basic conditions of causality and equilibrium, this notion of a healthy body extends beyond its physical constitution to include the atmospheric conditions of the polis and its public domain.

Anticipating the concept of *Umwelt* articulated by German biologist Jacob von Uexküll at the beginning of the twentieth century and later translated as "environment," Vitruvius understood the constitution of the body (inner-world) as dependent upon its surroundings (external-world)—the constructed polis.[38] To find examples of this elementary interdependency, Vitruvius suggested observing animals and reflecting on their behaviors:

> One form of mixture is proper to birds, another to fishes, and a far different form to land animals. Winged creatures have less of the earthy, less moisture, heat in moderation, air in large amount. Being made up, therefore, of the lighter elements, they can more readily soar away into the air.... Similarly, the land animals, being moderately supplied with the elements of air and heat, and having less of the earthy and a great deal of moisture, cannot long continue alive in the water, because their portion of moisture is already abundant.

In identifying the principles for a proto-environmental and bio-climatic relationship between the body and its all-enveloping atmosphere, Vitruvius noted the further interdependency inherent to the idea of the "commons," which is atmospherically constituted and mediated through sensation. As he elaborated: "Cold winds are disagreeable, hot winds enervating, moist winds unhealthy. We must, therefore, avoid mistakes in this matter and beware of the common experience of many communities."[39] A healthy atmosphere depended not only on the pre-existing climatic affordances of the site, but also on the design and construction of the city itself, in which the common experience is afforded by a variety of public, urban landscape elements: streets, plazas, alleys, colonnades, walkways, fora, and theaters. Constituting possibly the first instance of public health infrastructure, these public typologies provide the framework for a society to thrive. In this way the primordial "charged" clearing in the forest becomes the atmospheric blueprint for forming the polis as a complex and layered organism—one that affords nurturing sensations in a collectively shared anatomico-physiological domain.

How might these considerations help us reconsider the role of atmosphere in architecture, landscape architecture, and urbanism? Peter Sloterdijk, in his essay "Atmospheric Politics," posits an explicit relationship between urban and landscape practices and atmospheric conditioning: between the polis as a bio-meteorological construct and the acclimatizing work of the "English garden architects" in their nineteenth-century greenhouses.[40] In generating the favorable climatic conditions required for the biological nourishment of their "residents," the atmospheric formulations of the polis and the greenhouse reflect an understanding of the fundamental principle that bodies do not end at their physical boundaries but instead depend upon their surrounding atmospheres.

Although discussion of the atmosphere is often limited by its association with subjective or emotional impressions, "atmosphere" is, more significantly, a metonym for breath and for human sustenance. Accommodation of the human body implies an ontological understanding of the hosting environment, often deceptively referred to as "the void." Designing for the human body implies taking into account its atmospheres and sensually registered inputs—aural, thermal, haptic, olfactory, and visual. Sloterdijk makes the ecology of atmospherics explicit to individual well-being in the same way that Giorgione and Altdorfer rendered *things of a meteorological kind* apparent in the paintings they created during a period of heightened human awareness of the world. Much of Sloterdijk's thinking about the politico-ontological influences on his atmospheric thinking has been incorporated into the realm of architecture. As sealed containers that construct and envelop their own atmospheres, buildings are relatively autonomous in relation to the external environment. But how to "construct" atmospheres in the open when atmosphere is ubiquitous? How does one position the concept of atmospheric thinking within the realms of landscape architecture and urbanism? As noted earlier, landscape architecture and urban design have demonstrated a greater proclivity toward the visual, the solid, the vegetative, and the aqueous, than the aerial. If one shifts the lens of inquiry toward atmospheric qualities, including the anatomico-physiological mechanisms and their affiliated sensations, however, an important set of relations and projective possibilities emerges in these realms. The paradise garden, the polis, and the greenhouse are early manifestations of considering atmosphere and sensations as design mediums. In accordance with the human need for survival, physiological nurturing, and collective formation, these examples reify the importance of atmospheric elements in forming spaces to support human life. As spatial practices, landscape architecture and urbanism are intrinsic to the history of human vulnerability and alertness to the surrounding world. The present awareness of environmental degradation as a potential threat to human well-being signals the possibility for landscape to be understood as a fundamental medium for mediating the relationship between the sensate body and its immediate surroundings. Because the quality of environments that humans inhabit is dependent on the ontological affordances of the atmosphere, as Sloterdijk demonstrates, such consideration of its properties and meteorological behaviors is not merely conducive to a new epistemology of public space but also a prerequisite for re-evaluating the roles of landscape architecture and urban design as central to the making of pleasurable and healthy public realms to be sensed and desired, nurturing and beautiful.

Further examination of the question "Is space also atmosphere?" thus necessitates a paradigm shift: one that comprehends the human as a sensate being in osmotic exchange with the surrounding world and that being-in-space means becoming entangled with the weather-world, at times delightful and nourishing, and at other times toxic and threatening. Informed by evolving scientific knowledge about human anatomy, with its vulnerabilities and sensibilities, and its concurrent environmental dependency, such cognizance exposes the fallacy that atmosphere and its meteorological phenomena can escape perception... *because we feel the weather even when we are unaware that we do.*

1 Fernando Pessoa, *The Book of Disquiet,* Jerónimo Pizarro, ed., Margaret Jull Costa, trans. (New York: New Directions, 2017), 429.

2 See Anthony Ashley-Cooper, 3rd Earl of Shaftesbury, *The Moralists* (London: John Wyat, 1709), 124. "I shall no longer resist the Passion growing in me for Things of a *natural kind;* where neither Art nor the *Conceit* or *Caprice* of man has spoil'd their *genuine Order,* by breaking in upon that primitive State."

3 Luce Irigaray, *The Forgetting of Air in Martin Heidegger,* Mary Beth Mader, trans. (Austin: University of Texas Press, 1999), 14.

4 Hubert Damisch, *A Theory of /Cloud/: Toward a History of Painting* (Stanford, CA: Stanford University Press, 2002), 226.

5 Ignasi de Solà-Morales, "Terrain Vague," in *Anyplace,* Cynthia Davidson, ed. (Cambridge: MIT Press, 1995): 118–23, here 120.

6 Marcel Smets, "Grid, Casco, Clearing, Montage," *Topos* 38 (March 2002): 88–101, here 89, 90. Also see Marcel Smets, "Contemporary Landscape of European Infrastructures," *Lotus* 110 (September 2001): 116–43.

7 Martin Heidegger, "The Thing" [1971], *Poetry, Language, Thought,* Albert Hofstadter, trans. (New York: Harper & Row, 1975), 164.

8 Peter Sloterdijk, *Terror from the Air* (Los Angeles: Semiotext(e), 2009), 16, 15.

9 Aristotle wrote "Meteorologica" in 350 B.C.E.; Blaise Pascal, following Evangelista Torricelli's discovery of barometric pressure, rediscovered atmospheric pressure in 1648; Antoine Laurent Lavoisier discovered the air's composition in 1783; John Dalton explained the behavior of the water vapor in the atmosphere in 1800; and Nicolas Léonard Sadi Carnot laid the foundations for the second law of thermodynamics in 1825. See Gabrielle Walker, *An Ocean of Air* (London: Bloomsbury, 2007); Lucian Boia, *The Weather in the Imagination* (London: Reaktion, 2005).

10 Performance-based software for thermodynamic simulations includes Computational fluid dynamics, Flow design, Lady bug, Diva, Ecotect, Energy 2D, and ENVI-MET.

11 Stephen Rosen, *Weathering: How the Atmosphere Conditions Your Body, Your Mind, Your Moods—and Your Health* (New York: M. Evans, 1979), xi.

12 Davide Panagia, *The Political Life of Sensation* (Durham: Duke University Press, 2009), 3.

13 Philippe Rahm and Massimiliano Scuderi, *Philippe Rahm Architectes: Atmosfere Costruite: L'architettura Come Design Meteorologico = Constructed Atmospheres: Architecture as Meteorological Design* (Milan: Postmedia, 2014), 26

14 See Tim Ingold, "Landscape or the Weather-World?" in *Being Alive: Essays on Movement, Knowledge and Description* (London: Routledge, 2011), 126–35

15 Alison and Peter Smithson, *The Charged Void: Urbanism* (New York: Monacelli Press, 2005), 2.

16 Kenneth R. Olwig, "All That Is Landscape Is Melted into Air: The 'Aerography' of Ethereal Space," *Environment and Planning D: Society and Space* 29, no. 3 (June 2011): 519–32, here 526 [emphasis in original].

17 Richard Hartshorne, *The Nature of Geography: A Critical Survey of Current Thought in the Light of the Past* (Lancaster, PA: The Association, 1939), 163 [emphasis added].

18 Denis Cosgrove, "Landscape and Landschaft," *GHI Bulletin* 35 (Fall 2004): 57–71, here 61.

19 Denis Cosgrove, *Social Formation and Symbolic Landscape* (Madison, WI: University of Wisconsin Press, 1998), 102.

20 Damisch, *A Theory of /Cloud/* (2002), 186.

21 Hans Neuberger, "Climate in Art," *Weather* 25, no. 2 (1970): 46–56, here 54.

22 L. C. W. Bonacina, "Landscape Meteorology and Its Reflection in Art and Literature," *Quarterly Journal of the Royal Meteorological Society* 65, no. 282 (October 1939): 485–98, here 485, 489, 490.

23 Gerald Strauss, *Sixteenth-Century Germany: Its Topography and Topographers* (Madison: University of Wisconsin Press, 1959), 3.

24 See Denis Cosgrove, *The Palladian Landscape: Geographical Change and Its Cultural Representation in Sixteenth-Century Italy* (Leicester, UK: Leicester University Press, 1993); *Social Formation and Symbolic Landscape* (Madison, WI: University of Wisconsin Press, 1998).

25 Ernst Gombrich, "The Renaissance Theory of Art and the Rise of Landscape," *Norm and Form: Studies in the Art of the Renaissance* (London and New York: Phaidon, 1978), 109

26 In Italian, French, Portuguese, and Spanish, the word for "time" is the same as the word for "weather:" *il tempo, le temps, o tempo, el tiempo.*

27 Strauss, *Sixteenth-Century Germany* (1959), 6, 10.

28 Christopher S. Wood, *Albrecht Altdorfer and the Origins of Landscape* (Chicago: University of Chicago Press, 1993), 9.

29 Altdorfer's paintings include celestial phenomena, such as comet imagery and nova-like halos, that were unexplained at the time. See Larry Silver, "Nature and Nature's God: Landscape and Cosmos of Albrecht Altdorfer," *Art Bulletin* 81, no. 2 (June 1999): 194–214.

30 Vitruvius, *The Ten Books on Architecture,* M. H. Morgan, trans. (New York: Dover Publications, 1960), 3–6.

31 Christopher Thacker, *The History of Gardens* (Berkeley: University of California Press, 1979), 27.

32 *The Islamic Garden,* Elizabeth B. MacDougall and Richard Ettinghausen, eds. (Washington, D.C.: Dumbarton Oaks, Trustees for Harvard University, 1976), 7.

33 Marie Luise Schroeter Gothein, *A History of Garden Art,* Walter P. Wright, trans. (New York: Hacker Art Books, 1966), 10.

34 "The argument is a simple one: that beauty is a universal part of human experience, and that it provokes pleasure, rivets attention, and impels actions that help ensure survival of our genes." Nancy L. Etcoff, *Survival of the Prettiest: The Science of Beauty* (New York: Doubleday, 1999), 24.

35 Vitruvius Pollio, *The Ten Books on Architecture,* Morris Hickey Morgan, trans. (New York: Dover, 1960), 38, 17.

36 Hippocrates, "Airs, Waters, Places: An essay on the influence of climate, water supply and situation on health," *Hippocratic Writings,* J. Chadwick, W. N. Mann et al., trans. (Harmondsworth, New York: Penguin, 1983), 151.

37 Vitruvius, *The Ten Books on Architecture* (1960), 18.

38 See Jakob von Uexküll, *Umwelt und Innenwelt der Tiere* (Berlin: J. Springer, 1909).

39 Vitruvius, *The Ten Books on Architecture* (1960), 19, 24–25.

40 Peter Sloterdijk, "Atmospheric Politics," in *Making Things Public: Atmospheres of Democracy,* Bruno Latour and Peter Weibel, eds. (Cambridge, MA: MIT Press, 2005), 944–51, here 944.

Atmosphere as Immersive Jo

rney

ROUSHAM GARDEN, 1738–1741

William Kent: Architect, landscape designer, painter, and theater set designer (First scheme developed/implemented by Charles Bridgeman, c. 1720)
Oxfordshire, England

Accompanying project:

VILLA D'ESTE, c. 1549

Pirro Ligorio: Architect, landscape designer, antiquarian
Tivoli, Italy

The spatial condition of immersion in meteorological matter is intrinsic to the practices of landscape architects and urban designers in their shared capacity to address a city's open spaces: its parks, street networks, plazas, and gardens. After all, being in the outdoors implies inhabiting such open spaces and interacting with the forces and fluxes of the weather world. Inherent to designing these spaces is accordingly the *curation* of movement through them. Considerations such as how people walk through a landscape and what triggers the sequence of this journey are essential to a memorable experience. Indeed, John Dixon Hunt, in his essay "'Lordship of the Feet:' Toward a Poetics of Movement in the Garden," maintains that "no garden exists that cannot be explored on foot."[1] While walking is an indisputable activity in the aesthetic exploration and experience of outdoor space, the question of what motivates visitors is central to the design process and, therefore, requires further exploration. While variety and comfort are significant provocations to the act of walking, the question remains as to how such variety is constructed? The proposition of *Atmosphere as Immersive Journey* highlights projects in which the act of journeying, or moving through space, is supported by atmospheric moments: constructed situations that foreground the visitors' episodic, psychophysiological entanglements with the environmental elements of wind, sunlight, shade, humidity, and clouds, among others. Rather than providing unity, this way of conceiving of space prioritizes microclimatic compositions in an intermittent, ultimately disassembled manner—through tactical "on-and-off" engagements with the designed milieu relative to its sensual affordances and comfort, as engendered by cooling retreats, warming shelters, shaded rooms, humid and ventilated passages, wind-catchers, follies sheltering against the rain, and so forth. In a meteorological journey, the visitor moves through the varied atmospheric experiences of alternately cool, warm, wet, dark, bright, sheltered, aromatic, and windswept zones. The landscape is treated as a weather theater in which the amplification and/or amelioration of meteorological matter are significant design factors.

The theme of atmosphere as immersive journey hinges upon the effects of movement of the weather *and* the body in a reciprocal manner. On the one hand it acknowledges the relevance of weather's fluctuating nature as integral to the identity of a particular place, the *genius loci;* on the other, it recognizes psychophysiological stimuli from atmospheric moments and their capacity to trigger journeying throughout a spatial sequence. This kind of atmospheric reciprocity—one that is moving, another that "moves"—is found at Rousham Garden, in Oxfordshire, England, designed by William Kent at a time when the flux and mutability of meteorological phenomena were becoming sensory material for heightened stimuli of the newly discovered organ of the imagination: the nervous system. Embodying the poet Alexander Pope's allusion of the "great Shew of Nature," the garden at Rousham was conceived in terms of a sequence of scenarios animated by England's ever-changing weather and the visitors' perambulations through space.[2] Throughout the garden, Kent choreographed an atmospheric rhapsody in a tactical manner: diffuse light appears in clearings sculpted inside thick tunnels of tree canopies; wind-swept terraces intersect sheltered alleys; follies distributed throughout the garden host the visitors from unpredictable rainfalls; ponds and water rills humidify shaded grounds to amplify cooling temperatures; and alternating sunny and sheltered pockets soothe visitors as they experience chilly or warm weather conditions and contemplate the undisturbed prospects before them in anticipation of the next *discovery.*

The Villa d'Este at Tivoli, designed by Pirro Ligorio for a hillside site outside Rome, constitutes a tangible precedent for Rousham in various ways, particularly the principle of journeying through atmospheric moments. Kent is known to have visited the Villa d'Este, where he may have registered its microclimatic effects for soothing the body and prompting thermal delight while rambling through its multiple "conditioned" rooms.[3] Constructed as a place of symbolic relevance to its owner, Cardinal Ippolito II d'Este, who aspired to the papacy and thus welcomed the garden's multiple emblematic references to links with the city of Rome, the Villa d'Este is above all a fresh haven made for cooling during hot summer days in Tivoli, where air temperatures can reach 45°C (113°F). The conditioned environments were of particular importance to the Cardinal, who suffered from gout. Walking in shaded breezeways and in cooling environments was considered therapy for alleviating the symptoms of this disease. The Villa d'Este can be described as a sequence of such environments, involving thick shadows of dense canopy and tall hedges, multiple forms of water—in quiet pools, weirs, water stairs, cascades, waterfalls, a water organ, and fountain jets in multiple formats—grottoes and underground caves, cryptoporticus and ventilated passageways, wet walls and vegetated pergolas. Dominant winds that run along the principal terraces provide freshening breezes to shaded seats offering places for rest and outward prospects. In these environments the multiple forms of water and thickness of shade work with the varying wind and sounds to encourage constant motion. They stir the mind of the visitor in the same way that they promote physiological delight in retreat from the blazing temperatures.

1 John Dixon Hunt, "'Lordship of the Feet:' Toward a Poetics of Movement in the Garden," in *Landscape design and the experience of motion,* Michel Conan, ed. (Washington, D.C.: Dumbarton Oaks, 2003), 187–213, here 187.
2 George Sherburn, "Pope and 'The Great Shew of Nature,'" in Richard Foster Jones et al., *The Seventeenth Century: Studies in the History of English Thought and Literature from Bacon to Pope* (Stanford, CA: Stanford University Press, 1951), 306–15, here 306.
3 John Dixon Hunt, *William Kent, Landscape Garden Designer: An Assessment and Catalogue of His Designs* (London: A. Zwemmer, 1987), 26.

ROUSHAM GARDEN, 1738–1741

William Kent: Architect, landscape designer, painter, and theater set designer (First scheme developed/implemented by Charles Bridgeman, c. 1720)
Oxfordshire, England

Rousham Garden: A Meteorological Foray for the *Sensible* Body

> *Every smatterer in anatomy knows, that this pericardium, or case of the heart, contains in it a thin reddish liquor, supposed to be bred from the vapours which exhale out of the heart, and being stopped here, are condensed into this watery substance. Upon examining this liquor, we found that it had in it all the qualities of that spirit which is made use of in the thermometer, to show the change of weather.*
>
> —Joseph Addison, "Dissection of a Coquette's Heart" (1711–1712)[1]

In the candlelit scenes of Stanley Kubrick's *Barry Lyndon*—a 1975 film based on William Makepeace Thackeray's novel *The Luck of Barry Lyndon* (1844)—the actors perform in an atmosphere of near darkness. Rather than expose the whole setting to view, Kubrick illuminated each face and chest dimly, with disciplined restraint. Evoking the eighteenth-century aesthetic sensibility of controlled disclosure, these cinematic scenes construct a space of wonderment. In the diffuse light, Kubrick's characters unveil their desires and hopes in a restrained manner. These acts of concealment elicit the audience's imagination, prompting its participation in the space of suppressed light and partial thoughts. Audience and actors cohabit the darkened space that extends from the cinematic scene to the movie theater. The audience becomes an active participant, a reactive body seeking to uncover the whole of the concealed scene as mind and atmosphere intersect in the space of the imagination.

The role of the imagination, the medium of atmosphere, and the hosting environment of the newly found *sensible* body were central premises for the material embodiment of eighteenth- and ninetieth-century aesthetics. These premises, captured in the literature of poets Joseph Addison (1672–1719) and Alexander Pope (1688–1744), among others, found spatial expression in the emerging English picturesque landscape garden, such as that at Rousham in Oxfordshire, originally designed in 1720 by the gardener Charles Bridgeman (1690–1738). His series of straight and serpentine paths connecting two large square ponds and an amphitheater, set in a wilderness, was reconceived between 1738 and 1741 by the English architect, landscape architect, painter, and theater set designer William Kent (c.1685–1748).[2] By loosening the rigidity and imparting a measure of informality to the geometric aspects of Bridgeman's layout, Kent established a precedent for an emerging landscape sensibility that was rooted in spatial premises of ceaseless mutability and atmospheric variety—in ideas of curated disclosure and wonderment. These changes were not only formal; by introducing a variety of meteorological intensities to the garden, Kent stirred the visitor's cognizance of her bodily sensations and stimulated her imaginative capacities. In considering the apparent aspirations behind Kent's design, however, questions remain. Why were atmospheric variety and the evocation of wonderment so revered during Kent's time? What may have instigated such design motivations? This essay probes possible inspirations for Kent's design interventions, centered on the discovery of the body as a *nervous* self in physiological entanglement with its hosting environment and the emerging interest in meteorological phenomena as creative mediums, in response to the fluctuating qualities of the country's weather. These aspects are foundational to British cultural identity during a period when landscape was becoming both a surrogate for the dynamic living world and a meteorological analog for the newly found *sensible* body. Concurrently, landscape architecture developed as a professional practice in England, and Kent's design for Rousham represents a paradigmatic example of the emerging discipline.

Parallels can be established between *Barry Lyndon*'s dimly lit scenes and an eighteenth-century drawing of the poet Alexander Pope, attributed to Kent, which captures Pope working in the grotto at his rural London estate on the River Thames at Twickenham. Pope's face and body are faintly lit, conveying a sense of interiority, indicative of the poet's state of mind in his creative entanglement with the grotto's shimmering atmosphere that resulted from the reflective mirrors, shells, and crystals that he set amid its walls. As John Dixon Hunts points out, the allusion to the mind's creative process is further conveyed by the playful butterflies at the top of the drawing—symbols of the mind's soul.[3] Describing the grotto in a letter to Edward Blount, Pope noted that "when a lamp (of an orbicular figure of thin alabaster) is hung in the middle, a thousand pointed rays glitter.... When you shut the doors of this grotto, it becomes on the instant, from a luminous room, a *Camera Obscura;* on the walls of which all the objects of the river, hills, woods, and boats, are forming a moving picture in their visible radiations: and when you have a mind to light it up, it affords you a very different scene."[4] The allusion of a heightened atmosphere that stimulates higher states of wonderment is an essential premise of both Kent's drawing and Pope's description. Could Kent's heightened awareness of the imaginative potential of flexuous atmospheres have prompted his innovative design sensibility and, thus, the novel spatial effects in his garden layout for Rousham? If so, why was the imagination entitled to such eminence? Highlighting the intersection of aesthetic affinities and physiological advances in seventeenth and eighteenth centuries England, historian George S. Rousseau notes: "Without the stirrings of the new physiology, these aesthetic questions would never have been asked in the first place."[5]

I. The anatomy of the *sensible* body

During the seventeenth and early eighteenth centuries, anatomical study of the human body underwent an ontological revolution in which the body came be understood as a *sensible* self that was contingent upon movement for increased well-being. If the physiology of the nerves and the related idea of motion stirred the scientific community, these concepts also gained traction among the cultural elite. After all, to have "feelings" meant to have superior insights about the world. Like the philosopher and physician John Locke (1632–1704), who foregrounded human sensation in the empirical process of acquiring knowledge, William Kent and his intellectual circle, including Addison and Pope, were living in an era when concepts of the human body were evolving—from static to reactive and from stable to fluid and nervous. Locke's professor, the English doctor and neurologist Thomas Willis, contributed to this emerging conception. In his treatise *Cerebri Anatome* (1664), Willis introduced a groundbreaking neurophysiological view of the body as composed of a network of nervous fibers. Seeking to understand the "vital soul" acting upon the human brain and its physiological fabric, he declared that the anatomical study of the human brain could "unlock the secret places of Man's Mind and look into the living and breathing Chapel of the Deity."[6] In describing the anatomy of the brain and the nerves, Willis posited a link between anatomy and behavior, and Locke extended this medical concept to a philosophical and aesthetic premise based on human perception. Contrary to the prevailing Cartesian view that ideas associated with objects are innate and governed by laws of nature, fixed intrinsically by God, Locke claimed that sensibility to the outer world and the acquisition of ideas through the senses were the only ways to "furnish the yet empty cabinet."[7] The capacity to sense beauty did not result from the work of God alone, but was also formed through a sensitive and reactive body. The convergence of Willis's anatomy of the mind and Locke's understanding of sensibility contributed to the physiology of the imagination—the discovery of a network of sensitive fibers that could *feel* stimuli in reaction to the visible and invisible forces of the world. Such impressions would not only stimulate higher abstract ideas and specific emotions; they would also give agency to space as a vehicle for stirring the human imagination. "The discovery of the imagination," Rousseau explains, "does not imply that man suddenly realized he had one.... What he did discover was that the imagination was a real essence, as material in substance as any other part of the body, and that it therefore could be medically described."[8] The physiology of the mind, now understood to be composed of reactive and sensitive nervous fibers, was thus the seat of the creative process. It could affect one's disposition, such as being delighted, inspired, or irritated by the surrounding world, its meteorological events and atmospheric conditions. As Addition would later query: "why has Providence given [the mind] a Power of producing in us such imaginary Qualities, as Tastes and Colours, Sounds and Smells, Heat and Cold, but that Man, while he is conversant in the lower Stations of Nature, might have his Mind cheered and delighted with agreeable Sensations? In short, the whole Universe is a kind of Theatre filled with Objects [celestial phenomena] that either raise in us Pleasure, Amusement, or Admiration."[9] In the context of these physiological advancements, nature emerges as a "celestial" theater set before humans for greater pleasure, heightened sensibility, and moral improvement, in which the new human—now sensible and reactive—is an active agent rather than a distant observer. As historian Christopher Lawrence has noted: "Given the sensualist epistemology, the nervous system was clearly going to be of importance as the mediator between man and his environment."[10]

Whereas the newly discovered nervous apparatus enabled the body to be understood as a sensible organism, concurrent medical revelations on the human circulatory system viewed bodily movement as critical for increased health. The finding of the English physician William Harvey (1578–1657) that blood is pumped by the heart to flow in a continuous rhythm through a network of veins and valves led to the idea of walking in the open air as essential to human well-being.[11] Thus, belief in the act of walking to boost the circulation of blood became associated with a virtuous lifestyle. "Of all exercises that are or may be used for health," Dr. George Cheyne maintained in *An Essay of Health and Long Life* (1724), "*walking* is the most *natural.*"[12] Aware of these recent medical insights, the poet Joseph Addison observed: "Since the circulation of the blood has been found out and many other great discoveries have been made by our modern anatomists, we see new wonders in the human frame."[13] Paradoxically the act of walking in the *open air* as a prophylactic and social practice—manifested in the proliferation of dedicated eighteenth-century walks, including public routes, promenades, and pleasure gardens—also involved exposure of London residents to the increased airborne pollution that had been registered in the city from 1650 onward. Prominent among the physicians who were examining the effects of air on human well-being were Dr. Thomas Sydenham (1624–1689), known as the "English Hippocrates," and Dr. John Arbuthnot (1667–1735), a close friend of Pope. In *An Essay concerning the Effect of Air on Human Bodies* (1733), Arbuthnot urged "it is incumbent upon the Professors of our Art to know and assign, as far as they can, the true Causes of the Changes which happen in Human Bodies; and there are many more useless Inquiries than this, about the Effects of Air, which are daily the Subject of Human Curiosity." As Arbuthnot observed, the subject of air and its effects on human health, while vigorously discussed in the natural sciences, was being overlooked by medical practitioners: "Philosophers, Mathematicians, Chymists, the Professors of Agriculture and Gardening, have attended to the Effects of Air on the Subjects of their several Arts, more than the Physicians. The Reason of which Neglect may be, that Air is one of those *Ingesta,* or things taken inwardly, which neither can be forborn nor measur'd in Doses."[14]

Why were air and weather such lively subjects of investigation in the sciences and cultural domains? This attention to the quality of air and its constitution emerged in the context of two scales of atmospheric disturbance: on the local level, associated with the airborne pollution from the rapid industrialization in late seventeenth-century London; on the global scale, tied to the climatic decline associated with the extremely low solar activity between 1650 and 1715, later known as the "Little Ice Age."[15] Whereas the sulfurous smoke produced by burning coal gave the sky an unnatural and foul appearance, which Charles Dickens would refer to in *Bleak House* as "London Particular," comparable climatic incidents held the imagination of various authors who were trying to make sense of the weather. As landscape historian Mark Laird observes, "This was at a moment when Fellows of the Royal Society—Wren, Hooke, Locke, Boyle and Evelyn—began to develop the rain gauge, thermometers, barometers, the wind recorder and hygroscope for measuring the weather and the disease-weather relationship."[16]

John Evelyn (1620–1706), a zealous gardener and close friend of Dr. Arbuthnot, methodically registered the instability of weather during this period of atmospheric disturbances. In 1658, he recorded in his diary the "very cold & severe weather" and mourned the death of his servant under such conditions: "It was exceedingly mortal at this time; & the season was unsufferably cold. The Thames frozen, &c."[17] This combination of frigid temperatures and vaporous air fostered increased consciousness of the weather, its associated reductions in agricultural production, and its effects on the population's health, including that of the newly crowned King Charles II (1630–1685), who founded the Royal Society of London for Improving Natural Knowledge in 1660, claiming to be allergic to the "new" atmospheric environment. Aware of the King's vulnerability to the sulfurous vapors, Evelyn drew upon his own interest in the vagaries of weather to develop a design strategy for addressing these environmental concerns. He recommended rezoning the downwind periphery of London to accommodate all the city's polluting activities, such as coal-burning trades, graveyards, and slaughterhouses. To improve urban odor, Evelyn proposed introducing a one-hundred-fifty-foot wide zone of aromatic gardens that "would produce sweet-smelling and beautiful flowers and fill the air with their fragrant smell," elaborating that "Rosemary [is] the most important as it [is] reported to give off a scent for about thirty leagues at sea on the coast of Spain."[18] Because his proposal, *Fumifugium, or, The inconveniencie of the aer and smoak of London* (1661) privileged both the amelioration of air quality and the associated economic benefits, Evelyn claimed that its implementation would be an achievement of "far greater concern ... than draining a swamp or beautifying an aqueduct." Although Evelyn never developed his proposal further, it is nonetheless a pertinent example of comprehending the design significance of air and weather. It registers the cultural sensibilities and converging concerns of a period in which landscape architecture was about to set its professional foundations: premises embodied in the garden at Rousham. Could these physiological considerations and alertness to meteorological phenomena have influenced William Kent's design sensibility?

II. Stirring the imagination

A wide range of studies has accounted for Kent's design for the garden at Rousham as informed by multiple contexts during his lifetime: political, economic, symbolic, iconographic, and so forth. What concerns us here is whether other influences from Kent's cultural milieu might be relevant to an understanding of his design in its atmospheric capacity to activate the senses and stir the imagination. Could Kent's motivation to design for "variety" have been triggered by the emerging notions about the body and the attentiveness to meteorological fluxes, in particular by the physiological findings on the anatomy of the nerves and their receptiveness to the surrounding atmospheres? If one accepts that the theater-like meteorological effects of nature trigger one's mind and sensations, could this causal relation have motivated a novel design culture, sensitive to the spatial implications of such sensations? These innovations in medicine and physiology certainly influenced the cultural elite of the time, including the influential poets Addison and Pope, who were central authorities in establishing the new design protocols for a national language with landscape at its forefront. Their ideas are widely understood to have inspired Kent's design for Rousham.

Pope and Addison were avid proponents of the Royal Society's scientific activities and informed consumers of medical experiments and advancements. Both partook in the Italian Grand Tours that began during the mid-seventeenth century, and they were loyal devotees of classical antiquity. This last affiliation suggests an awareness of the relationship between the body and its immediate surroundings established and explored by such classical authors as Hippocrates, Galen of Pergamon, Aristotle,

Pliny the Younger, and Vitruvius, to name just a few. Their writings, rediscovered and translated during this period in England, set forth causal dependencies between climate and health, air and constitution, meteorological elements and temperament, and, lastly, design for human well-being and delight. Influential among members of the British medical and intellectual communities were the writings of Hippocrates, in particular his treatise "On Air, Water, and Places," considered to be the first to recognize the potential for disease arising from poor environmental qualities. Just as the classical authors imagined that the influence of their immediate surroundings was driven by the *Pneuma,* the "vital spirit" that runs through the body's hollow "tubes" and animates the soul, so such sensitivity was physiologically understood in eighteenth-century England to derive from the newly found nervous system—the "fabric" responsible for stirring the imagination of the newly discovered sensible audience. The impulse to adapt these classical references to English soil reflects a growing interest in acclimatizing the temperate Mediterranean climate associated with classical Arcadia to the cold, wet, and windy climate of England—an issue that did present its challenges.

Although Kent never wrote about his design motivations, he was familiar with Addison and Pope's reflections on nature, the human body, and the imagination. His friendship with Pope is well documented; both had the same patron, Lord Burlington, and they collaborated on Pope's estate at Twickenham during the early 1730s. Although Addison's influence on Kent's design sensibility is less established, his acclaim of nature as an aesthetic principle was fundamental to the emerging English landscape movement. Moreover, Kent's design efforts at Richmond for Queen Caroline, an advocate of Addison's writings, and his illustrations for James Thomson's *The Seasons* (1730)—a tribute to the rural landscape with origins in Addison's empirical philosophy—may have exposed him to the poet's interest in meteorological phenomena. *The Seasons* extends the literary interest in relating weather with life cycles (economical, emotional, and social) as registered by the Classic poet Virgil in *The Georgics* (circa 29 BCE), which was translated into English with an introduction by Addison in 1697. *The Seasons* depicts seasonal variability as a creative force affecting agricultural production, animal and vegetal life, artistic production, and people's dispositions. In his four frontispieces, Kent framed the power of the weather's engulfing forces as if he were composing a meteorological act. Characters engaging in different activities occupy each of the seasonal scenes, except Winter—a possible acknowledgement of its adverse climate.[19] In the other three images, each character or group of characters alertly interacts with the corresponding seasonal cycle and elements. Some find refuge from the fierce wind; others rejoice under a warming sun; still others hunt or harvest wheat. Wild and irregular nature accommodates human life that is evocatively attuned to a landscape animated by atmospheric fluxes and meteorological phenomena. The British literary critic Samuel Johnson (1709–1784) maintained that the atmospheric mutability captured in the poem (and, by extension, in Kent's illustrations) "leads us through the appearances of things as they are successively varied by the vicissitudes of the year, and imparts to us so much of his own enthusiasm, that our thoughts expand with his imagery, and kindle with his sentiments."[20] This "appearance of things as they are successively varied" could equally apply to the meteorological "scenes" that Kent construed a few years later at Rousham.

A consistent spectator of anatomical dissections, Addison reported his amazement at the era's medical discoveries in his collection of essays, "The Pleasures of the Imagination," published in *The Spectator* in 1712. There he elaborated on the imaginative potential wrought by "the authors of the new philosophy, whether we consider their theories of the earth or heavens, the discoveries they have made by glasses [i.e., microscopes], or any other of their contemplations on nature."[21] Moreover, in his satirical sketch of "a Sett of merry Fellows, who are passing their Summer together in the Country," the human body appears as a kind of a meteorological instrument in its capacity to register the phenomena of weather. Addison calls these Fellows "human barometers," as they are physiologically affected by the fluctuations of weather.[22]

Pope, infirm since childhood, had a specific interest in making the anatomy of the mind, that is, the physiology of the nerves, the locus of creation—as opposed to his "crazy constitution."[23] The meteorological elements and their fluctuations, which he described as the "great Shew of Nature," also gained relevance in the poet's writings, where they promote delight and nurture the human mind.[24] Alluding to the therapeutic capacities of weather in stirring his spirit and soothing his body, Pope expanded on his concept of pleasure: "In fair weather when my heart is cheered, and I feel that exaltation of spirits which results from light and warmth, … I regard myself as one placed, by the hand of God, in the midst of an ample theatre, in which the sun, moon, and stars … perpetually changing their positions, or their aspects, exhibit an elegant entertainment to the understanding."[25]

Just as the picturesque garden emerged in this innovative literary context, so its form served to elaborate on the notion of an earthly surrogate for a wider world—a constructed space to host, legitimize, and foment knowledge.[26] The underlying entanglement of the self and the world seems to be an analog for Pope's "ample theater"—a site where fluctuating phenomena are revealed without artifice, where humans meander immersed in the caprices of a changing atmosphere. With disdain for the excessive use of artifice in contemporary French gardens, Pope enthused over the unadorned aesthetic that Anthony Ashley-Cooper, 3rd Earl of Shaftesbury associated with the ancient classical garden. Suggesting that "genius" is a gift from nature that is, in return, nurtured through exposure to nature, Pope proclaimed: "I believe it is no wrong observation, that persons of genius, and those who are most capable of art, are always most fond of nature."[27] If genius, as both intellectual capacity and heightened taste, refers to a greater empathy for *natura naturans* (nature behaving like nature), the same genius relies upon entanglement both with that form of nature and with the ability to sense its phenomena. The idea of the new garden accordingly arose with reference to a world in flux, waiting to be discovered and sensed, a process in which the wondering mind would be nourished and cultivated to achieve a higher intellectual state.

Among the founders of the Royal Society of London, the English natural philosopher John Wilkins used the term "atmosphere" to explain the envelope (sphere) made out of vaporous air (atmos) surrounding the moon. Described as an *appearance,* this envelope was evocative of a space and an effect, revealed to the subject, that alluded to the powers of the imagination.[28] The relation between the body and its surrounding sphere, furthered by the discovery of the nervous system—the legitimate *locus* for sensorial stimuli—was a central interest in early eighteenth-century England. "The progression is clear," notes George Rousseau: "medicine, built on the anatomy learned in the schools, presented nerves first; thereafter fiction imported their medical theories ... and only after early fiction had vivified nervous protagonists ... did they migrate further afield to infuse philosophy."[29] In this progression from anatomical knowledge to its absorption by other disciplinary practices, was this new knowledge of the body also assimilated into design practice as a novel spatial sensibility?

III. Rousham: A meteorological foray

Given Addison and Pope's influences on Kent's work and the latter's intellectual affiliation with the new "sensualist epistemology," a question remains: How might these affinities have elicited a new spatial ethos in the garden at Rousham? On the one hand, the design reflects a predilection for shifting formal attributes; it is less rigidly laid out than earlier, more geometric examples. On the other hand, it not only materializes the intellectual processes involved in the new ways the world was being "sensed" but also reflects radical ideas about the human circulatory system and neurological apparatus—the supporting organs of the imagination. Attesting to such a premise is the spatial variety in the garden's extensive pedestrian routes. But what type of variety is registered at Rousham? And why was variety such a revered spatial concept, particularly as manifested in Kent's work? If one assumes that landscapes of this period reflect the possibility of reproducing *natura naturans* and its mutability, then the question of

The Bowling Green
and woodland path

purpose—for variety, dramatic contrast, or delicious ambiguity—remains. In the literary journal *The Tatler,* Addison alluded to the juxtaposition of landscape, its atmospheres, and its associated sensations: "I dreamed that I was in a wood, of so prodigious an extent, and cut unto such a variety of walks and alleys, that all mankind were lost and bewildered in it.... The Walks which we marched up, for Thickness of Shades, Embroidery of Flowers, and Melody of Birds, with the distant purling of Streams, and Falls of Water, was so wonderfully delightful, that it charmed our Senses, and intoxicated our Minds with Pleasure."[30] For Addison such variety derived less from the physical attributes of a space than its immaterial and atmospheric qualities—the sensory material and "fabric" for bewildering stimuli.

In the garden at Rousham the visitor becomes an active participant in an ever-changing scene of atmospheric performances. These may be visual, but they are above all aural, olfactory, haptic, and thermal. In acknowledgment of nature's ever-changing rhythms, the elements of wind, clouds, heat, and cold, as well as forms of water in fountains, rivers, rills, and spray, appear as design "substance" for engaging an audience; thus, they seem deliberately constructed. But how are the notions of ambience and atmosphere—and particularly the integration of weather as a design medium—constructed spatially to trigger the imagination? This analysis follows one of the many possible routes through the garden to focus on moments of heightened atmospheric phenomena: those synonymous with intense microclimates and related thermal sensations. The chosen walk is a circuit that Rousham's head gardener, John MacClary, described in a letter of 1750 to entice the estate's absent owners to "set their faces toward Rousham."[31] This examination expands upon MacClary's description in the form of a meteorological foray, in which the body acts as a moving "barometer," eliciting Addison's account of his characters being physiologically affected by atmospheric variability.

To describe his route, MacClary drew upon a set of five concave slopes that constitute a network in which the visitor could meander: the Great Slope by the Bowling Green, the slope at the Praeneste Arcade, one at the Gothic Seat toward the Oval Fishpond, another facing the Temple of Echo (or Townsend's Building), and, finally, that at the Venus Vale. Drawing upon these topographical configurations, Kent devised tactical moments of interaction between solar orientation and the prevailing winds at opportune points along the circuit. With a dominant northeast outlook, the garden rises fifteen meters above the valley of the River Cherwell. This topographical difference results in a continual interaction in which the prevailing winds come from southwest, while the humidity, concentrated along the river, combines with the heated slopes to promote a northeastern upslope airflow. These opposing air currents amplify the variety of climatic conditions along the meandering river and among the concave slopes, which operate as receptacles for wind, mist, light, and heat, thereby amplifying the visitor's sense of meteorological immersion in a series of chambers of delight.

As MacClary describes the first slope: "When you walk out at the Hall Door you come into a Large parterre, the middle of which is a Large Bowlingreen ... when your eyes drops upon a very fine Concave Slope, at the Bottom of which runs the Beautiful River Charwell." On the flat plane of the Bowling Green, the prevailing southwest winds gently blow toward the visitor's back, which is simultaneously warmed by the sun. The Grand Slope promotes convection as the humid air rises along its heated surfaces, forming an eddy that is strongest at the slope's edge, where, with two carefully placed seats, Kent offers the visitor the "prettiest view in the whole World."[32]

Contrasting the open, bright, warm, and breezy qualities of the Bowling Green and the Grand Slope, the next space in MacClary's sequence is a path through a dense woodland composed of "fine Open Grove of Oaks, Elms, Beachs, and Black Cherrys, Thirty feet Hight, backt with a very fine close Beach Hedge, which brings [the visitor] to a pleasant opening."[33] The path is cool and dark, shaded and enclosed, with a thick canopy that affords protection from the wind and the drizzling rain, making the visitor's pupils adjust to the diminished light to gain a glimpse of a light-filled clearing in the distance. Proceeding to the clearing, she encounters a terrace with the statue of a Dying Gladiator. Here, the view opens to the far rural landscape, and the visitor experiences another contrasting meteorological moment: a warmer, brighter pocket of air. The terrace, while open to the sky, is unexpectedly sheltered from the wind. She either feels the heat from the southern exposure or is cooled by intermittent rainfall, while a ha-ha on the downward side of the terrace lifts the dominant southwestern wind upward, so that it glides overhead and back down to the river. → p. 51 Ⓐ

Standing at the parapet that edges the terrace, the visitor experiences an increase in airflow from the breezes that rise up along the concave slope, carrying cold air stored in the sunken Praeneste Arcade, which is tucked into the topography below. Here the sun is on the visitor's back as she faces the upslope breezes from the river valley. A jetty formed by a moment of low pressure at the bottom of the Arcade increases the air velocity at the terrace edge, and the wind picks up the aroma of the scented plantings at the base of the Dying Gladiator statue. From this vantage point the visitor apprehends a portal to larger worlds, as the intense atmospheric entanglement of the meteorological elements and rhythms upon which the rural ambience and agricultural cycles depend—wind, rain, heat, and light—accompany the sweeping vistas and the immense sky, where weather is in endless flux. This dynamic is referenced not only in many classic writings, such as Virgil's *Georgics,* but also, as noted earlier, in Kent's illustrations for Thomson's *The Seasons,* made only a few years before he began his design for Rousham.

The visitor following MacClary's circuit would next turn west along "a pleasant green Walk, backt with all sorts of Flowers, and Flowering Shrubs," where the view opens eastward to the paddock, the main house, and the previously experienced sequence of meteorological sensations.[34] The route leads to an architectural folly, the Gothic Seat: an enclosed structure with thick masonry walls and a bench that invites visitors to enjoy a moment of rest. This is one of a number of follies that Kent devised at Rousham, which John Dixon Hunt terms "carefully inserted *fabriques.*"[35] Instead of facing the main house to the east, the Gothic Seat faces north to a forested area. This orientation, while surprising, is not random; it is the same as the other follies at Rousham: the Temple of Echo (Townsend's Building), and the Pyramid. These structures not only arrest the attention of the visitor when viewed from afar but also offer valuable shelter from the inclement weather, reflecting Kent's sensitivity to the body's vulnerability in confronting the vagaries of the English climate. As he expressed in a note written upon his return from a trip to Italy, his "Italian constitution" could not endure the winter weather of "this Gothick country."[36] The northern orientation of these follies not only affords shelter from the dominant southwest winds—reducing the chances for further cooling during the

A Terrace with Dying Gladiator above Praeneste Arcade

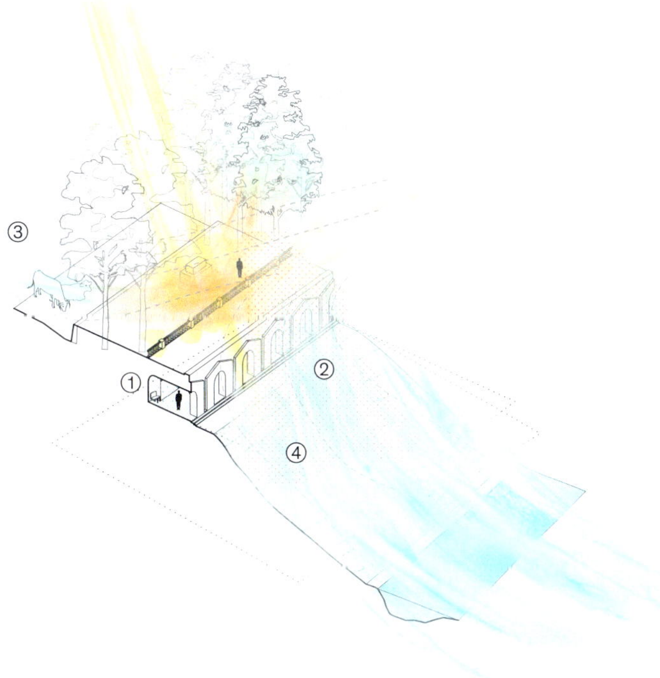

Thermodynamic performance:

1) Thermal mass / radiant cooling: shaded structure tucked into terrain stores cold (geothermal)
2) Forced convection / anabatic flow: upslope breezes from river
3) Forced convection: prevailing winds from south
4) Solar radiation (exposed): heated grassy surface increases humid air that rises

B Gothic Seat

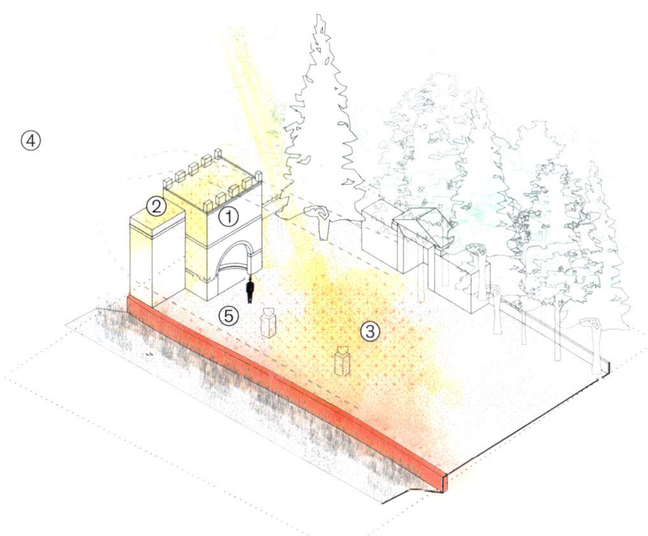

Thermodynamic performance:

1) Rain shelter (architectural folly): shelters visitors during inclement weather
2) Thermal mass / radiant heating: exposed walls store heat and release it at night
3) Solar radiation (exposed): unobstructed solar exposure to the west, east, and south
4) Forced convection: prevailing winds from south
5) Forced convection (reduced): architectural folly blocks winds

colder seasons—but also complies with Pope's account of the orientation he associated with Gothic garden structures. "Westward, a sumptuous frontispiece appear'd," Pope elaborated: "The eastern front was glorious to behold.... But on the south, a long majestic race," and finally: "Of Gothic Structure was the Northern Side."[37] Furthermore, owing to the cooling afforded by its thermal mass, Kent's Gothic Seat also provides a cooler environment during the hot summer hours. From this resting point, the visitor's view is directed northward to the next sequence of the walk—a thick woodland. ← p. 51 B

Leaving the Gothic Seat, the visitor gradually descends a gentle, winding pathway that MacClary describes as "one of the noblest Green Serpentine Walks that was ever seen, or ever made." His description continues: "You walk forward down a pretty concave Slope, which brings you to a fine Large oval Fish pond."[38] A strong hedge of *Buxus* and *Laurus* evergreens holds the right side of the path, which is wide enough to admit the setting sun that streams into the space, illuminating the bright leaves with a soft, green, immersive glow that reverberates along the route. To the left, the shade is dramatic and dark, affording the visitor a cooler environment. The path is buffered from the wind, yet the canopy picks up the prevailing breezes that animate the route as they channel down toward the river valley. The asymmetrical configuration of solar and wind exposure provides a contrasting set of thermal possibilities: dark and humid; bright and warm. At the end of this serpentine walk, Kent positioned another bench that faces south for the visitor to catch the midday sun or to look back up the route she has just traversed, reinforcing the dialogue between bodily experience and visual perception.

After pausing for a moment, the visitor following MacClary's circuit would continue through a densely planted woodland before turning "down a little Serpentine Gravil Walk, into a little opening, made with Yew and other Evergreens as dark and melencholly as it was posable to make it."[39] The path, replete with dense evergreens intermingled with flowers, leads to one of Rousham's most memorable features: the Watery Walk. This is Kent's master stroke: a narrow, meandering water rill formalized from an existing stream that bifurcates the path. The walk is, in turn, framed by dense edges of laurel and a tightly knitted canopy of evergreen and deciduous trees, in which tactical clearings produce varied light effects and thermal gradients. Just as the robust laurel border accentuates the rill, contributing to the intimate scale of the ensemble, so the watercourse's twisting configuration invites the visitor to seek out its concealed destination. As the water passes languorously through the rill, it reflects the diaphanous light filtered in various intensities by the dense canopy. In the darker moments of the path, the cooling sensation increases and the aroma of wet soil becomes more apparent. → p. 54 C

A small clearing opens up to reveal a "Large Octogon Basson" and a "little Building."[40] The latter structure is formed as a ruin; embedded in the topography, it provides a grotto like environment with intensified cooling effects. Its atmosphere is dark and damp, cold and mysterious, in contrast to the bright and airy conditions in the clearing. The effects of weathering and ruination—aesthetically valued during this period—expand the structure's metaphorical meaning in relation to an imagined, undisclosed past and trigger the visitor's imagination. The water in the basin reflects the bordering canopy, infusing the clearing with an overall tint of green and immersing the visitor in the woodland environment as if she were inhabiting the elemental *locus* of primordial England. In the midst of this thick and intimate woodland, the act of bathing would cleanse the body and host the visitor within its atmospheric elements. This primordial atmosphere recalls Pliny the Younger's description of his Roman villa at *Laurentinum:* "in the gardens of the first Ages, they seem to have been no more than select, well-water'd Spots of Ground, irregularly producing all sorts of Plants and Trees, grateful either to the Sight, Smell, or Taste, and refreshed by Shade and Water."[41] This translation, commissioned by Kent's patron, Lord Burlington, was published as *The Villas of the Ancients Illustrated* in 1728—ten years before the work at Rousham began.[42]

To the west of the basin, the shadows lift to reveal the Temple of Echo (or Townsend's Building) and the third concave slope leading down

Ⓒ Clearing in the Watery Walk with "Large Octogon Basson" and "little Building"

→ p. 336

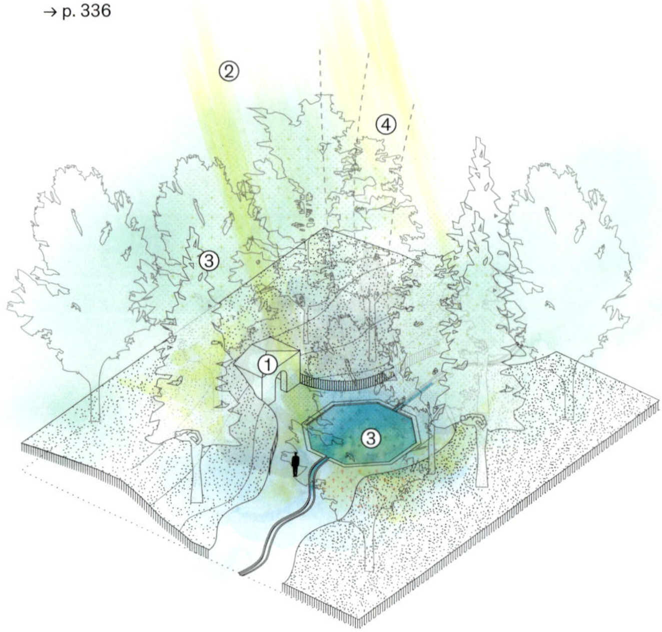

Thermodynamic performance:

① Thermal mass / radiant cooling: shaded folly tucked into terrain stores cold (geothermal)
② Solar radiation (exposed): ground and water surface in clearing
③ Evaporative cooling / isothermal evaporation: thick tree canopy and water surface
④ Free convection: humid air in clearing rises

to the River Cherwell—an airy, sun-filled space affording distant views to the countryside that is one of the "prettiest concave Slopes in England," according to MacClary. Here stands the second folly in the gardener's circuit, a "pavilion, built in the Tuscan order where you goe in & sett down." This temple affords the visitor a broad prospect to the distant landscape, sheltering her during moments of drizzly rain or encompassing wind and revealing "a very fine Echo" from the buoyant upslope breezes that it captures. → p. 56 Ⓓ Ⓔ

From the Temple of Echo, the visitor would descend the slope to follow a path along the river through a dark and scented grove composed of "Oaks, Elms, Beach, Alder, plains, and Horsechestnuts, all in Flower now.... [T]his Grove is a Hundred feet Broad, and five Hundred feet Long, one side runs the River, the other is Backt with all sorts of Evergreens, and Flowering shrubs entermixt."[43] At the end of this shaded walk, she would arrive at the confluence of the final two concave slopes in the circuit—that which develops from the Praeneste Arcade and the Venus Vale. Whereas the former integrates the airflow in the manner of the other valleys, the latter adds the dramatic effects of water and humidity interacting with the sunlight and the upslope breezes. The Venus Vale, flanked by thick and dense woodlands, is the longest and the most animated concave slope in the garden. Kent formed its topography to augment the drama of the water, with a pair of cascades that he constructed in the valley, where he imagined water spouts—an impression reflected in Kent's drawing of the cascades. Although they are no longer operating, these jetting spouts would produce a theatrical setting of vaporous and fleeting materiality, aided by the northeastern upslope breezes from the river through the elongated clearing. The upward airflow would carry the humidity and water sprays along with it, enabling the water mist to reflect and refract the sunlight and create an effect of rainbows flickering in the space. In this scenario of swirling airflow, the spectacle of sunlight striking the water droplets, released by the buoyant fountains, holds the prospect of a dramatic scene for the visitor glancing up from her position at the river's edge. → p. 57 F

As the visitor ascends toward the water cascades, a long, dark walk, known as the "Elm Walk," emerges to the right, displaying, at its end, the back of a statue of Apollo. This walk, with its deep contrasts of light and dark, wet and dry, hot and cold, incorporates the most striking atmospheric signature of Kent's spatial effects. Clearings of varied dimensions carved out from the thick woodland bring varying intensities of light to the walk. During a drizzling rain, a glittering atmosphere forms in front of the visitor. The accentuated effects achieved through the topographical manipulation and planting—the clearings carved from the thick canopy, the varied tints of green and grays as sunlight illuminates the walk, the airflow stirring the humidity produced by the intense vegetation—provide the visitor with the experience of an ever-changing atmospheric theater. This orchestrated sequence, illuminated then darkened, moist then dry, prompts an awareness of time that is in turn associated with an appreciation of weather, as the fleeting cycles of meteorological elements confront and entangle the visitor. The author William Gilpin (1725–1804) would later comment on the meteorological elements and phenomena that informed the distinctive qualities of the picturesque landscape: "The moisture, and vapory heaviness of our atmosphere, which produces the rich verdure of our lawns; gives birth also to another peculiar feature in English landscape—that obscurity, which is often thrown over distance…."[44] This "style," meteorological at its core, expresses a novel spatial sensibility that is attentive to the visitor's sensitivity to the effects of weather and atmosphere. This meteorological sensibility—above and beyond the often acknowledged symbolic, iconographic, political, or economic motivations of the picturesque landscape garden—constitutes a central foundation from which landscape architecture emerged as a recognized design practice. → p. 57 G

The visitor returns to the river's edge, where she encounters the last concave slope in the garden that rises to the north-facing Praeneste Arcade, followed in turn by the terrace with the Dying Gladiator statue. The thick evergreen and deciduous woodland that lines the valley accentuates the airflow that derives from a combination of the humidity generated by the River Cherwell and the heat stored on its concave slope. This buoyant

D Temple of Echo (Townsend's building)

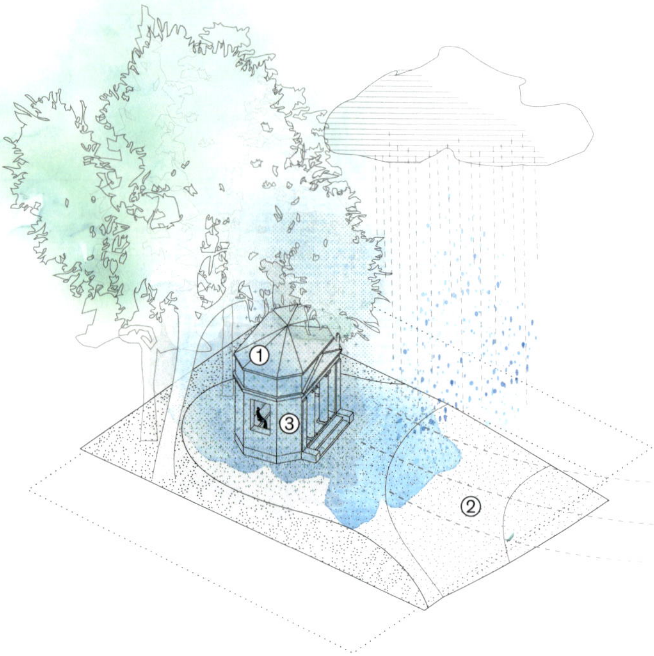

Thermodynamic performance:
① Rain shelter (architectural folly): shelters visitors during inclement weather
② Free convection / anabatic: folly captures upslope breezes (warm air on soil rises and drags cold air from the river in the morning until afternoon)
③ Thermal mass / radiant cooling: shaded surface of folly

E Third concave slope

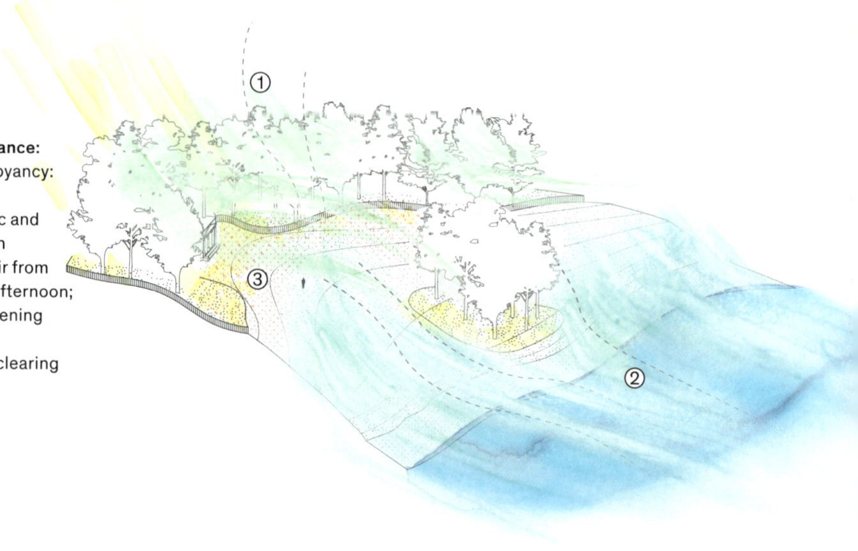

Thermodynamic performance:
① Free convection / free buoyancy: warm air lifts in clearing
② Free convection / anabatic and katabatic flow: warm air on soil rises and drags cold air from river in the morning until afternoon; process reverses in the evening
③ Solar radiation (exposed): heated ground surface in clearing

F Venus Vale

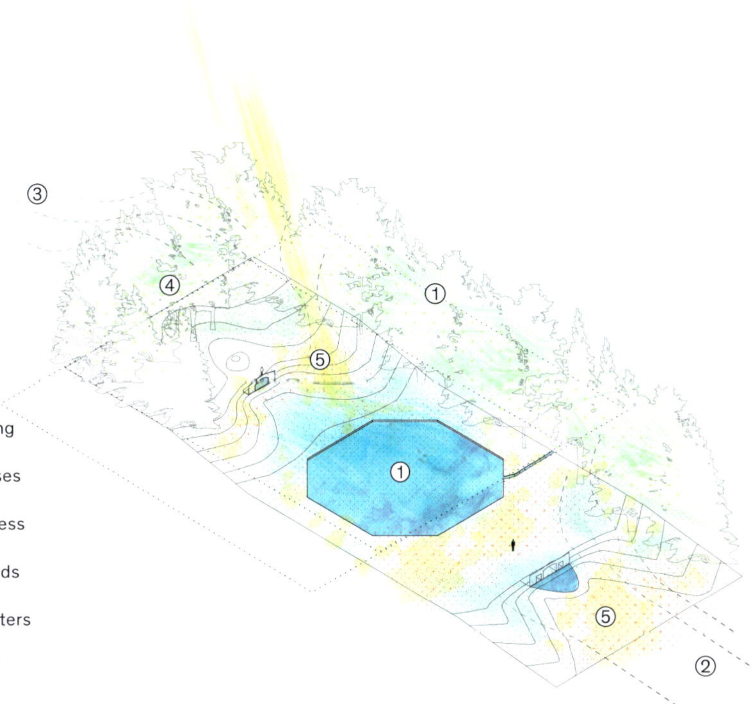

Thermodynamic performance:

1) Evaporative cooling / isothermal evaporation: water surface and thick vegetation bordering clearing
2) Free convection / anabatic and katabatic flow: warm air on soil rises and drags cold air from river in the morning until afternoon; process reverses in the evening
3) Forced convection: prevailing winds from south
4) Wind deflection: tree canopy shelters against winds
5) Solar radiation (exposed): ground and water surface in clearing

G Elm Walk

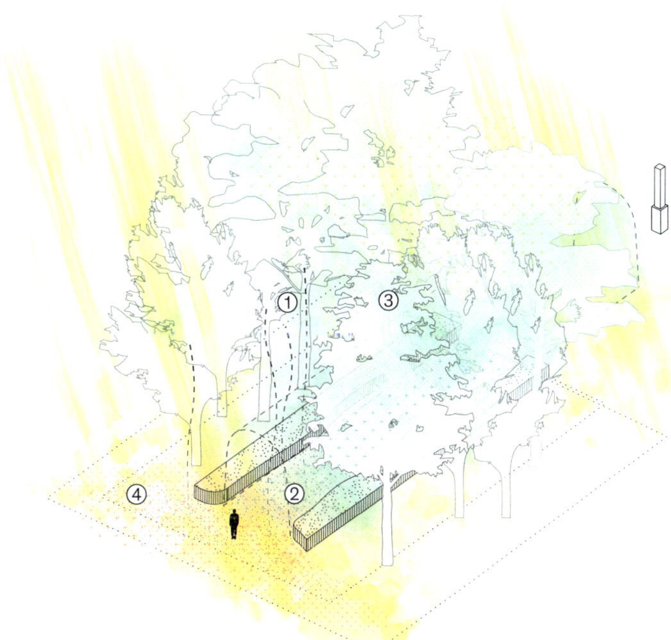

Thermodynamic performance:

1) Free convection: humid air rises
2) Radiant cooling: shaded surfaces and ground from tree canopy
3) Evaporative cooling / isothermal evaporation: tree canopy
4) Solar radiation (reduced): thick tree canopy creates dappled light

From Elm Walk to the Praeneste Arcade

From the Praeneste Arcade to the Cherwell River

upward movement of air interacts with the dominant southwest winds, which are in turn captured in the niches of the Praeneste Arcade. A significant low pressure at the base of the arcade accentuates this upward airflow, while its interior is cold, with an earthy scent that derives from its northeastern aspect and its integration into the topography. The designation "Praeneste" may refer to these specific airflow and thermal phenomena. John Dixon Hunt highlights a parallel between the topographical positioning of the Praeneste Arcade at Rousham and that of the ancient Greek temple of Fortuna Primigenia in Praeneste, Italy. As Hunt notes, Addison remarked that "Palaestrina stands very high, like most other towns in Italy, for the advantage of the cool breezes, for which reason Virgil calls it *Altum,* and Horace *Frigidum Praeneste.* Statius calls it *Praeneste Sacrum,* because of the famous temple of Fortune that stood in it."[45] The translation of such admired Italian structures to the English context was prompted by the belief in the physical existence of the imagination. Just as this notion of translation implied the identification of Kent's arcade with its historic antecedent, so the creative mind would open up such examples to a stream of conceptual possibilities and reinterpretations. Rather than simply a viewing platform or a feature to be seen from the approach, Kent's arcade operates as a *Frigidarium* in its spatial performance. Thus, it not only bridges the valley overlooking the River Cherwell but also captures airflow rising from the riverbed to accentuate its cooling effect. Aware of the scent of wet soil, the visitor would look to the far rolling hills and the meteorological phenomena that signal the sublime existence of a larger world beyond the immediate boundaries of the physical and physiological, emotional and sensorial realms. ← p. 51 Ⓐ

Leaving the Praeneste Arch and the last concave slope in the circuit, the visitor would turn into another "Serpentine Gravel Walk" that passes through a theater that was designed by Charles Bridgeman and altered by Kent. The route continues through sequence of loose and dense woodlands, where she again encounters the currents of air rising from the river. Further along this path is "a large nich, that makes a very handsom Garden Seat, where you set down, and view the River, and Garden, from one end to the other." As MacClary describes it, the route then proceeds through dense woodlands to an "Egyptian pyrimade," the last of Kent's follies, also oriented to the north and where one "goe in and set down."[46] From this vantage point, the visitor would look down the meadow toward the river and recall the sensations she had experienced previously. MacClary's description ends here, where another serpentine gravel walk brings the visitor to an irregularly clipped box hedge that marks the east side of the house and conceals the final stretch of the walk—the Bowling Green and the Grand Slope—the spot where the circuit began.

In foregrounding the atmospheric impetuses behind Kent's design for the garden at Rousham, this analysis draws attention to the importance of the body as a reactive self—the moving "barometer" that Addison cited in his *Spectator* chronicle. The sensations and imaginative capabilities of this sensible audience were stirred in turn by the power of England's weather vagaries. As the art historian Nikolaus Pevsner reminds us, "any account of landscape gardening must start from the English climate."[47]

Conclusion

Novel and exhilarating, Kent's garden at Rousham provides an experience for all the senses, fully supporting eighteenth-century ideas of flux and variability. It emerged in the context of the newfound sensible body, for which meteorological phenomena were both sensory material and "fabric" for heightened stimuli. While the garden is often discussed as a choreographed sequence of paths and vantage points, its form derives equally from a consideration of the relationships between its spatial qualities and the potential for higher levels of physiological response to its alternately cool, warm, wet, dark, bright, sheltered, aromatic, and windswept zones. The episodic rhythms of ever-changing meteorological appearances and effects are integral to Kent's spatial script, in which varied sequences of light and darkness, evergreen corridors, scented pathways, temperature differences, water sprays, wind exposure, and the shelter afforded by architectural follies artfully immerse the visitor in the garden's spatial circuits.

Kent's innovation in his garden at Rousham is in transcending the representational aspects of the picturesque garden by focusing on its sensory dimension, using fluctuating meteorological phenomena as design media. The era's scientific discourse on the nerves provided a way of articulating how weather and its meteorological manifestations alter inner states of mind, stirring the creative imagination and enhancing delight. Exercising these internal states through external stimuli was presumed to affect the activity of the nerves, resulting in a refinement of the mind. Kent's new design language also benefited from the possibilities associated with the discovery of blood circulation. Encouraging constant motion through its dynamic environments, the design supports the axiom that if blood flows in the body, then the same body requires movement to support such flux. From both perspectives, the act of walking and the associated external stimuli nurture the body while stirring the mind to higher imaginative states. By placing the visitor in the very midst of this meteorological activity, Kent created an interactive "theater" of landscape: a sequence of living scenes of meteorological amplifications directed to the newly revealed *sensible* body in a state of constant mental and physical engagement with the world. Like Kubrick, Kent transformed his audience into an active and reactive participant in the scene. At Rousham, the visitor responds to the garden's contrived atmospheric states in the space of her imagination.

1 Joseph Addison, "The Spectator 281," January 22, 1711-1712 [sic], *The Spectator with Notes and a General Index: The Eight Volumes comprised in One* (Philadelphia: Hickman & Hazzard, 1822), 333.

2 Oxford architect William Townsend designed the house at Rousham, a bowling green and a raised terrace, while Kent was responsible for extensions to the house and the stable block, as well as major revisions to Bridgeman's garden layout. See Gerhard Bissell, "Rousham inside and out," *Studies in the History of Gardens & Designed Landscapes* 29, no. 1–2 (2009): 33–43.

3 John Dixon Hunt, email to author, 05/01/2019.

4 Alexander Pope to Edward Blount, June 2, 1725, letter XIV, "A Description of a Grotto," *The Works of Alexander Pope Esq: Volume VII* (Dublin: George Faulkner, 1753), 27.

5 George S. Rousseau, *Nervous Acts: Essays on Literature, Culture and Sensibility* (New York: Palgrave Macmillan, 2004), 90.

6 James O'Connor, "Thomas Willis and the background to Cerebri Anatome," *Journal of the Royal Society of Medicine* 96, no. 3 (March 2003): 139–43, here 140. See Thomas Willis, *The Anatomy of the Brain and Nerves*, William Feindel, ed., Samuel Pordage, trans. of *Cerebri Anatome, cui accessit Nervorum descriptio et usus* (Montreal: McGill University Press, 1965).

7 John Locke and Alexander Fraser, *An Essay Concerning Human Understanding*, Vol. 1 (Oxford: Clarendon Press, 1894), 48.

8 Rousseau, *Nervous Acts* (2004), 86.

9 Joseph Addison, "The Spectator 387," May 24, 1712, *The Spectator with Notes* (1822), 469.

10 Christopher Lawrence, "The Nervous System and Society in the Scottish Enlightenment," in *Natural Order: Historical Studies of Scientific Culture*, Barry Barnes and Steven Shapin, eds. (Beverly Hills: Sage Publications, 1979), 24.

11 See William Harvey, *On the Motion of the Heart and Blood in Animals* [1628] (Chicago: H. Regnery, 1962).

12 George Cheyne, *An Essay of Health and Long Life* (London: G. Strahan and J. Leake, 1724), 94.

13 Joseph Addison, "The Spectator 543," November 22, 1712, *The Spectator with Notes* (1822), 651.

14 John Arbuthnot, *An Essay Concerning the Effects of Air on Human Bodies* (London: J. Tonson, 1751), vi. See Marjorie Hope Nicolson and G. S Rousseau, *"This Long Disease, My Life:" Alexander Pope and the Sciences* (Princeton: Princeton University Press, 1968).

15 See Mathew J. Owens et al., "The Maunder minimum and the Little Ice Age: an update from recent reconstructions and climate simulations," *Journal of Space Weather and Space Climate* 7, A33 (January 2017).

16 Mark Laird, *A Natural History of English Gardening, 1650–1800* (New Haven: Yale University Press, 2015), 43.

17 John Evelyn, *The Diary of John Evelyn*, Guy de la Bédoyère, ed. (Woodbridge, UK, and Rochester, N.Y.: Boydell Press, 1995), 266.

18 John Evelyn, *Fumifugium: Or, the Inconvenience of the Aer, and Smoake of London Dissipated. Together with Some Remedies Humbly* Proposed [1661] (London: B. White, 1772), 22.

19 John Dixon Hunt, *William Kent: Landscape Garden Designer* (London: Zwemmer, 1987), 37.

20 Samuel Johnson, *The Lives of the Most Eminent English Poets: with Critical Observations on Their Works* (Edinburgh: J. Sawers, 1819), 104.

21 Joseph Addison, "The Spectator 420" ["The Pleasures of the Imagination"], July 2, 1712, *The Spectator with Notes* (1822), 506.
22 Addison, "The Spectator 440," July 25, 1712, Ibid., 529.
23 Alexander Pope, *The Works of Alexander Pope*, New Edition, Vol. 1, John Wilson Croker, ed. (London: John Murray, 1871), 314.
24 George Sherburn, "Pope and 'The Great Shew of Nature,'" in Richard Foster Jones et al., *The Seventeenth Century: Studies in the History of English Thought and Literature from Bacon to Pope* (Stanford, CA: Stanford University Press, 1951), 306–15, here 306.
25 Alexander Pope, "Guardian #169" (September 24, 1713), in Alexander Chalmers, *The British Essayists: with Prefaces, Historical and Biographical* (Boston: Little, Brown, 1866), 237.
26 The first essay to establish the aesthetic concept of the picturesque was Sir Uvedale Price, "Essay on the Picturesque" (1790). An earlier document defining picturesque beauty as a visual quality is William Gilpin's anonymously published paper, "A dialogue upon the gardens of the Right Honourable the Lord Viscount Cobham, at Stow in Buckinghamshire" (1748). See John Dixon Hunt, *The Picturesque Garden in Europe* (London: Thames and Hudson, 2002).
27 Alexander Pope, "Guardian #173," September 29, 1713, in Alexander Chalmers, *The British Essayists: with Prefaces, Historical and Biographical* (Boston: Little, Brown, 1866), 261. See Anthony Ashley-Cooper, 3rd Earl of Shaftesbury, *The Moralists: a philosophical rhapsody* (London: John Wyat, 1709), 205.
28 See John Wilkins, *The Discovery of a World in the Moone* [1638] (Delmar, NY: Scholars' Facsimiles and Reprints, 1973).
29 G. S. Rousseau, *Nervous Act: Essays on literature culture, and sensibility* (Basingstoke: Palgrave Macmillan, 2004), 16–17.
30 Joseph Addison, *The Tatler* Vol. III (January 13, 1709–10 [sic]), George A. Aitken, ed. (London: Duckworth & Co, 1899), 32–33.
31 Mavis Batey, "The Way to View Rousham by Kent's Gardener," *Garden History* 11, no. 2 (1983): 125–32, here, 132. The date of this letter has been recently been reassigned to approximately ten years later. See Hal Moggridge, "Notes on Kent's Garden at Rousham," *The Journal of Garden History* 6, no. 3 (1986): 187–226.
32 Batey, "The Way to View Rousham" (1983): 127.
33 Ibid., 128.
34 Ibid., 128.
35 See John Dixon Hunt, "Folly in the Garden," *The Hopkins Review* 1, no. 2 (2008): 227–62, here 243.
36 Kent note of January 30, 1720, cited in John Dixon Hunt, *William Kent: Landscape Garden Designer: an Assessment and Catalogue of His Designs* (London: Zwemmer, 1987), 51.
37 Alexander Pope, "The Temple of Fame," *The Works of Alexander Pope, Esq. in Verse and Prose: with a Selection of Explanatory Notes, and the Account of His Life by Dr. Johnson*, Vol. II (London: Nichols and Son, 1812): 89-109, here 94. David Coffin explained the orientation of follies relative to their style: "Gothic toward the north, Egyptian at the east, and ancient Roman at the south." David Coffin, "The Elysian Fields of Rousham," *Proceedings of the American Philosophical Society* 130 (1986): 406–23, here 420.
38 Batey, "The Way to View Rousham" (1983): 128.
39 Ibid., 129.
40 Ibid. See Michel Baridon, "Ruins as a mental construct," *Journal of Garden History* 5, no. 1 (1985): 84–96.
41 Robert Castell, *The Villas of the Ancients Illustrated* (London: R. Castell, 1728), 116.
42 Hunt, *William Kent, Landscape Garden Designer* (1987), 23–24.
43 Batey, "The Way to View Rousham" (1983): 129.
44 William Gilpin, *Observations, Relative Chiefly to Picturesque Beauty, Made in the Year 1772, on Several Parts of England* (London: R. Blamire, 1786), 165.
45 Hunt, *William Kent, Landscape Garden Designer* (1987), 84. See Joseph Addison, *The Works of the Right Honourable Joseph Addison*, Vol. II (London: George Bell and Sons, 1891), 308.
46 Batey, "The Way to View Rousham" (1983): 130.
47 Nikolaus Pevsner, *The Englishness of English Art* (London: The Architectural Press, 1956), 173.

Rousham House and the Paddock

Vegetated hedge on the eastern side of the Bowling Green

e the vegetated hedge

Walled garden and fruit wall

From the “little Building” looking at the “Large Octogon Basson”

Elm Walk, view to Praeneste Arcade

Accompanying project:

VILLA D'ESTE, c. 1549

Pirro Ligorio: Architect, landscape designer, antiquarian
Tivoli, Italy

- A Enclosed passageway (cryptoporticus) on lower level of the palace
- B Cardinal's Walk
- C Loggia of Pandora in the Cardinal's Walk
- D Oval Fountain and cryptoporticus
- E Terrace of the Hundred Fountains
- F Stairs of the Bubbling Fountains
- G Fountain of the Organ above Neptune Fountain
- H Grotto of the Sybil under Fountain of the Organ
- I Humid Terrace and observation turret atop the Neptune Fountain

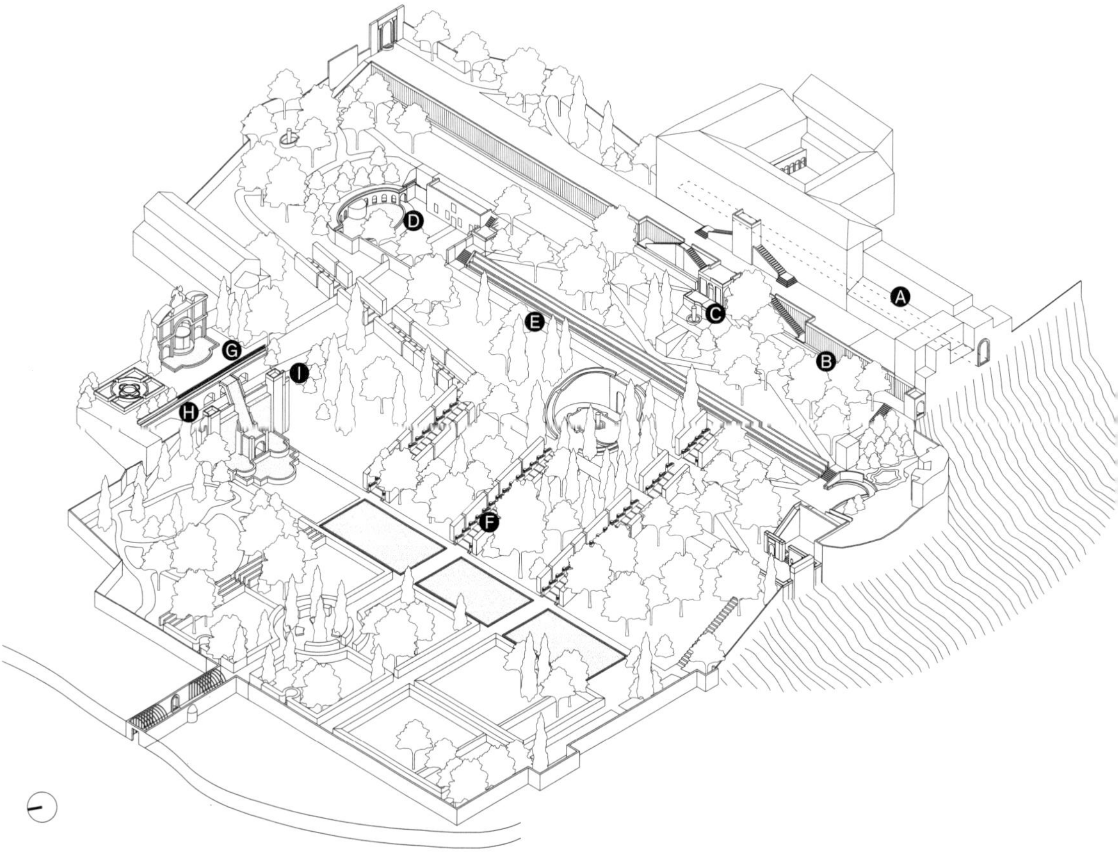

Like Rousham Garden, Pirro Ligorio's garden at the Villa D'Este in Tivoli comprises a meteorological journey that is intensified by episodic microclimatic performances. The steeply sloping hillside garden incorporates exuberant water features, dense tree canopies, humid grottoes, breezy passageways, and wet walls—each with a particular role in eliciting this journey. Sequential climatic moments, memorable in their capacity to cool and delight the visitors during Tivoli's unhospitable hot and dry summer days, are central to the villa's spatial identity.

A Enclosed passageway (cryptoporticus) on lower level of the palace

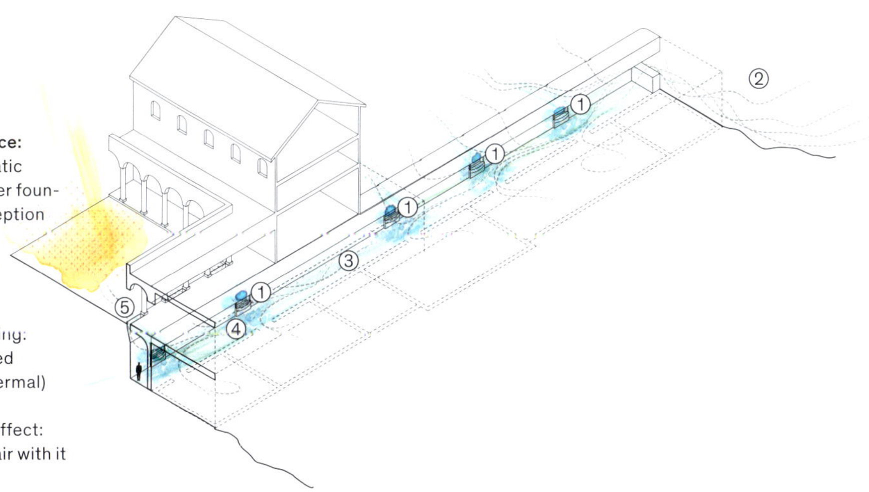

Thermodynamic performance:

① Evaporative cooling / adiabatic evaporation: spray from water fountains (sound enhances perception of cooling)

② Forced convection: opening at end of cryptoporticus captures prevailing winds

③ Thermal mass / radiant cooling: shaded cryptoporticus tucked in terrain stores cold (geothermal)

④ Solar radiation (reduced)

⑤ Free convection / chimney effect: hot air rises and drags cold air with it

B Cardinal's Walk

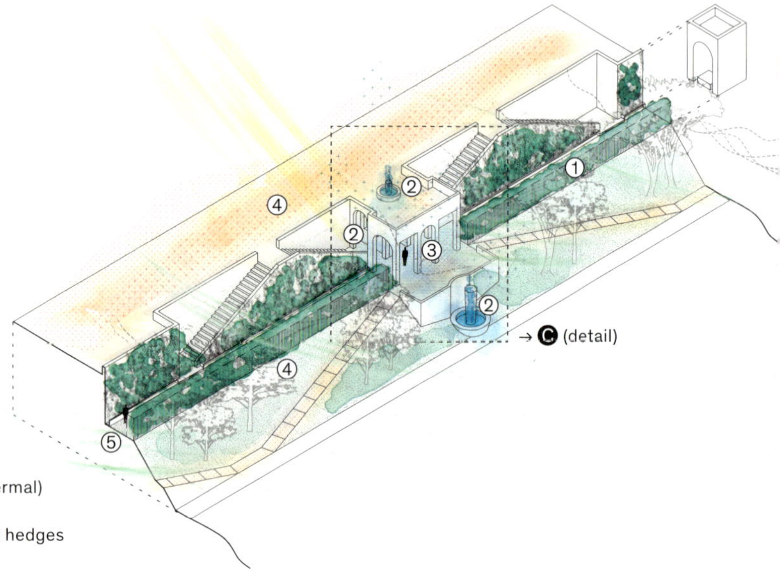

Thermodynamic performance:
① Evaporative cooling / isothermal evaporation: vegetation
② Evaporative cooling / adiabatic evaporation: spray from water fountains (sound enhances perception of cooling)
③ Thermal mass / radiant cooling: shaded surfaces and structure tucked in terrain store cold (geothermal)
④ Solar radiation (exposed)
⑤ Solar radiation (reduced): walls and hedges
⑥ Forced convection: portico at end of walk captures prevailing winds

C Loggia of Pandora in the Cardinal's Walk

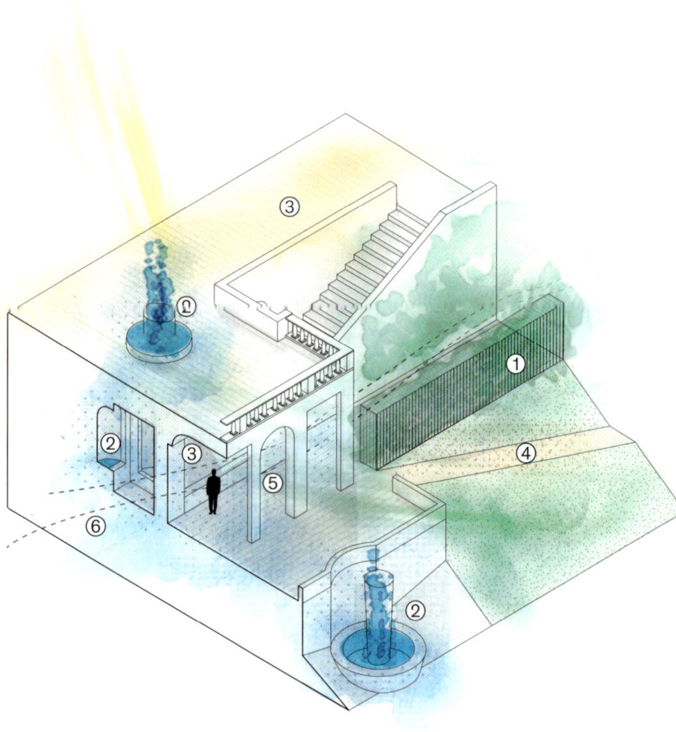

Thermodynamic performance:
① Evaporative cooling / isothermal evaporation: grassy surface and hedge
② Evaporative cooling / adiabatic evaporation: spray from water fountains (sound enhances perception of cooling)
③ Thermal mass / radiant cooling: shaded room with thick walls tucked in terrain stores cold (geothermal)
④ Solar radiation (exposed)
⑤ Solar radiation (reduced): walls
⑥ Forced convection: portico at end of walk captures prevailing winds

D Oval Fountain and cryptoporticus

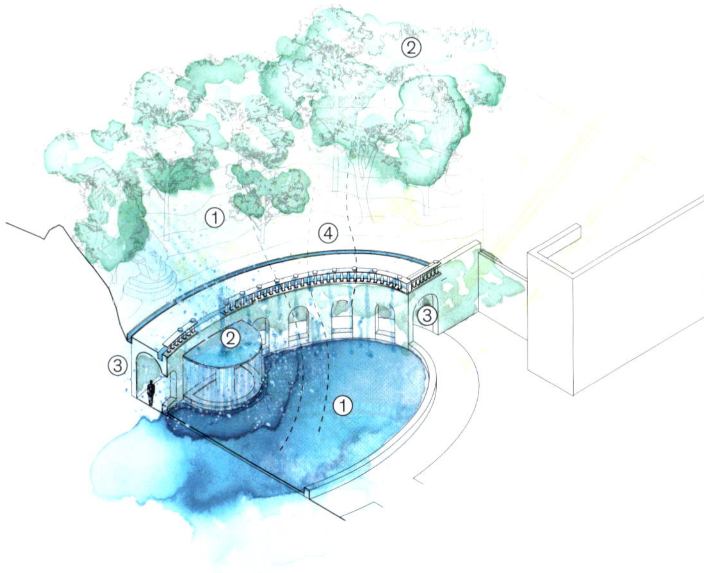

Thermodynamic performance:
) Evaporative cooling / isothermal evaporation: water surface, tree canopy, and grassy surface
) Evaporative cooling / adiabatic evaporation: spray from water fountain (sound enhances perception of cooling)
) Thermal mass / radiant cooling: shaded cryptoporticus tucked in terrain stores cold (geothermal)
) Free convection: humid air rises, promoted by fountain

E Terrace of the Hundred Fountains

→ p. 337

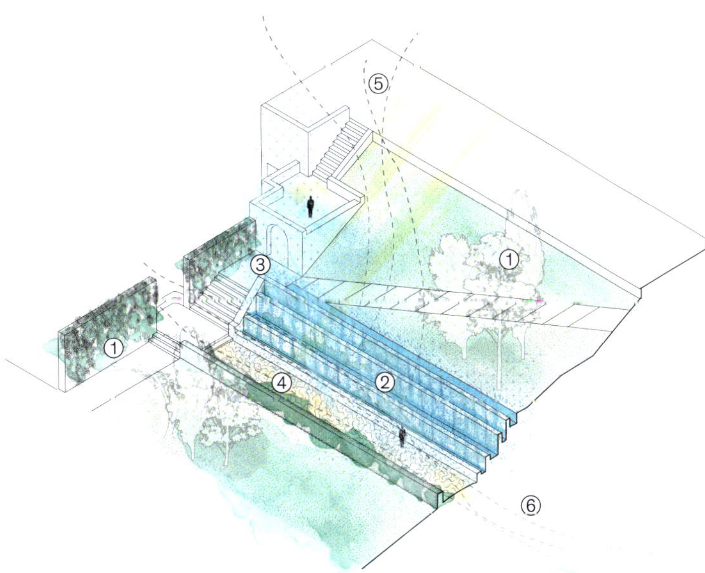

Thermodynamic performance:
) Evaporative cooling / isothermal evaporation: grassy surface, tree canopy, hedges, and vines
) Evaporative cooling / adiabatic evaporation: spray from water fountains (sound enhances perception of cooling)
) Solar radiation (reduced)
) Solar radiation (exposed)
) Free convection: hot air rises
) Forced convection: walkway captures prevailing winds

F Stairs of the Bubbling Fountains

Thermodynamic performance:
① Evaporative cooling / isothermal evaporation: grassy surface, tree canopy, and side hedges
② Evaporative cooling / adiabatic evaporation: water descending and splashing in channel (sound enhances perception of cooling)
③ Solar radiation (reduced)

G Fountain of the Organ above Neptune Fountain

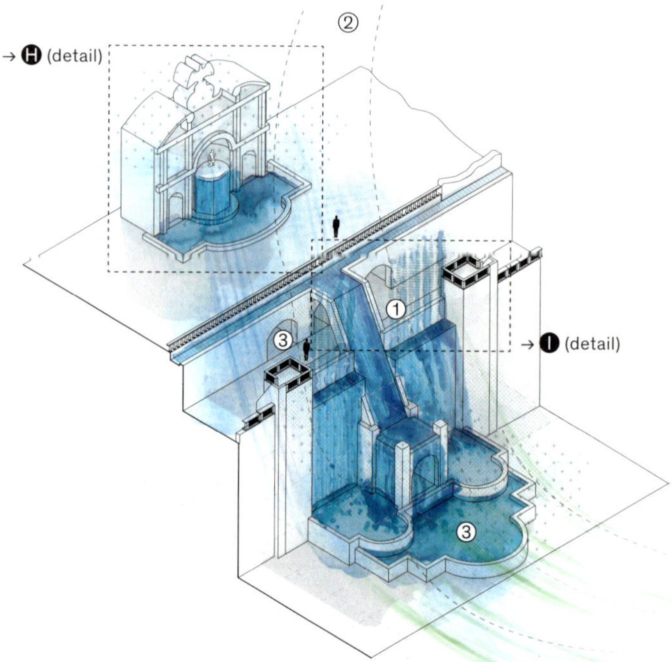

Thermodynamic performance:
① Evaporative cooling / adiabatic evaporation: spray from water fountains (sound of water enhances perception of cooling)
② Free convection: humid air rises, promoted by fountains
③ Radiant cooling: shaded surfaces (walls and water)

H Grotto of the Sybil under Fountain of the Organ

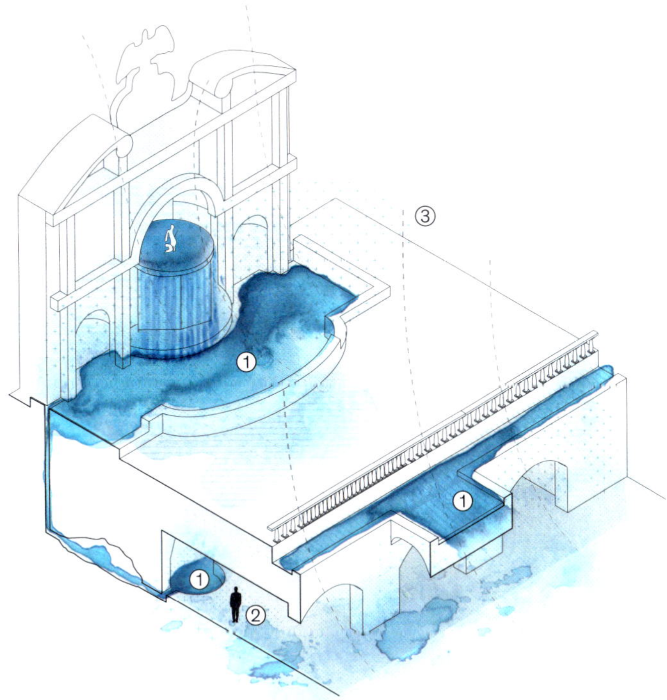

Thermodynamic performance:

1) Evaporative cooling / adiabatic evaporation: spray from water fountains (sound enhances perception of cooling)
2) Thermal mass / radiant cooling: shaded room tucked in terrain stores cold (geothermal)
3) Free convection: humid air rises, promoted by fountains

I Humid Terrace and observation turret atop the Neptune Fountain

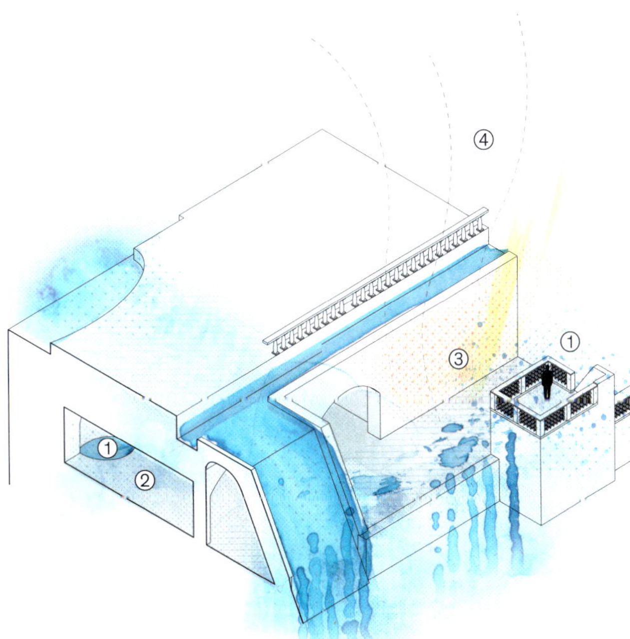

Thermodynamic performance:

1) Evaporative cooling / adiabatic evaporation: spray from water fountains (sound enhances perception of cooling)
2) Thermal mass / radiant cooling: shaded room tucked in terrain stores cold (geothermal)
3) Thermal mass / radiant heating: wall stores heat and releases it at night
4) Free convection: humid air rises, promoted by fountains, and drags cold air from tucked in Grotto of the Sybil

Viewing terrace looking northwest to the garden

From the Neptune Fountain to the Fish Ponds

Pond

Courtyard of the Oval Fountain

tune Fountain from the level of the Fish Ponds

Stairs of the Bubbling Fountains leading to the Fountain of the Dragons

Hundred Fountains

Drinking fountain in the Loggia of Pandora (in the Cardinal's Walk)

Stairs to the Fountain of the Dragons

Cryptoporticus of the Oval Fountain

Atmosphere as Thermal Thre

hold

CHANDIGARH, 1951–1966

Le Corbusier: Architect, urban designer, painter
(with Pierre Jeanneret, Jane B. Drew, and E. Maxwell Fry)
Chandigarh, India

Accompanying projects:

ORTEGA HOUSE AND GARDEN, 1943

THE GARDENS OF EL PEDREGAL RESIDENTIAL SUBDIVISION, 1947–1962

LAS ARBOLEDAS RESIDENTIAL SUBDIVISION, 1958–1961

LOS CLUBES RESIDENTIAL SUBDIVISION, 1963–1964

Luis Barragán: Architect and civil engineer
Mexico City, Mexico

The proposition of *Atmosphere as Thermal Threshold* recognizes the microclimatic potential of the spatial boundary between indoors and outdoors—the site of exchange between the private and public domains that lies at the disciplinary intersection of architecture and landscape architecture. The capacity for this boundary to both ameliorate climatic excesses and provide zones with varied thermal characteristics has economic, health, and civic significance. This means more energy-efficient buildings, increased users exposure to natural environments, and more comfortable outdoor places for the community to gather and interact. Recognized typologies of such spatial boundaries include verandahs, courtyards, patios, porticos, arcades, terraces, passageways, arbors, pergolas, loggias, brises-soleil (sun-breakers), and open pavilions. In these thresholds, landscape extends to the architectural boundary and vice versa. Gradients of shade and exposure to breezes ameliorate heat loads at the building scale and reduce thermal stress in the psychophysiological domain. These thresholds provide shelter against humidity, solar radiation, rain, or snow, just as the microclimatic conditions they create promote individual relaxation and civic interaction. Owing in part to the simplicity of their thermal purposes, these thresholds promote sensations of comfort, safety, delight, retreat, and nourishment. They are accordingly central to the experience of space and constitute sites of disciplinary reinterpretation.

Chandigarh, the new capital for the States of Punjab and Haryana in India, developed by Le Corbusier and his design team of Pierre Jeanneret, Jane Drew, and E. Maxwell Fry, is a paradigmatic example of the potential of such threshold spaces at the scale of the city as well as the building. The assimilation of these in-between spaces was vital to ameliorating the extreme meteorological conditions of the Punjab, with its temperatures ranging between 35 degrees and 40 degrees Celsius (95–104 degrees Fahrenheit) from March to May, followed by the humid monsoon season from June to October. Aware of the economic and technical constraints on addressing such needs, Le Corbusier drew upon local vernacular building traditions, declaring the verandah to be the "architectural answer" to the region's climatic challenges.[1] The potential for the verandah to both negotiate climatic events and host civic life led him to thicken his architectural membranes and integrate landscape as a bioclimatic medium. Working closely with the climate control specialist and engineer André Missenard and the horticulturalist Dr. M. S. Randhawa, Le Corbusier found a technical rationale for "sculpting" the physical and sensual capacities of climate. He accordingly expanded his architectural repertoire not only to ameliorate the physical environment but also to honor weather as a creative force in the daily life of the community.

To thicken these thresholds, Le Corbusier included detached roofs, parasols, sleeping terraces, projecting shades, and supersize scuppers on his buildings, as well as landscape elements such as rills, ponds, reflecting pools, canals, groves, follies, green belts, artificial hills, and water basins—all in service to spiritual and physiological nourishment.

Influenced both by Le Corbusier and by the Islamic gardens of the Alhambra in Spain, the work of the Mexican architect Luis Barragán reflects a similar interest in the microclimatic and affective potential of spatial thresholds. Dedicated to the play of shadows and sunlight on solid and liquid volumes, Barragán created "gardens for the clouds," as Emilio Ambasz evocatively observes.[2] Lacking in extreme ranges of temperature and humidity, Mexico City has a climate that is mild, yet incandescently sunny and dry. To integrate bioclimatic objectives in his architecture, Barragán produced a series of thresholds that expand domestic spaces into the outdoors through landscape elements such as walled enclosures, courtyards, vegetated trellises, semi-covered terraces, water features, and patios that serve as comfortable spaces for eating, relaxing, and luxuriating amid the vagaries of weather. As Keith Eggener notes, "The colors, sounds, smells, light, and atmospheric conditions of the world beyond the house entered it through the mediating agency of the patio."[3] This thickening of the architectural membrane filters the sun's burning luminosity and affords shelter from strong winds and short-term heavy rains. In the public domains of his residential subdivisions of El Pedregal, Los Clubes, and Las Arboledas, Barragán created a series of threshold zones along the network of streets and parks, including vegetated walls, cold and shaded retreats, water channels, and fountains where water splashes from atop brightly painted walls. Humidifying the air, providing aroma, and creating areas for civic cooling, these intermediary zones offer both spiritual and physiological delight. The adiabatic cooling produced by the wind in combination with the continual water spray—a transitional state between liquid and vapor—establishes a system of zones for thermal amelioration in the thin, dry atmosphere of Mexico City, while the persistent sound of splashing moderates the street noise to affect a sense of refuge in these designed landscapes.

1 Le Corbusier, Sketchbook "Album Punjab Simla I," 1951, FLC W1-5-33.
2 Emilio Ambasz, *The Architecture of Luis Barragán* (New York: Museum of Modern Art, 1976), 73.
3 Keith Eggener, "Postwar Modernism in Mexico: Luis Barragán's Jardines Del Pedregal and the International Discourse on Architecture and Place," *Journal of the Society of Architectural Historians* 58, no. 2 (June 1999): 122–45, here 129.

CHANDIGARH, 1951–1966

Le Corbusier: Architect, urban designer, painter
(with Pierre Jeanneret, Jane B. Drew, and E. Maxwell Fry)
Chandigarh, India

- A "Leisure Valley" public park
- B Government housing, Sector 23, by Maxwell Fry
- C Government housing (Peon's House), Sector 22, by Pierre Jeanneret
- D V4 (bazaar street) and commercial strip
- E Vertical V3 (sector-defining street) tunnel of shade
- F V6 neighborhood inner access lane
- G Assembly building
- H The Open Hand
- I Lake Sukhna promenade
- J Lake Sukhna

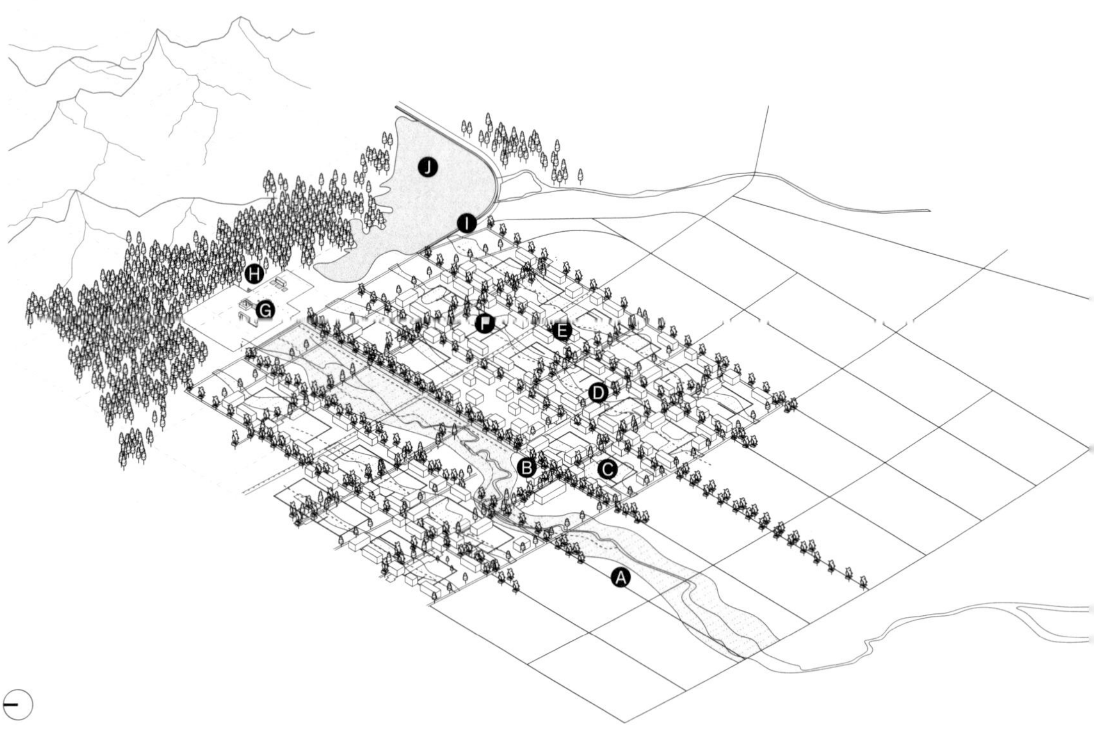

Chandigarh: On Breathing, Landscape, and Bioclimatic Space

Our purpose is to say: to new times, new times. It's not just about amenities anymore. We must designate the objective: these amenities are intended for men! The human factor is introduced into the equation!

The human?

One biology

One psychology.

Who will plan for this biology and psychology?

... This architecture and this urbanism are and remain one—and are but one—a single person.

—Le Corbusier, 1960[1]

The idea of cities as biological entities abounds in Le Corbusier's oeuvre. In *Creation Is a Patient Search* (1960), for example, he paired illustrations of the respiratory system (heart, lung, and pulmonary tissue), digestive organs, and skin membranes with those of city sections, declaring: "A plan arranges *organs* in order, thus creating *an organism* or *organisms* ... BIOLOGY! The great new word in architecture and planning."[2] Le Corbusier's intersection of architecture, the body, and biology, while often examined in terms of its anthropomorphic and symbolic associations, induces a systematic set of correspondences between the built environment and the well-being of humankind in which landscape and climate emerge as essential to the design enterprise. These correspondences are particularly poignant at Chandigarh, his new capital for the states of Punjab and Haryana, India. In a letter of December 1951 to the project's administrative manager, Prem Nath Thapar, Le Corbusier noted: "My conviction is that India must treat the modern architectural form according to its sun, hygrometry and wind regulations." In response to the region's extreme climate, he framed the "problem of breathing" as a biological vulnerability.[3]

In accepting the imperative of "breathing" as foundational to his design process, Le Corbusier indicated his awareness of the climate's affordances—biological, cultural, and spiritual—and its effects on human psychophysiological well-being. With this project he expanded his concept of the architectural membrane to engage a new biotechnical scope that includes landscape as a bioclimatic medium. To reflect his design process, he established two new grids associated with the Congrès Internationaux d'Architecture Moderne (CIAM): *la grille climatique* (climatic grid) and *la grille d'arborization* (tree-planting grid). With the support of engineer André Missenard and the city's first chief commissioner, the horticulturalist Dr. Mohinder Singh Randhawa, Le Corbusier found a technical rationale to express his new design sensibility and a spatial repertoire appropriate to such an enterprise. Rather than resorting to anthropomorphic associations or symbolic values, he embraced an understanding of the human body as a biological entity conditioned by its milieu, which led him to a new disciplinary synthesis, one that is worthy of scrutiny in light of today's heightened alertness to climate.

I. Breathing: An urban prompt

Breathing is a recurrent metaphor in Le Corbusier's evolving design methodology. In his urban proposal *La Ville Radieuse* of 1933, he invoked breathing as a therapeutic response to the pathological conditions of nineteenth-century cities, proclaiming "To live! To Breathe." This architectural and urbanistic response implied the release of the urban dweller from her confinement "in an envelope of solid materials belonging to a static system" to accommodate her modern lifestyle, centered on experiencing the qualitative conditions of the outdoors. As he elaborated: "The basic pleasures, by which I mean sun, greenery and space, penetrate into the uttermost depths of our physiological and psychological being."[4] Despite the promise of living among these fluctuating external states, Le Corbusier initially centered his technical attention on developing controlled atmospheres supported by mechanical means: "one single building for all nations and climates, the house with *respiration exacte*," with a constant air temperature of 18 degrees Celsius and supported by an "arterial system."[5] Urban living replete with sun, space, and greenery thus entailed an amplified exposure to sunlight inside a manufactured atmosphere—*l'air exact*—contained within all-glass façades—*murs neutralisant.* "The invention?" Le Corbusier explained, "the discovery that if architecture follows certain paths, it can provide city dwellers with good, true God-given air, for the salvation of their lungs." The realization that urban environments were dusty and unhealthy prompted internalized climates controlled by what Le Corbusier playfully called "machines of childish simplicity," such as filters, humidifiers, and disinfectors, intended to cultivate the physiological body with medical precision—the *Corps Nouveau* of the new era, as endorsed by his doctor, Pierre-André-Eugène Winter (1891–1952).[6] At this stage in Le Corbusier's career, landscape and the natural elements of sunlight and buoyant air, while foundational to the modern zeitgeist, were borrowed, mediated, or accessed indirectly.

Within thirty years, however, Le Corbusier would expand these propositions to include a wider range of climatic parameters for the design of Chandigarh—where, as his collaborators Jane Drew and Maxwell Fry explained, one could find six climates: "Cold, dust, rain, wind, wet or dry heat."[7] In an early letter to his design team in India, Le Corbusier declared that the "urbanistic problem of Chandigarh has been solved on doctrinal bases so obvious and unquestionable that the drawings are clear, harmonious and real." The urbanistic problem in question concerns "the breathing problem," he elaborated, conditioned by the meteorological parameters of "sun, shade, winds, hygrometry, temperature."[8] What implications does breathing have for the design work relative to Chandigarh's extreme climatic conditions? In foregrounding Le Corbusier's alertness to the biological effects of climate on psychophysiological well-being, this essay probes the design integration of landscape as a bioclimatic medium at both an urban and an architectural scale.

During the economic decline of the early 1930s, the architectural scope for breathing within sealed building envelopes underwent limited development in Le Corbusier's work. The presumed need for controlled environments augmented budgets for mechanized ventilation, while solar exposure in building interiors resulted in increased heat gain, making healthful breathing not only expensive but also physiologically challenging. With his growing attentiveness to economic limitations and his reduced access to new commissions, Le Corbusier initiated a serious of transatlantic travels to deliver public lectures in nontemperate zones.[9] During visits to South America and North Africa, he began to recognize the potential for vernacular design techniques to address hostile environments and for the architectural boundary to affect an interplay between interior and external atmospheres in order to engage a broader set of sensations: aural, thermal, kinesthetic, and olfactory. By 1933, Le Corbusier expressed a new intellectual affiliation with the "natural order" of things: "I can keep a large range of relations in space by means of this basic binomial: man and nature." But what did Le Corbusier mean by "relations in space" between humankind and nature?

During his travels in North African cities and deserts, Le Corbusier drew extensively in his sketchbooks, evocatively describing spatial conditions where daily life occurs: amid gutters, filtering walls, the coolness and quiet of private dwellings, liminal zones of luminous gradients, luscious greenery of gardens, and in villages surrounded by "palm groves and stuffed with all the trees of paradise on earth."[10] In these drawings architectural space emerges as an environment—an interplay of various conditions beyond the customized and controlled settings of his earlier *respiration exacte.* His published travelogue, "Rétours … ou l'enseignement du voyage," describes cities that accommodate their residents to seasonal flux. In the oasis of Algeria's capital city of Ghardaïa, for example, he observed that the summer compounds are protected and sheltered in palm groves, and the winter housing lies in the hills, exposed to the sunlight—"a masterpiece," he concluded.[11] In the M'Zab Saharan region, Le Corbusier discovered living environments in which landscape and architecture merge to address climatic extremes in service to human biological, emotional needs, and in tune with the rhythms of nature: "Whereas everything seemed to go against man: desert, stoniness, the sun's infernal blaze, suddenly the most lilting melody is heard: architecture and paradisiacal verdure, streaming waters, coolness, flowers and fruit: palm trees, orange groves, apricot and pomegranate trees, green shadow and starry nights to worship, filtered through the date palms."[12] Because he came to understand microclimates and landscapes as vehicles for transforming once punitive and inhospitable environments into spaces capable of accommodating and nurturing human life, the possibilities for his architectural repertoire also expanded—from the therapeutic environment to the biologically supportive, or what Le Corbusier termed "*urbanisme complet.*"[13] The embodied knowledge that he gleaned from these visits to territories outside the temperate and developed zones would inform the sensibility that directed his work in Chandigarh.

This progression was supported intellectually by a critical reference in his career: the biologist and physiologist Dr. Alexis Carrel (1873–1944), author of the best-selling book *L'Homme, cet inconnu* (*Man, The Unknown,* 1935) and regent of the French Foundation for Human Research during the Vichy Regime. Critical of "artificial modes of existence," including sealed building envelopes and "*l'air exact,*" Carrel declared: "It appears that the individuals accustomed to natural bodily exercise, to hardships, and to the inclemency of the weather, as were their fathers, are capable of harder and more sustained efforts than our athletes.... Perhaps the triumphs of hygiene, medicine and modern education are not so advantageous as we are led to believe."[14] Despite the controversies surrounding Carrel's eugenics theory, Le Corbusier came to embrace the potential for an increased alliance between human biology and the elements of nature, including a growing awareness of the climate's effect on human life and well-being. In *La Maison des hommes* (1942), written in response to Carrel's book, Le Corbusier sought to formulate a design approach appropriate to both the new form of living and the new form of man. There he portrayed the human body with its various physiological layers—skeleton, skin, digestive and circulatory system—along with paradisiacal retreats in the form of gardens and parks, solariums and floating gardens, skies of changing intensities, shading veils (*brises-soleil*), primordial forests, and "trees with astonishing forms,... a variety of species: play of forms and of colors, of denseness and heaviness, of lightness and fitness." Endowing nature with an active role for biological revitalization, Le Corbusier concluded: "Nature is entered in the lease."[15]

Carrel's collaborator, the French climate control specialist (*thermicien*) André Missenard (1901–1989), was equally critical of Le Corbusier's earlier embrace of artificially controlled environments, maintaining: "It is to be feared that the great picture window of Le Corbusier, 'incorporating the landscape into the rent,' gives a dangerous illusion of life in the open, and thus an advantage becomes a disadvantage through ignorance." He added: "Dr. Carrel used to say, half facetiously, that 'houses should be built with very small windows so that people would feel the urge to go out more.'" In Missenard's unapologetic critique of the scientification of the architectural milieu, including all-glass walls and thermal regimes based on maintaining a constant indoor temperature, he rejected such unified environments through his concern for health, asserting: "Man must struggle against the monotony of environment in the widest sense of the term."[16] He considered the constant internal environments at 18°C—"what technicians call comfort temperature"—to be the zone of "thermal neutrality of physiologists" because it maintains "the minimum forces necessary to keep the internal temperature of the body constant ... without it being necessary to thermo-regulate through transpiration."[17] Missenard was committed to forming a "doctrine" that would support human health by boosting the immune system through a continual activation of the body's homeostatic regulation. This would mean interacting with "colder environments that evolve in their temperature according to the outside variations."[18] Describing this as the "*doctrine des climats artificiels*" (doctrine of artificial climates) in his book *L'Homme et le climat* (1937), Missenard elaborated that thermal sensation is not solely dependent on the hygienist principles of maximized solar exposure and parameters for healthful air. Instead, it results from a combination of various factors: humidity levels, thermal performance of adjacent materials, wind velocity, and human activity. Rather than a standardized internal climate, Missenard called for greater human contact with the outdoors, with architectural implications for creating a range of spatial transitions between inside and outside. In associating psychophysiological strength with climatic gradients, Missenard appears to have ascribed central importance to the threshold between the interior and exterior space—the *in-between*—an idea that implies not only the integration of architecture and landscape but also a deeper entanglement with weather. Le Corbusier saw in Missenard's climatic doctrine an opportunity to translate his empirical understanding of the spaces he had experienced in North African oases into a biotechnical protocol for a new architectural ethos. Although he did not meet Missenard until 1943, Le Corbusier owned a copy of *L'Homme et le climat,* in which he inserted numerous comments that indicate a growing alliance with the atmospheric qualities of space. Words such as "interior milieu," "intuition," and "ambient" are scribbled beside paragraphs on thermo-regulation and the "*sensibilisation de l'espirit,*" the physiological effects of light, the influence of the cosmic world, and the effects climate on human's psychophysiological well-being.[19]

To capture this emerging spatial sensibility, Le Corbusier published an essay "L'Espace indicible" (Ineffable Space, 1946), which he expanded into book form and published in English as *New World of Space* (1948); this quasi-mystical concept marks the foundation of his new design philosophy.[20] Driven by the various physiological and emotional responses to space, including its atmospheric phenomena, he described space as an entity in which living things, humans and animals, plants and clouds, are interdependent, as he elaborated: "We pause, struck by such interrelation in nature, and we gaze, moved by this harmonious orchestration of space, and we realize that we are looking at the reflection of light." Like a biological composition, these elements appear ineffably and extend their "influences around them.... A phenomenon of concordance occurs." The role of the architect is to make this "appearance" palpable through design. "Then," Le Corbusier concluded, "a boundless depth opens up, effaces the walls, drives away contingent presences, *accomplishes the miracle of ineffable space.*"[21] In this new ethos, the body also responds to the ever-present forces of weather, breathing, and perspiring according to the conditions of air—its temperature, humidity, wind, pressure, and sound. Architectural boundaries that Le Corbusier had once imagined as containers for space become complex thresholds, capable of negotiating between inside and outside conditions, like organic membranes endowed with life. These thresholds gain spatial magnitude and thermal variance—all in support of breathing. In this pursuit, landscape evolves from a mediated medium into one endowed with bioclimatic roles for psychophysiological sustenance and delight. While Le Corbusier's concept of ineffable space testifies to his new spatial alliances, Missenard's doctrine of artificial climates provided the architect with a techno-scientific rational for addressing Chandigarh's climatic constraints and the "problem of breathing." As Roberto Gargiani and Anna Rosellini maintain, Chandigarh's climate is the "generating function of [a] new architecture of a 'biological order.'"[22] But how does this spatial sensibility and concern for a biological order, including breathing, find its expression in Le Corbusier's design for Chandigarh?

II. Chandigarh: Formative design impressions

With a new spatial sensibility committed to the effective qualities of space and disciplinary alliances with the climatic sciences and with landscape, Le Corbusier and his partner Pierre Jeanneret arrived at their initial quarters for living and working, a rest-house in Simla, the former British summer resort area in the Himalayan foothills, on February 20, 1951. The future site of Chandigarh, about seventy-five miles away, lay "under a splendid sky, in the midst of an eternal landscape," Le Corbusier wrote to his wife, Yvonne.[23] In his sketchbooks dedicated to this initial contact with the site for the new capital city, Le Corbusier captured the agrarian landscape with a network of footpaths and irrigation canals throughout its agricultural clusters and cultivated fields.[24] In his sketches, adobe houses and mango trees (*Mangifera indica*) that blot the sloping ground plane can be seen against the skyline of the Shivalik Hills, while the site's eroded valley reveals the forceful results of the annual monsoons. → p. 104 Ⓐ

Inspired by this meteorological theater, Le Corbusier drew scenes from domestic life—houses and furniture, peasants and animals—in an Arcadian setting amid the rhythms of nature, as he noted: "affectionately linking men, woman, children, dogs, cows, buffalo, donkeys, goats, crows, vultures, songbirds, God's trees, sun, shade, water ... ALL VISIBLE, present, close, united."[25] Under the heading of "Vie domestique" (domestic life), he listed the meteorological conditions and their effects on daily life—too cold, hot, windy, rainy, humid, or, alternately, good weather. He observed that in the hot month of May, "everyone sleeps outside," and in September, the air is "madly" damp with simultaneously refreshing and pleasant "Southeast breezes." The key, the "architectural answer" to both, he realized, was the verandah.[26]

If in Simla, Le Corbusier discovered the rhythms of daily life influenced by meteorological conditions, his visit to Jantar Mantar, the eighteenth-century astronomical observatory in New Delhi, revealed the intersection of architectural space and the meteorological elements, binding humankind to the cosmos. With a revelatory tone he noted that these structures "point to a new way" as "precise adaptations of forms and organisms to the sun, rain, air, etc."[27] Recalling his experiences in the North African oasis, Le Corbusier sketched again the M'Zab's courtyard house, conveying its spatial depth with deep shadows that reflect the interplay between the architectural boundary and the harsh sun of the desert climate. He was already revisiting the possibility of a disciplinary synthesis in which elements of landscape, climate, and architecture combine to foster a nurturing environment—one that both breathes and supports human breathing.

For the High Court building in Chandigarh's capitol complex, he imagined and sketched an architectural wall resembling a layered membrane—the first such instance of his evolving concept. This membrane has deep, burrowed notches and projecting fins that suggest shade- and windcatchers, capable of moderating the light and guiding the penetrating airflow. The liminal space provides for the wider thermal variances that Missenard theorized while simultaneously rendering the boundary between

Ⓐ "Leisure Valley" public park

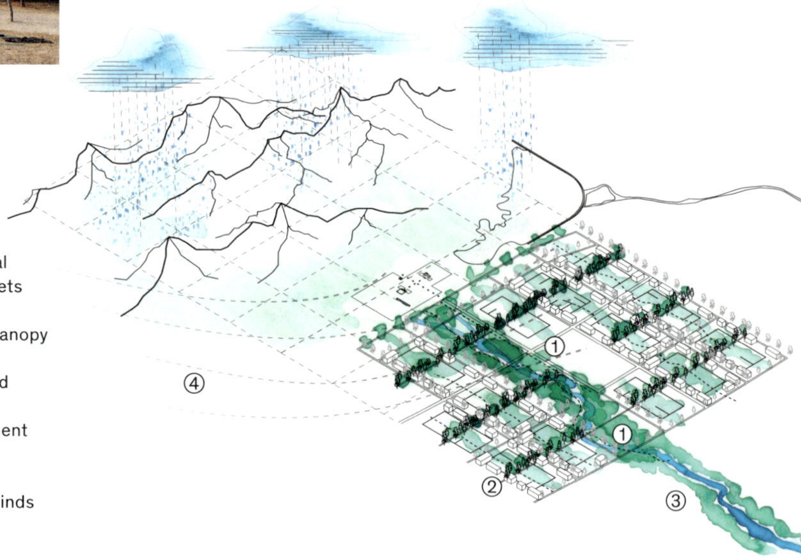

Thermodynamic performance:

① Evaporative cooling / isothermal evaporation: vegetation on streets and parks

② Solar radiation (reduced): tree canopy on streets provides shade and reduces sun glare for drivers and pedestrians

③ Leisure park as water management infrastructure during monsoon season (June–September)

④ Forced convection: prevailing winds from northwest

inside and outside ambiguous. Writing on Le Corbusier's initial studies of the High Court building, architect Michael Graves noted "how the porosity of the wall allows one to engage the landscape with the substance of the architectural surface."[28] The opposite relation is also valid; the porosity of the walls enables the architecture to engage the substance of the landscape—including its weather. Thus, one might think of Le Corbusier's early concept for the High Court building as a version of Delhi's astronomical instruments—an architectural organism tailored to the meteorological forces of the sun, the rain, and the air.

On the High Court sketch, Le Corbusier wrote "*murs isothermes*" (insulated walls) to describe this type of façade, which appears in his design nomenclature as a potential substitute for his earlier "*murs neutralisants*" (neutralizing walls). As he advised: "Do not hesitate to make grand empty naves full of shadow, generators of air currents, … kids play there in the evening and the inhabitants sit all around."[29] He was similarly inspired by the "Baradari"—the arched open-air pavilions in the region's historic Moghul gardens—for their spatial integration with the landscape and their potential use for refuge from the sudden rains.[30] His *murs isothermes,* with their holes, fins, and notches, similarly host people during the rainy season, when they can enjoy the fresh breezes and watch the black clouds on the horizon, as they embrace their delight at being immersed in the caprices of weather.

The space that resulted from this astronomical "reinterpretation," while monumental and symbolic, constitutes a possible proxy for Missenard's doctrine of artificial climates and points to the evolution in Le Corbusier's thinking in which he came to understand architecture, landscape, and weather as integrated domains. The cavernous membranes of the *murs isothermes* moderate the thermal differences between interior and exterior atmospheres by affording spaces of transition—the spaces that Missenard eulogized as vital to healthy thermo-regulation and increased psychophysiological well-being. This shift in Le Corbusier's thinking is fundamentally responsive to the extreme meteorological conditions of the Punjab, with its temperatures ranging between 35 degrees and 40 degrees Celsius from March through May, followed by the humid monsoon season from June to October, and a cooler period from November to February.

Upon his return to Paris, Le Corbusier contacted Missenard to solicit his help in resolving the urbanistic problem of Chandigarh—one concerning breathing, as he conveyed in a letter to Prem Nath Thapar, the administrative manager of the capital project. Committed to including Missenard on the design team, Le Corbusier explained: "Yesterday took place the first meeting with Mr. Missenard, a polytechnician, biologist and physician, to discuss the problems of breathing and climate.... My conviction is that India must treat the modern architectural form according to its sun, hygrometry, and wind regulations."[31] For Le Corbusier, climate was at once physical and emotional, mathematical and biological, cultural and social. Importantly, he identified climate as a directive for new modes of architectural expression, as he elaborated: "The symphonic problem of climate has not yet been grasped by modern architecture. Modern architecture, foraging through manuals and magazines from all over the world, blindly absorbs French, American, Indian, German, English or Scandinavian discoveries and forms. Confronted with this inconsistency, we felt the need for a *grille climatique,* and we have created it, checked by Mr. Missenard. ... [T]his climatic grid allows us to bring order to the problems of human breathing and behavior in extreme climates; it automatically prepares the architectural answer."[32]

III. The climatic grid: Design principles for breathing

Le Corbusier's formative impressions from his first visit to the site for the new capital city, together with his emerging design sensibility and collaboration with Missenard, provided the basis for his new grid: the *grille climatique,* which emerged early in the design for Chandigarh as a means to address the problem of breathing conditioned by the meteorological parameters of "sun, shade, winds, hygrometry, and temperature."[33] Since Le Corbusier viewed the biological sustenance of breathing as contingent upon a design doctrine suited to the climate, the grid was a vital mechanism in the design process. He described it as the "key to research and the solution."[34] Consistent with the grids he deployed to structure urban challenges for CIAM, Le Corbusier understood the climatic grid as "a working tool that makes it possible to reduce the complexity of the data of a problem and thus prepares technicians, architects, town planners, and engineers, to answer questions based on ambient conditions and limits advised by the biologist."[35] As it was developed between December 1951 and January 1952 by Le Corbusier's Parisian collaborators Iannis Xenakis (1922–2001) and German Samper (1924–), the climatic grid took the form of a matrix in which meteorological data (air temperature, relative humidity, wind direction and velocity, and thermal radiation of adjacent surfaces) are plotted in three categories: bioclimatic diagnoses, the "physico-biological rectifications" or adjustments necessary to ensure human comfort and well-being, and related architectural solutions.[36] Each category is subdivided in turn according to monthly climatic conditions over the course of a year. Missenard worked closely with Le Corbusier's atelier to determine the relevant climatic parameters and the psychophysiological effects that the architecture would presumably foster. For instance, the rectification for increased human comfort during the hot and dry month of June includes the "decrease of temperature by 12° to 14°C," while the humidity could be "increased by 10% to 15%." To reduce the radiant temperature, the document asserts that it would be necessary to "shut-off everything."[37] The architectural components associated with these physico-biological rectifications include a "layer of greenery on the walls with espaliers, green carpet with herbs and flowers"; a "fine dust of water droplets in the garden, roof and walls"; operable fins to allow for free airflow; sunshades or *brises-soleil,* vegetal mats supported on trellises, and a "parasol painted white to reflect hot sun rays"; as well as the insertion of "dampened calico at the point where wind enters to increase moisture in the air." Architectural elements in support of "the optimal and theoretical variations of the environment to conserve or to augment VITAL EFFICIENCY" include overhangs and loggias as well as the thickened thresholds of the *murs isothermes.*[38] In addition to their bioclimatic performance, these transitional spaces would also comprise spaces for social and civic interaction, particularly significant for the housing type he proposed for Chandigarh's low-income villages, the "*Maison des Péons.*"

As one of the first urban components to be elaborated, the social housing districts for the city's poorest inhabitants was the basis for testing the climatic grid.[39] This prototypical governmental housing project of 110 square meters is comprised of single-floor units and gardens. Prime Minster Nehru supported a modern residential model that would integrate climate, sanitation, lighting, and water. "Nothing is more horrible," he acknowledged, "than the 'peasant' or 'servants' quarters that were standard during the English era and continue to be built with a few variations.... We should think about what Mr. Corbusier has suggested, i.e., that our buildings, whether big or small, should be designed to meet Indian conditions."[40] To address restricted budgets and improve living conditions in the demanding climate required an alliance of the available know-how and the vernacular building practices that Le Corbusier observed during his first trip to the site. Indeed, he sought to offer equitable climatic conditions to all of the city's residents by equipping every housing unit with a verandah, a ventilated interior, and front and back gardens. "Do not have any qualms about the classes!" he declared. "Up to now the peon has led an extremely primitive existence without a dwelling house. But now he has a dwelling planned and built with the same love and care lavished on the homes of the ministers."[41]

In Le Corbusier's initial sketches for the quarter incorporating the *Maison des Péons,* dating from March 1951, the complex is a compact, single-story block for seven hundred fifty residents, with interior gardens, courtyards, and access roads oriented east–west to avoid direct sunlight and maximize exposure to the dominant winds.[42] Each dwelling has a private garden, with lush vegetation, a trellis, and a detached roof that undulates above the roof slab to catch the breezes for enhanced cooling. Honeycombed partition walls allow the wind to move thorough the units, slender partitions support sunshades, and verandahs open to a tree canopy.[43] Beside each verandah, a water tank collects rainfall, and a bed for sleeping is included in the garden to take advantage of the nocturnal cooling and the grandeur of the nighttime sky. "Each evening," Le Corbusier observed, "Indians like taking their bed out into the grass ... under the stars."[44] As the architect Harris Sobin notes, using "his own bodily reactions as the 'measuring instrument,'" Le Corbusier captured this experience in sketches made at the rest house in Simla and at the Taj Hotel in Bombay.[45] Inspired by the dark ceiling of the rest-house, which, Le Corbusier noted, forms an immersive "blue-black sky, an interesting 'interior-exterior,'" he proposed to paint the ceilings of the peon dwellings black.[46] In addition to augmenting cooling, the penumbra of their darkened interiors would provide a striking contrast to the dazzling sunlight bearing down on the city.

As part of the first attempt to translate Le Corbusier's sketches for the *Maison des Péons* into measured drawings, the "Insolation Diagram for the Summer Solstice" depicts a figure in the unit's garden under thermal stress produced by a combination of the exposure to direct sunlight and the heat radiating from the walls.[47] To further ameliorate the thermal stress, a layer of clay and perforated water pipes covers the flat roof to increase evaporation and reduce heat loads. A pair of oversize scuppers grace the edges of the roof to capture the dramatic effects of the monsoon. One directs the rainwater to an outdoor shower in the back garden, while the other sends it into the front garden for irrigation.[48] The outdoor shower is open to the sky and set beside a fireplace at the center of the garden, symbolizing the spiritual union of air and earth, water and fire.[49] A trellis above the verandah is covered in vegetative mats to increase shade during the summer months. *Jaali* walls of perforated brick provide porous edges, filtering the western light and admitting the breezes to the interior through adjustable wooden shutters, while the compound is oriented north–west to take advantage of the cooling summer breezes. In a letter to Mr. Thapar, Le Corbusier declared: "I have found the best method to face the two climatic problems of Chandigarh: sun and rain.... I think I detain [sic] an Indian architectural truth that can be realized easily and cheaply.... I have the feeling of having erected an architectural esthetic that falls in with the traditions, the landscape and the modern spirit."[50]

This early version of the peon house type provided a basis for subsequent design iterations, based on Le Corbusier's discussions of the architectural tactics with Missenard, which led in turn to design revisions based on the climatic grid protocols.[51] The most pertinent changes include the addition of a "parasol," a curved plane that is elevated above the vaulted roof and painted white to "reflect the thermal rays."[52] The parasol would reduce the temperature on the interior by diminishing direct light incidence and heat transfer to the roof and increasing airflow through the intervening space. The roof vault is extended in both directions to reduce solar incidence on the façades, or, as an alternative, mats are provided in frames that project from the ends of the vaults to further this aim, just as operable fins on the southwestern façade generate seasonal shade.[53] Finally, the garden is made greener and wetter by its layers of trees, ground cover, and espaliers on the walls that contribute to the sense of a sheltered oasis, while a system of sprinklers would serve to amplify the humidity during the dryer months. Extolling these modifications, Le Corbusier claimed: "Sun, space, greenery, part covered, part open in shade, and part completely in the open air with the inevitable variety of the nearby street ... is a new [solution] in housing design."[54] → p. 109 D C

By the end of January 1952 Le Corbusier sent his final version of the climatic grid with the drawings for the *Maison des Péons* to the design team in Chandigarh (Pierre Jeanneret, Jane Drew, and Maxwell Fry) as well as to the Punjab's Chief Engineer, P. L. Varma. The team agreed that the integration of landscape and architecture was one of the most positive measures to ameliorate the site's extreme climatic conditions of heat and dryness, while Drew suggested that it was "possibly practical to grow grass on the roof and occasionally humidify."[55] Following the process elaborated in the "Program of Priorities for Construction," the team developed designs for the housing units and the remaining fabric in each city sector, while Le Corbusier turned his attention to the capitol complex and the city's landscape.[56]

B Government housing, Sector 23, by Maxwell Fry

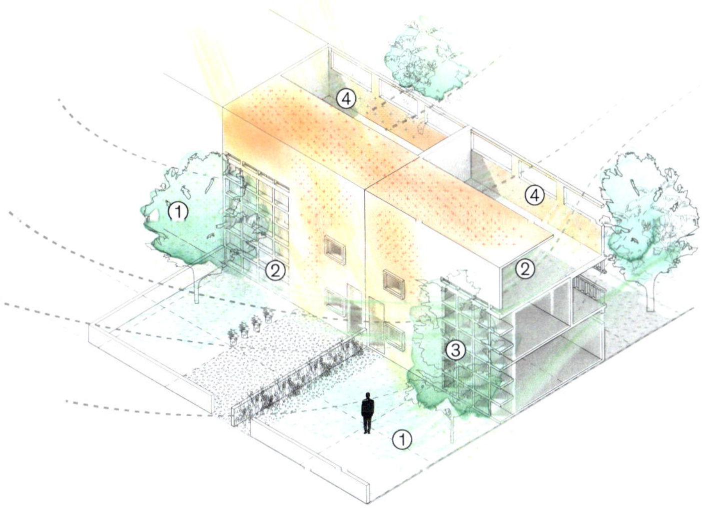

Thermodynamic performance:

- Evaporative cooling / isothermal evaporation: tree canopy, domestic gardens, and vegetated courtyards
- Solar radiation (blocked): roofs, verandas, parasols, and jaalis (perforated screen walls) block sunlight
- Forced convection / cross ventilation: jaalis and screens allow breezes to flow
- Radiant cooling: barsati (rooftop room and terrace) allows exposure to breezes and cold night sky

C Government housing (Peon's House), Sector 22, by Pierre Jeanneret

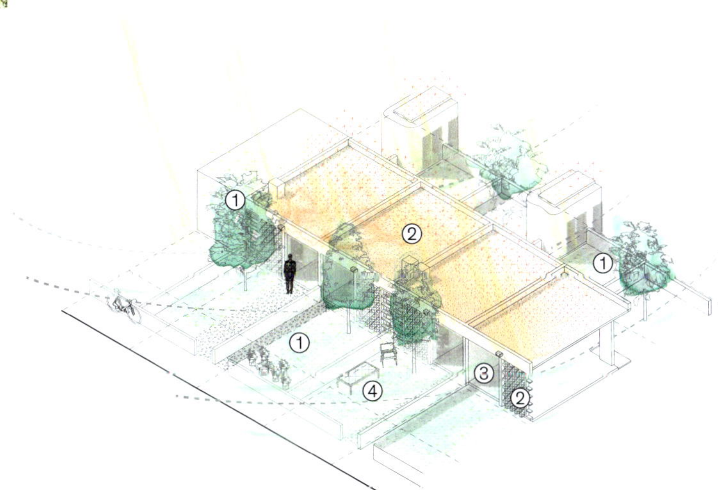

Thermodynamic performance:

- Evaporative cooling / isothermal evaporation: tree canopy, domestic gardens and vegetated courtyards
- Solar radiation (blocked): roofs, verandas, parasols, and jaalis
- Forced convection / cross ventilation: jaalis and screens allow breezes to flow
- "Convective" furniture: charpai (Indian day bed) allows air to flow for body cooling

During his second trip to India, in October 1951, Le Corbusier acknowledged that a "transformation is taking place: the global fusion of needs and means, of economic plans and of spiritual and intellectual points of view."[57] With the climatic grid and his ideas for the *Maisons des Péons,* Le Corbusier merged architecture and landscape, a disciplinary synthesis that embodied his aim of determining a new architectural doctrine for India.

IV. *Grille d'arborisation:* Landscape for bioclimatic amelioration

The disciplinary hybridization that characterizes Le Corbusier's development of the *Maisons des Péons* would also propel his extensive use of landscape to address Chandigarh's public realm. Acknowledging the importance of public space for the Indians' social life, Le Corbusier wrote: "I am confident, after observing life in Bombay and in Ahmedabad, as well as Mongolian architecture in Delhi and elsewhere, that in this country *life happens outdoors* ... in the gardens, verandahs, and arcades."[58] Among his concerns were heat amelioration, the cooling of public areas, providing shelter from the sand and dust, directing view sheds, managing the monsoon rains, and preserving some "scenery during winter," or simply offering color and a "great living fantasy" for the residents. To address the implications of these concerns for the Chandigarh landscape, he devised a new protocol: *la grille d'arborisation* (the tree-planting grid). On August 1, 1952, several months after he submitted the climatic grid and the *Maisons des Péons* drawings to the design team and Varma in India, Le Corbusier sent his tree-planting grid, composed of nineteen sheets. As he noted in a letter to Jane Drew: "Following a very meticulous study, I am giving you, in the form of a grid, my instructions relative to the landscape of the Capital."[59] This set of drawings includes a "Tableau de Synthese" (Synthesis Table)—a matrix addressing the tree arrangements, both "architectural" and "natural," for the various areas of the city, including the Leisure Valley, the Capitol complex, the commercial center, the University, and the network of vehicular streets and pedestrian paths (referred to as the 7V system).[60] In the Synthesis Table, trees disposed in an "architectural" manner appear ordered in single, double, or multiple rows. In the "natural" configurations, they are either isolated or disposed in homogeneous or heterogeneous groves or forests. In both of these arrangements, however, trees are treated as sculptural elements with bioclimatic affordances and categorized according to their canopy characteristics, or "shapes"—irregularly rounded, regularly rounded, irregular column, regular column, conical, and drooping branch. Further considerations include heights, rates of growth, evergreen or deciduous foliage, and density of flowers.

The tree-planting grid addresses the city's hierarchical circulation system relative to solar orientation. For instance, the street grid is organized so that "no motorists will be driving into the setting sun."[61] Asymmetrical street profiles in the commercial and pedestrian areas also showcase the need to augment thermal comfort. The bazaar streets (V4) at the mid-crossing of each residential sector are coupled with wider sidewalks on their northern sides with multiple rows of trees in diverse "shapes," mixed with deciduous and evergreen foliage to provide shade in summer and admit sunlight in winter. The wide sidewalks and thickened tree canopies provide shade in support of commercial activities, reflecting Le Corbusier's aim of making "gathering space[s] of intense activity in the city life of the sectors." He accordingly instructed Jane Drew: "The V4s must be alive."[62] Each of these streets, which run parallel to the mountains, has a consistent color of flowers—"one is yellow, another one red, another one blue."[63] → p. 112 D

The sector-defining streets, or V3s, provide access to the residential districts by running either "vertically" (northeast and southwest) toward the Shivalik Hills and the Capitol complex or "horizontally" (northwest and southeast), parallel to the hills. Le Corbusier explained that the tree-planting grid for these two directions "must be studied to give the best conditions in particular to the sun glare" and to simultaneously "allow the users to know automatically in which direction they circulate."[64] The selection of tree "shapes" for the V3s resulted from a cosmologically driven analysis of sun angles for both summer and winter scenarios, with particular focus on the extremes at the solstices. For instance, at the winter solstice, the tempered afternoon sun would align with the vertical V3s, leading to potential sun blindness. A low and wide canopy with evergreen foliage would thus form an overarching shade tunnel, protecting the drivers from glare and framing the year-round view to the mountains. The horizontal V3s are less challenging, as they align with the sun when it is low on the horizon only during late winter afternoons. Here the road section indicates a tree canopy with drooping branches, resulting in rhythmical, long, and diaphanous shadows during the mornings and afternoons. → p. 112 E

In the residential sectors, where vehicular traffic is restricted to encourage social life, there are three further categories of the network of streets and paths: looping neighborhood streets (V5s), inner access lanes (V6s), and pedestrian and bike paths (V7s). The V6s provide access to the residential sectors, not only for pedestrians but also for wheeled wooden carts—the "*thele*" used for produce-vending—and cycle-rickshaws for human transport. As Maxwell Fry and Jane Drew observed, the V7s that thread through the linear parks of the residential sectors are "dedicated to the other side of life: to recreation and relaxation … under the shady trees."[65] In accordance with Le Corbusier's principle of providing open space for sleeping as well as leisure activities, the planting in these zones would provide "fantasy and color throughout the year in various forms and formats."[66] → p. 113 F

D V4 (bazaar street) and commercial strip

Thermodynamic performance:
① Evaporative cooling / isothermal evaporation: thick tree canopy
② Solar radiation (reduced): thick tree canopy
③ Radiant cooling: shaded walls, ground, and tree leaves

E Vertical V3 (sector-defining street) tunnel of shade

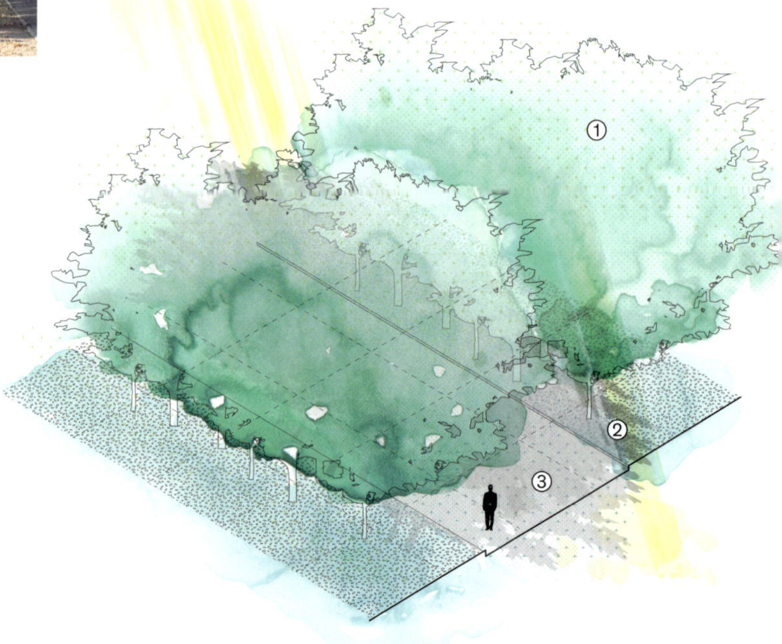

Thermodynamic performance:
① Evaporative cooling / isothermal evaporation: thick tree canopy (tunnel of shade)
② Solar radiation (reduced) prevents heat and glare from southwest exposure
③ Radiant cooling: shaded ground and tree leaves

F V6 neighborhood inner access lane

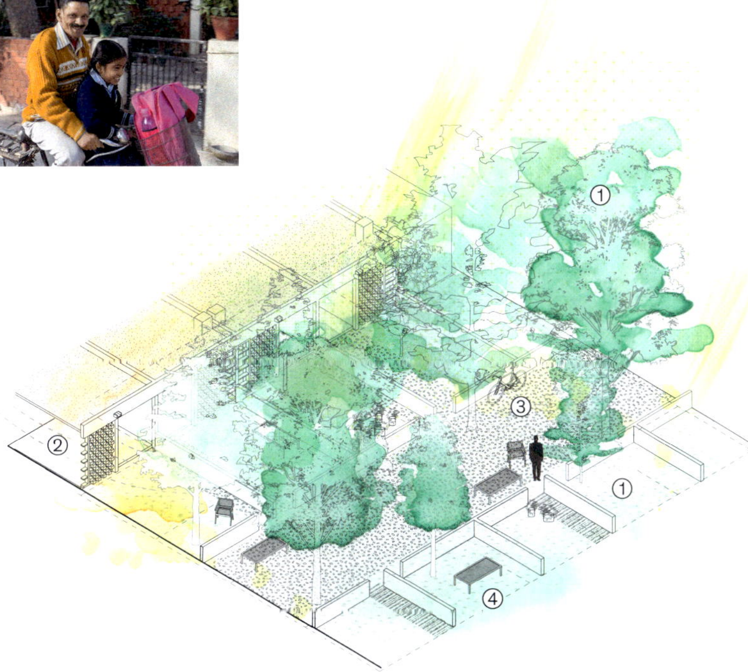

Thermodynamic performance:

- Evaporative cooling / isothermal evaporation: tree canopy and domestic gardens
- Forced convection / cross ventilation: jaalis and screens allow breezes to flow
- Solar radiation (reduced): shaded street by tree canopy activates social life
- "Convective" furniture: charpai (Indian day bed) allows air to flow through for body cooling

G Assembly building

→ p. 338

Thermodynamic performance:

- Evaporative cooling / isothermal evaporation: humidification through solar radiation on water surface
- Evaporative cooling / adiabatic evaporation: water falling from roof ("cascade")
- Radiant cooling: water surface
- Radiant heating: concrete surfaces heated by sunlight
- Free convection: humid air rises
- Forced convection: prevailing winds from northwest move through parasol and holes in walls
- Solar radiation (reduced): large parasol and walls creates shade

For the city's most symbolic architectural compound, the Capitol complex, the tree-planting grid addresses the psychophysiological effects of the landscape on its users in the complex's artificial mounds, and sunken gardens in addition to tree "shapes" and planting arrangements. Moreover, it identifies meteorological elements—light, wind, shade, and water—as substances for design expression. This complexity derives in part from Le Corbusier's source of inspiration: the traditional landscapes of India's Moghul gardens, in which microclimatic conditions moderate adversities of the weather.[67] Indeed, as Maxwell Fry claimed of the Capitol complex: "This group of buildings is a subtle asymmetrical arrangement within a Moghul-like park of lawn, lagoon and sculpture."[68]

During Le Corbusier's initial trips to India, he visited several of these historic compounds and gardens. In an early notebook, he sketched the "garden of the Maharaja of Patiala" and its features: two contiguous squares of different sizes. These are subdivided into quadrants and linked by a wide central axis flanked by water channels that culminates in a main pavilion.[69] Moreover, a subsequent sketch in this notebook depicts an early version of the Capitol's planimetric layout organized as a coherent organism, evoking a Moghul garden in homeostatic regulation with its climate. Building footprints are set among square plots of grass and mineral surfaces, just as water canals and reflecting pools punctuate an orderly quadrangular ground plane, replete with sunken courts, enclosing walls, elevated walkways, promenades, earthworks, and shaded rooms made of trees.

As realized, the design of this "organism"—a biological entity itself—constitutes a lyrical response to the meteorological cycles of solar orientation, monsoon rains, and wind. For example, rainwater collected on the surface of the vast pedestrian plaza reflects the sky during rainy intervals. The capitol complex is permeated with landscape features, including groves of trees, tree-rooms, water basins, sunken courts, and densely planted earthworks, or "artificial hills" as Le Corbusier termed them.[70] Together with the capitol buildings, these features interrupt the vast expanse and create moments of psychophysiological intensity. Here, Le Corbusier's interest in composing with shadows, reflections, and ineffable manifestations of atmospheric qualities led him to render the capitol complex as an orchestration of cooling moments composed of shade, buoyant air, and water in varied forms. Just as the as *murs isothermes* of the main capitol buildings—the Legislative Assembly, the Secretariat, and the High Court—deepen the climatic threshold through their arches, parasols, notches, and fins that afford shelter from the sun, direct the wind, and form spaces of deep shadows, so the encompassing landscape was envisioned to expand the complex's bioclimatic effects. In conjunction with the work on the Capitol complex, a new typology of walls emerged in Le Corbusier's nomenclature: "*murs de verdure*" (walls of greenery). These are dense walls of trees, intended not only to amplify the shaded hollowness of the *murs isothermes,* but also to break up the spatial continuity of the capitol complex and shelter its walkways. He envisioned using these walls of trees to create "*chambres de verdure*" (rooms of greenery) as spaces of cooling refuge.[71] For example, to extend the scale and rhythm of the Assembly building arches, Le Corbusier proposed "walls alternating with rings of cypresses," and he extolled the spaces within these cypress walls as "chambers of dark shadows."[72]

Le Corbusier intended the steep earthworks of the artificial hills created south of the Assembly building to be densely planted, adding moments of forceful lushness to the varied mineral surfaces of the pedestrian plaza, the buildings, and even the Himalayan foothills, visible on the horizon. In sharp contrast to the flat, open terrain of the capitol complex, Le Corbusier noted, these hills "will create a play of forms with the buildings of the Capitol and will be covered with evergreen trees of different types."[73] Although only partially realized, the planting on these artificial hills was intended to provide shade and amplify the humidity to counteract the site's prevailing aridity, while visually isolating the complex from the city under construction to the south and its associated dust and noise. He intended these steep topographical formations to curate more profound, even metaphysical, connections between the capitol complex and its broader milieu, as registered in the sketches he made during his first visit to the site. Moreover, at the southern end of the complex Le Corbusier imagined a "*glacis*"—a continuous horizontal embankment—to augment this sense of physical separation from the city while enhancing its connections to the distant mountains and the sky.[74]

Le Corbusier fostered the bioclimatic composition of the capitol complex by introducing shallow reflecting pools that instigate a sense of freshness. Inspired by the water courses and terraces in the Moghul gardens, he reasoned that one must "compose using all levels for composed reflections."[75] The diaphanous quality of its reflections make water a medium for spatial deception—an effect that Le Corbusier created by exploiting water's multiple forms of appearance, including that which results from the cyclical monsoon rainfall. Enlarged scuppers with affinities to gargoyles are attached to the parasols atop the Assembly and High Court buildings, symbolically highlighting the transitory presence of the monsoons. These scuppers form seasonal fountains as the water gushes into basins far below, emitting a fine spray in a kind of meteorological spectacle of "Capitol Cascades," as Le Corbusier termed them.[76] During such prolonged periods of intense rain, the esplanade surface is replete with water basins and canals that echoes the spirit of New Delhi's astronomical observatory in its physical embodiment of cosmic events. The cyclical nature of the monsoon would activate the appearance of a hidden footprint made of a network of canals to collect and lead the rain, similar to a fleeting tattoo scored on the Capitol's esplanade. Intermittently, the esplanade becomes a vast stage for nature to perform in an orchestrated manner. ← p. 113 G

With the various "Monuments" in the Capitol complex dedicated to the elements of wind, sun, and shadow, Le Corbusier's impetus for sculpting space with respect to climate and its meteorological forces rose to metaphysical dimensions. These monuments—the Open Hand, the Tower of Shadows, the 24-Hour Solar Cycle, and the Geometric Hill—register and react to climatic forces, embodying the architect's commitment to extolling the meteorological elements for orchestrating "the relations between men and his surroundings: *men-nature* and *cosmos.*" Attributing the origins of these artifacts to Jane Drew, Le Corbusier recounted her advice: "why do you not set up between the edifices of the Capitol certain of the signs evoked by you which symbolize your strongest preoccupations.... This was the starting point."[77]

The Open Hand, symbolizing the acts of giving and receiving in a postwar context, operates as a weathervane: an anemometer revealing the direction of the wind and cooling breezes so fundamental to achieving psychophysiological balance in the region. The Tower of Shadows makes palpable the "Insolation Techniques" developed in Le Corbusier's Parisian atelier for the *Maisons de Péon.*[78] Oriented to the "4 horizons" and bounded by variably spaced horizontal and vertical *brises-soleil,* the Tower of the Shadows demonstrates that "the sun can be controlled at all four cardinal points of an edifice and even manipulated in a hot country to reduce temperature."[79] Le Corbusier intended that a diagram of the 24-Hour Solar Cycle be scored on the angled surface of the Geometric Hill—the steep artificial mound that rises directly from the esplanade—to eulogize the human dependency on the sun in its diurnal rhythms.[80] Reminding visitors of their vertical axis, this monumental embankment reflects the earth's upward orchestration toward the celestial sphere. "The cosmic laws outside of Man," declared Le Corbusier, are "the rule."[81] → p. 118 H

Immediately southeast of the capitol complex is Lake Sukhna, a reservoir reflecting a similar climatic sensibility, constructed to epitomize the meteorological apogee in Chandigarh. With the guidance of Chief Engineer Varma, the lake was developed as a sanctuary, an urban refuge for the city's residents. Visitors perambulating on its twenty-four-meter-wide esplanade are exposed to the cooling breezes from the mountains (katabatic flow), the reflective surface of the water, and the early morning fog rising from its surface, viewed against the ever-present background of the Shivalik Hills. The lake operates on a larger scale as bioclimatic infrastructure, sheltering the city against dust storms and providing humidity during the dry seasons. Indeed, Le Corbusier claimed, it "has transformed the local climatic conditions."[82] Fed by the seasonal rivulets in the Shivalik Hills, the lake is “sufficiently large to create the spectacle of the mountains and sky reflected in the water.”[83] Various individuals have testified to the lake’s memorable effects. Among those, the British architect Maxwell Fry wrote that its embankment, “made ten times wider than was strictly necessary,” makes the most memorable promenade in the city under the diurnal-nocturnal solar cycles.[84] Dr. Randhawa described the air surrounding the lake as being “like champagne, bracing and invigorating.”[85] In the early morning, when the sun rises behind the mountains and slowly emerges on the open horizon, the view is often foregrounded by a thick layer of fog hovering on the water’s surface. During the late afternoon, when the sun casts its last rays on the lake, the result is an enveloping atmosphere of red hues and shimmering light. The pervading quiet provides an opportunity for spiritual retreat and meditative physical exercise. Because Le Corbusier considered silence and slow movement to be priorities in supporting a greater spiritual embodiment with the solar cycles and the mountains, he allowed no buildings to be erected in the view shed to the mountainous horizon and forbade the use of vehicles of any kind (including bikes and motorboats) along the promenade and on the lake. → p. 118 I, → p. 119 J

During the decade following the publication of Le Corbusier’s article on “L’Espace indicible” (1946), the psychophysiological effects afforded by the atmospheric qualities of the spaces surrounding the body began to assume multiple dimensions in his work: bioclimatic, affective, and symbolic. This evolving sensibility is captured in a series of drawings Le Corbusier made during his third trip to India, in March and April 1952: a period when the architectural and landscape repertoire of the capitol complex was in development. This collection of drawings evokes a cross-fertilization of sky and the earth, animals and humans, conjoining humans and the built environment in a unified figure—hybrid forms that Le Corbusier referred to as “bestiaries.”[86] The capitol complex would accordingly reflect a hybridization of the numerous references he had accumulated during his prior visits, when he experienced a range of examples in which humankind intersects with meteorological forces in an unbounded manner. In Simla he discovered the meteorological conditions affecting the rhythms of daily life; his visit to the eighteenth-century astronomical observatory in New Delhi revealed the intersection of architectural space and the meteorological elements of the solar system, binding humankind to the cosmos; and the Moghul-like paradise garden showcased a space of effect and climatic amelioration for civic interplay. At Chandigarh the “machine for living” that Le Corbusier postulated during the early 1920s became an organic instrument—a “bestiary” in tune with landscape and weather.[87]

Ⓗ The Open Hand

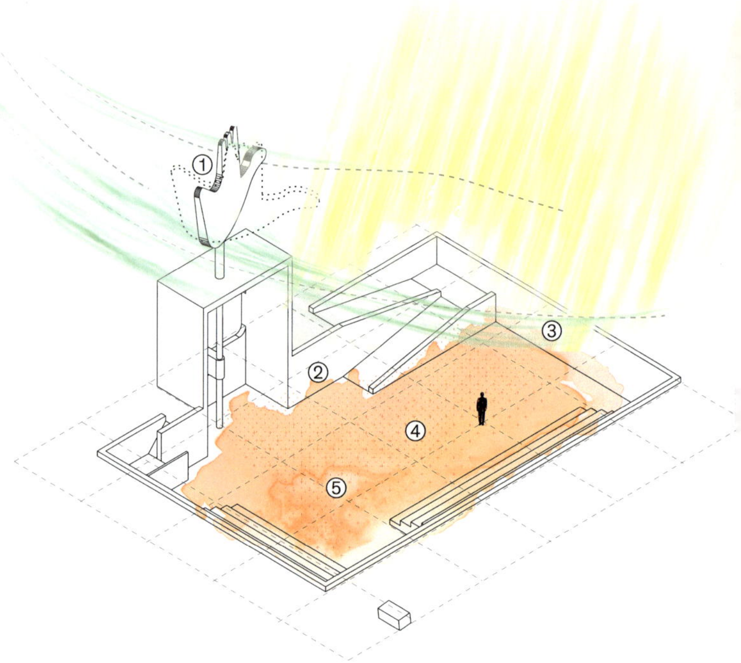

Thermodynamic performance:

① Wind vane: rotating "hand" registers wind direction
② Wind protection: sunken plaza
③ "Heat trap": sunken surfaces reduce convective heat transfer from ground to air
④ Radiant heating: solar exposure to concrete walls and ground plane and release of heat at night
⑤ Solar radiation (exposed)

Ⓘ Lake Sukhna promenade

Thermodynamic performance:

① Evaporative cooling / isothermal evaporation: vegetation and lake (humidification through solar radiation on water surface)
② Evaporative cooling / adiabatic evaporation: water splashing on promenade walls
③ Free convection / anabatic and katabatic flow: warm air on mountain slopes rises and drags cold air from lake in the morning until afternoon; process reverses in the evening
④ Radiant cooling: lake surface
⑤ Thermal mass / radiant heating: promenade walls and ground store heat during the day and release it at night
⑥ Solar radiation (reduced): thick tree canopy

J Lake Sukhna

Thermodynamic performance:

1) Green belt: barrier against sand and dust storms during hot and dry season (March–June)
2) Radiant cooling: lake surface
3) Evaporative cooling / isothermal evaporation: humidification through solar radiation on water surface
4) Forced convection: prevailing winds from northwest
5) Free convection / anabatic and katabatic flow: warm air on mountain slopes rises and drags cold air from lake in the morning until afternoon; process reverses in the evening

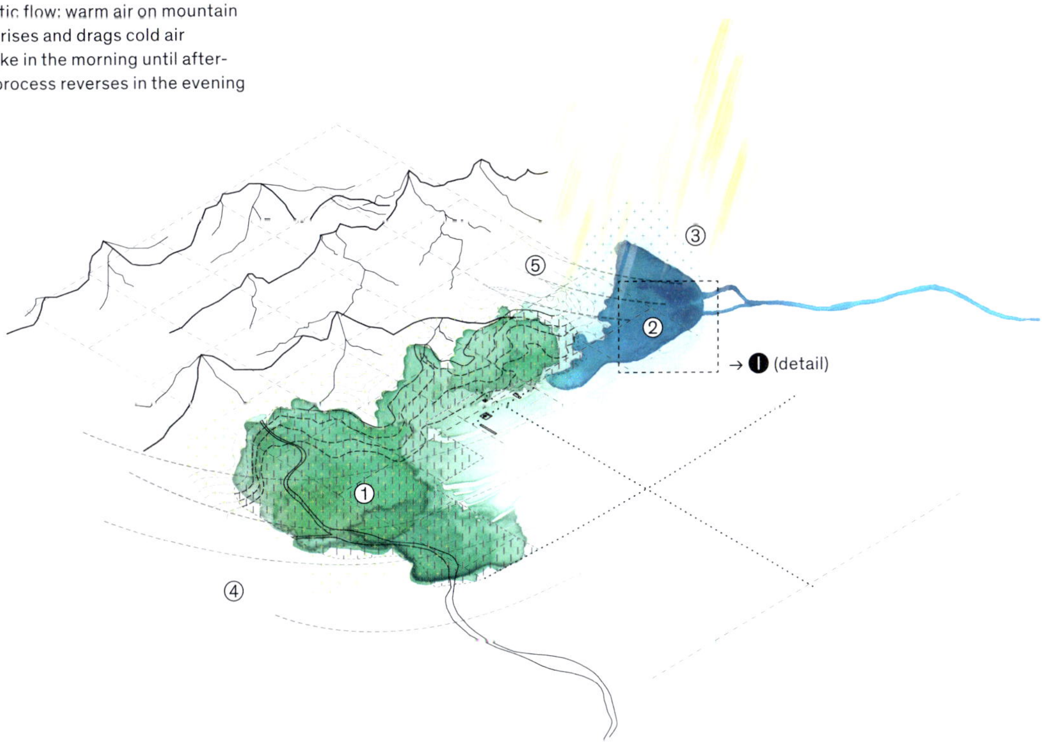

V. Dr. Randhawa and implementation of the tree-planting grid

To Le Corbusier the tree-planting grid reflected an "order of architectural nature"—a guide to form, volume, branch structure, color, and aroma that lacked horticultural specification. "I am neither an arborist nor a gardener," he explained, and thus not competent "to intervene in any way in the choice of the tree species."[88] To coordinate the team of architects, town planners, engineers, horticulturalists, and foresters involved in the capitol project, a Landscape Advisory Commission was established in July 1953 under the chairmanship of horticulturalist Mohinder Singh Randhawa. With the participation of Le Corbusier and the design team, along with Chief Engineer Varma and the Divisional Conservator of Forests, the Commission was to be responsible for the horticultural definition of the project relative to climate, cultural practices, and botanical features. Under its purview the Tree Preservation Act was formulated and enacted to protect and retain many of the existing trees on the site, such as the "venerable mango trees, clumps of date palms and groves of the Flame of the Forest (*Butea monosperma*) ... thus creating an illusion of great age." In addition, the commission was responsible for supervising the capital nursery, which supplied plant material for the capital landscape and managed the innumerable seeds and tree saplings that were "collected from the ancient state gardens of Patiala, Amritsar, Attari, Bhunga and the Moghul Garden at Pinjore," as well as a wide array of foreign trees.[89] Dr. Randhawa's horticultural knowledge, together with his prominent position as vice-president of the Indian Council of Agricultural Research, made his input essential to forming Chandigarh's landscape.

Like Le Corbusier, Randhawa believed that that unless the conditions of nature are re-established in people's lives, humankind cannot be healthy in body and spirit. Framing this concept as "bio-aesthetic planning," Randhawa highlighted the "utilitarian and aesthetic aspects" of trees in the city fabric.[90] Trees in urban areas, he noted, "constitute an effective buffer against dust and noise and also act as wind breaks and shelter-belts.... [They] link up individual masses of buildings in a harmonious whole."[91] Inspired by the Moghul gardens in India and the New Delhi landscapes of Edwin Lutyens, Randhawa imagined a luxuriant Chandigarh, "clothed in a mantle of vegetation."[92] Highlighting the significance of relating plant ecology with anthropological and bioclimatic values, he wrote: "Where philosophy has failed, Biology has come to our rescue, and the inquiry into the cause of beauty has moved from the realm of speculation to the realm of objective observation of facts and phenomena, dissociated from anthropomorphism."[93] Randhawa's concept of bio-aesthetic planning strengthened the spatial and bioclimatic affiliations in Le Corbusier's tree-planting grid, leading to the replacement of the initial Syntheses Table by another chart classifying "all the beautiful ornamental, flowering and foliage trees in India—the basis of all tree planting which is to be done in Chandigarh ... for establishing avenues, shrubberies, and parks as well as compounds of residential buildings and offices." Integral to this chart is a list of ornamental trees arranged according to size, height, spread of crown, rate of growth, foliage, color of flowers, and spread of root system, thus extending well beyond Le Corbusier's classification system. Flowering trees, and their blooming cycles, were of great importance to Dr. Randhawa's principle of bio-aesthetic planning. For the vertical V3, the continuous tunnel of shade, he specified evergreens with the large umbrella-like crowns—*Ficus infectoria, Schleichera trijuga, Sapium sebiferum* and *Cedrela tuna*—so that their young leaves would provide "many shades of colors ranging from bright scarlet to pink in the months of May and June." The chart indicates a border of high trees along the Capitol Avenue to demarcate one side of the vehicular highway. On the other side a dense canopy of *Cassia javanica, Jacaranda mimosaefolia, Albizzia procesa, Eugenia cuspidate, Lagerstroemia flos-reginae, and Grevillea robusta,* as well as "many varieties of bougainvillea" would shelter pedestrian movement. As Randhawa subsequently elaborated: "In the months of November and April this strip provides a striking color scheme of magenta, red and orange.... At the flanks are clumps of *Poinsettia pulcherrima,* a beautiful shrub with showy bracts of three colors, viz., scarlet, yellow and pink, which make a sticking display in winter months."[94] The lively and active bazaar streets were to include "trees with a regular shape such as cypresses, Lombardy Poplar, *asoka,* and chorisia."[95] In the residential roads evergreens and flowering trees to one side would shade the pedestrian and bike pathway. Along the inner sector roads, the V5's, the sidewalks were to include trees with "beautiful flowers and foliage, such as kachnar, jacaranda, coral trees, amaltas, gulmohur, pink cassia, silver oak, and the Pride of India."[96] The sector's inner parks were to be planted informally with an emphasis on forming shaded pedestrian pathways and horticultural clusters of different colors, shapes, and textures. Here, the solar orientation according to the season was calculated to increase comfort. For instance, shade trees planted on the western side would enable the shade to fall on the maximum area of use in summer.[97]

While endorsing the ornamental values of trees, Randhawa also argued for their "utilitarian" contribution—particularly within the city's residential areas and surrounding greenbelts. In a critical tone, he pointed out that too much emphasis has been laid on "mere ornamentals" in the residential compounds of New Delhi's bungalows, where fruit and medicinal trees are "totally ignored."[98] Considering the residential landscape there to be as important as the city's public parks and the open spaces among its public buildings, Randhawa noted that "the tree planting scheme of New Delhi could have been very much improved if fruit trees like citrus, figs, and papayas have been planted in the back yards, thus achieving a happy compromise between beauty and utility." This view prompted a guiding principle for Chandigarh's residences: that utilitarian plants should be planted in the back gardens and ornamental flowerings trees in the front yards. In a letter to Varma, Randhawa advised: "I suggest that we should collect fruit plants and bud-wood of different fruit plants such as citrus, *ber,* grapefruit, etc., so that sufficient number of plants are available for planting in the compounds of houses."[99]

Landscape as a "utilitarian" medium also characterizes the bioclimatic objectives of the large-scale landscape projects in Chandigarh: the planting of shelterbelts along the monsoon rivulets on both sides of the city—the Patiali Rao and Sukhna Choe—and the reforestation on the north side of Capitol complex, including the banks of Lake Sukhna. Following Le Corbusier's proposal to form a continuous greenbelt at a five-mile radius around the city (later extended to ten miles), the Punjabi government approved the Periphery Control Act in 1952 to protect the city from dust storms and environmental pollution, limit its expansion, and shield the adjacent rural communities from potential distress from the urban environment. Rows of *Dalbergia sissoo* (North Indian rosewood) were planted along the monsoon riverbeds to structure the slopes, reduce erosion, and provide shelter from the blowing sand during the dry and hot months of May and June. By 1958, during a Landscape Committee meeting that included Le Corbusier and Randhawa, Varma noted: "the forest belt along the Patiala Choe had proved to be very useful in preventing sand coming into the Capitol area."[100] For Randhawa, these planted zones also provided an additional opportunity to support the social and economic milieus of the rural residents. He maintained that subservient agriculture could supply Chandigarh "with food, grains, fruits, vegetables and milk."[101] Toward this end, an order was passed stressing the Commission's duty in promoting "agriculture, particularly horticulture and vegetable cultivation in the periphery area so that it serves as a green belt."[102] Randhawa noted that "this green belt would be really green" and that fostering its cultivation would "protect the crops in the farm from hot and dry winds."[103]

The "Leisure Valley," which Le Corbusier described as the *Valleé d'Erosion* during his initial visit to the site, is both the city's major urban park and the catchment area for the monsoon stream N-Choe. Conceived of as a series of "theme gardens" and intermixed with the residential sectors, the park runs northeast to southwest through the city.[104] Adjacent to the Government Arts Schools and Museums, the commercial core, and the Colleges, the Leisure Valley terminates in Rajendra Park next to the Capitol complex, where it spreads over four hundred acres east of the Secretariat.[105] Rajendra Park was intended to protect the capitol complex from adverse microclimatic conditions, including the scorching dust during the dry and hot seasons. To that end extensive mango groves were added to those that existed without impeding the view to the mountains. Their rounded, evergreen canopy proved suitable to arresting the dust rising from the dry riverbeds and restraining the effects of the hot and cold winds. Moreover, as Rajnish Wattas, former principal of the Chandigarh College of Architecture, notes: "More than 4,000 plants were planted in this park.... Viewed from the tall buildings in the Capitol area ... the entire space has the look of a green carpet."[106] Nevertheless the park has suffered from prolonged neglect and incompliant plantings.

In 1957, acclaiming the successes achieved at Chandigarh, Randhawa remarked: "The marriage of the tree and the building has taken place. The result is harmony, and the link between nature and man is established."[107] Chandigarh is the only systematically planted city in India—or, as Randhawa expressed it, "the only city in India which has adopted land planting with vegetation as a matter of policy" in response to the region's extreme climate and its effects on psychophysiological well-being.[108] Nearly ten years after starting work, Le Corbusier reminded Prime Minister Nehru that "the construction of the 'Capitol' and its lateral elements has brought to Chandigarh such a marvelous landscape (lake and mountain) which no city in the world possesses. Let us not destroy it!"[109] Nevertheless, the various reports produced by the Landscape Advisory Commission up to 1966 indicate a number of concerns. These include a lack of funds to complete the landscape in the sectors, the repeated damage to seedlings by stray cattle, unregulated construction in Chandigarh's greenbelts, and insufficient landscape maintenance. Despite these issues and the incompleteness of such a large enterprise, residents continue to voice their appreciation for living in a city that is safe, green, and unpolluted. Lacking the urban intensity of Ahmedabad, Delhi, or Mumbai, Chandigarh has from its very inception benefitted from Le Corbusier's approach to landscape as an integral bioclimatic medium. The city has one of the highest records in health and education in India. As noted in *The Indian Express*, "the understanding of the city as a whole organism with many interconnected parts—including housing and climate, social integration and community living, well-being and supporting infrastructure—can be accountable for its success."[110]

Conclusion

Chandigarh culminates Le Corbusier's design itinerary focused on nature. Whereas his projects from the early 1930s were concerned largely with sunlight, the challenges of Chandigarh—one concerning breathing as a biological mechanism—demanded an expanded set of climatic parameters, such as heat, wind, humidity, and temperature. With increased awareness of the psychophysiological potentials of the human body, Le Corbusier wrote: "The problem was no longer one of reasoning but of sensation."[111] While acknowledging humankind's psychophysiological vulnerability amid the region's climatic extremes, Le Corbusier became increasingly aware of the intersection between architecture and landscape to temper the environment in order to promote sustained physical and emotional well-being. At Chandigarh he turned the architectural membrane, previously sealed and "neutralizing," into a deep space that includes landscape, broadening his understanding of the scope of the discipline. In *New World of Space,* he invoked space as a "whole environment," where boundaries dissolve and an "unbounded depth opens up." Space is permeable and cavernous, physical and emotional, and, importantly, "in service of social health."[112] Just as this spatial concept attests to an emerging sensibility centered on the fleeting qualities of meteorological elements and their effects, so Le Corbusier's collaboration with Missenard and Randhawa provided the design principles for their implementation in the form of his two new CIAM grids: the climatic grid and the tree-planting grid. In reconciling evidence from science with emotional aims, these grids reflect the principles of a disciplinary synthesis where architecture, landscape, and climate converge into a unified idea of space for human nurturing. They translate Le Corbusier's revised idea of breathing into a wider homeostatic relationship with the inhabited space. "The exterior also becomes an interior," Le Corbusier had declared in *Vers une architecture* (1923).[113] At Chandigarh he materialized this interdependence with a refined spatial choreography at various scales and temporal domains: from the region to the sector; from the building compound to the individual structure; from the public to the private domain; and from the meteorological rhythms—annual, diurnal, and nocturnal cycles—to human interaction. At the regional and sector scales, Lake Sukhna and the planted greenbelts protect the city from the seasonal sand storms, scorching winds, and dry air. The Leisure Valley and the neighborhood parks direct the cooling winds from the mountains, acting simultaneously as civic anchors and as catchment areas during the annual monsoons. The streetscape, often asymmetrical in section, moderates the heat and protects against solar glare during the summer. The horticultural differentiation among the bazaar streets contributes to a sense of locality, and the domestic gardens sustain an active social and civic life in the core of the residential sectors. The architectural envelopes—*murs isothermes*—operate as thick thresholds and spaces of thermal regulation. In homeostatic exchange with the exterior, these walls breathe and support breathing through their thermo-regulative "physiology," just as the detached roofs, verandahs, parasols, *jaalis,* operable *brises-soleil,* sleeping terraces, projecting roofs, and *murs de verdure.* Some features register the diaphanous presence of meteorological forces for cyclical recharge: cooling vaults, reflecting basins, canals, supersize scuppers, and folly-like signs and symbols. Others expand on this repertoire, including embankments, tree groves, pedestrian promenades, artificial hills, water basins, and topographical manipulations of the ground. The recognition of breathing as a biological act equalizes climate and space, physiology and emotion, broadening Le Corbusier's understanding of living atmospheres as contingent upon a disciplinary symbiosis. At Chandigarh, the "machine for living" evolved into a climatic "bestiary"—a spatial orchestration of architecture and landscape, weather and psychophysiological well-being, that is both physical and ineffable.

1 Le Corbusier, "Preface" (Chandigarh, November 12, 1960), 2 [typescript for publication in Didier Gompel Netter, *L'Engineering. Contribution à la vulgarization et à son développement* (1961)], Fondation Le Corbusier [FLC] U3-09-21 [emphasis in original].
2 Le Corbusier, *Creation Is a Patient Search* (New York: Frederick Praeger, 1960), 155.
3 Le Corbusier to P. N. Thapar, December 9, 1951, FLC P2-17-183.
4 Le Corbusier, *The Radiant City: Elements of a Doctrine of Urbanism to Be Used as the Basis of Our Machine-age Civilization* [1933], Pamela Knight, Eleanor Levieux, and Derek Coltman, trans. (New York: Orion, 1967), 101, 29, 86.
5 Le Corbusier, *Precisions sur un état present de l'architecture et de l'urbanisme* (Paris: G. Crès, 1930), 64.
6 Le Corbusier, *The Radiant City* (1967), 40, 42. See Pierre Winter, "Le Corps nouveau," *L'Esprit Nouveau* no. 15 (February 1922): 1755–58, here 1758.
7 Jane Drew and Maxwell Fry, "Chandigarh and Planning Development in India," *Journal of the Royal Society of Arts* 103, no. 4948 (April 1955): 315–33, here 329.
Jane Drew and Maxwell Fry, who had construction experience in the tropical climates of West Africa, played crucial roles in the design and execution of the housing and landscape types in the residential sectors of Chandigarh. With her expertise in social integration and climatic awareness, Drew led "extensive consultation with the local populace to align the architecture with what she thought of as a local *custom* and *tradition*." Iain Jackson, "Maxwell Fry and Jane Drew's Early Housing and Neighborhood Planning in Sector-22, Chandigarh," *Planning Perspectives* 28, no. 1 (2013): 1–26, here 5 [emphasis in original].
8 Le Corbusier to Jane Drew, December 21, 1951, FLC P2-11-152.
9 Le Corbusier's travels included Argentina and Brazil (1929), Morocco and Algeria (1931), and the United States (1935). He returned to Brazil in 1936, and in 1947 he visited Bogota, Colombia.
10 Le Corbusier, *The Radiant City* (1967), 6.
11 Le Corbusier, "Rétours ... ou l'enseignement du voyage. Coupe en travers: Espagne. Maroc. Algérie. Territoires du Sud," *Plans* 8 (October 1931): 92–108, here 105.
12 Le Corbusier, *The Radiant City* (1967), 232.
13 Le Corbusier, "Rétours ... ou l'enseignement du voyage" (1931): 101.
14 Alexis Carrel, *L'Homme, cet inconnu* (Paris: Plon, 1935), 17. Carrel was a French biologist and physiologist who received the Nobel Prize in Physiology and Medicine in 1912. The eugenics theory of biological order was part of fascist ideology, which endorsed racist discourse, sexism, and euthanasia procedures for criminals and mentally diseased, or so-called "defective" individuals. The French Foundation for Human Research proposed a "New Science of Man," defined as strictly dependent on the physicochemical and physiological environment. The foundation was "dedicated to the safeguarding, improving and developing of the French population." See Alain Drouard, "Les trois âges de la Fondation française pour l'étude des problèmes humains," *Population* 38, no. 6 (November–December 1983): 1017–47.
15 Le Corbusier and François de Pierrefeu, *The Home of Man* [1942] (London: Architectural Press, 1948), 24, 96 [emphasis in original].
16 André Missenard, *In Search of Man* [*À la recherche de l'homme,* 1954], Lawrence G. Blochan, trans. (New York: Hawthorn, 1957), 218.
17 André Missenard, "Le Chauffage des habitations du point de vue physiologique et higiénique," *La Presse Médicale* 81 (8 October 1938): 1495–97.
18 I. Requena-Ruiz and D. Siret, "Experiments on Thermal Comfort and Modern Architecture: The Contributions of André Missenard and Le Corbusier," in *Investigating and Writing Architectural History: Subjects, Methodologies and Frontiers. Papers from the Third Eahn International Meeting,* Michela Rosso, ed. (Torino: EAHN, 2014), 651–63, here 654.
19 Le Corbusier, annotated copy of Missenard, À *la recherche de l'homme* (1954), FLC.
20 Le Corbusier, "L'Espace indicible," *Architecture d'Aujourd'hui* (April 1946): 9–17; special issue devoted to Le Corbusier.
21 *Le Corbusier: New World of Space* (New York: Reynal & Hitchcock, 1948), 7, 8.
22 Roberto Gargiani and Anna Rosellini, *Le Corbusier: Béton Brut and Ineffable Space, 1940–1965: Surface Materials and Psychophysiology of Vision* (New York: Routledge, 2011), 219.
23 Le Corbusier to Yvonne Gallis, Chandigarh, February 25, 1951, FLC R1-12-96.
24 These footpaths, irrigation canals, and trees are indicated as features to maintain in the "Album Punjab," FLC W1-5-3, W1-5-6.
25 Le Corbusier, Sketchbook "Album Punjab Simla I," February 25, 1951, FLC W1-5-22.
26 Ibid., FLC W1-5-18.
27 *Le Corbusier Sketchbooks,* vol. 2, 1950–1954 (Cambridge: MIT Press and New York: Architectural History Foundation, 1982), E18: 330.
28 Michael Graves, "Le Corbusier's Drawn References," in *Le Corbusier: Selected Drawings* (New York: Rizzoli, 1981), 8–25, here 24.

29 *Le Corbusier Sketchbooks,* vol. 2 (1982), E19: 403. While the Unité d'Habitation in Marseille (1947–1952) includes thick walls serving as *brises-soleil* (sun breakers), he achieved such spatial and thermal complexity only with the concurrent projects of Ronchamp (1955) and Chandigarh (1951–1965). For Le Corbusier's use of the *brise-soleil,* see Harris Sobin, "Veils and Shadows: Le Corbusier in North Africa, 1928–1936," *Proceedings of the French Colonial Historical Society* 19 (1994): 187–99; Harris Sobin, "Masters of Light: Le Corbusier," *AIA Journal* 68, no. 11 (September 1979): 56–59.

30 Nivola Sketchbooks I, FLC W1-8-87. Le Corbusier sketched the "Baradari" of the Diwan-i-Am, or the "Hall of Public Audience," during his visit to the Red Fort in Delhi. His sketch emphasizes its shaded arches, the landscape to either side, and a water basin in the foreground.

31 Le Corbusier to P. N. Thapar, December 9, 1951, FLC P2-17-183.

32 Le Corbusier, "Reportage sur l'Inde" (fait par L. C. pour Lucien Hervé pour être publié dans 'Point de Vue'), November 10, 1952, FLC U3-7.

33 Le Corbusier to the Chandigarh Design Team, December 12, 1951, FLC P2-22-149/153. See the correlation of human temperaments with the cosmological forces of the sun, the earth, and the moon in Drs. Pierre Winter and M. Martiny, "Le grille cosmique de l'homme," *Plans,* no. 4 (April 1931): 43–47.

34 Le Corbusier to Takamasa Yoshizaka, December 19, 1951, FLC G2-11-1117-2.

35 Le Corbusier, "Grille CIAM applied to Chandigarh," April 17, 1952, FLC P2-13-5-12.

36 See drawings FLC 5612, –5624, –5623.

37 "Climatic Grid of the Atelier Le Corbusier," January 31, 1952, FLC P2-1-3.

38 Iannis Xenakis, "Programme d'études des Conditions Climatiques Optima et des Moyens Architecturaux de correction," December 16, 1951, FLC P2-1-1.

39 See the development sequence documented in FLC P2-1-10.

40 Prime Minister J. Nehru to the Indian Planning Commission, April 4, 1952, cited in Jean Louis Cohen and Tim Benton, *Le Corbusier le grand* (London: Phaidon, 2008), 466.

41 *Le Corbusier Oeuvre Complète, Vol. 6: 1952–1957,* Willy Boesigner, ed. (Basel: Birkhäuser, 1995), 51.

42 Le Corbusier, Carnet Nivola I, FLC W1-8-100 and 101.

43 Ibid., FLC W1-8-93 and 94.

44 Le Corbusier to J. P. Keller, April 27, 1953, FLC T1-4-163.

45 Sobin, "From l'Air Exact to l'Aerateur" (1996), 223.

46 *Le Corbusier Sketchbooks,* Vol. 2 (1982), E21: 398.

47 Le Corbusier, "Insolation diagram at summer solstice. Four floor plans and five transverse sections with insolation diagram according to time of the day" [drawing by Maisonnier], April 12, 1951, DVD #11 FLC 31145.

48 Le Corbusier, "Floor plan and sections through typical cell with dimensions and interior layout, orientation / Plan of terrace with water runoff, gargoyle" [drawing by Maisonnier], April 13, 1951, DVD #11 FLC 29091.

49 Le Corbusier, Sketchbook "Album Punjab Simla I" (February 25, 1951), FLC W1-5-19, FLC.

50 Le Corbusier to P. N. Thapar, May 5, 1951, FLC G2-11-492.

51 Le Corbusier, Plans, January 16, 1952, DVD #11 FLC 29089.

52 Le Corbusier, Plans, DVD #11 FLC 05603.

53 Le Corbusier, Plans, DVD #11 FLC 05601, 05603, 05605, 05607, 05608, 05611.

54 *Le Corbusier Oeuvre Complète, Vol. 5: 1945–1952,* Willy Boesigner, ed. (Basel: Birkhäuser, 1995), 158.

55 Jane Drew, "Minutes of the meeting held on 8th March 1952 at 10.30am," FLC P2-8-28.

56 P. L. Varma, "Program and Priorities for Construction," in "Selection of Architects and Town Planners for Chandigarh, Visit of P. N. Thapar and P. L Varma to Europe," sent to the Secretary, Secretaries Committee, Simla, February 17, 1950, Professional archives of Dr. M.S. Randhawa, Archive of Chandigarh's Government Museum and Art Gallery [GMAG].

57 *Le Corbusier Sketchbooks,* vol. 2 (1982), E23: 662.

58 Le Corbusier to Pierre Jeanneret, June 2, 1951, FLC P1-20-25, -26.

59 "A la suite d'une très minutieuse étude, je vous remete inclus, sous forme d'une grille, mes instructions relatives à l'arborisation de la Capitale." Le Corbusier to Jane Drew, "OBJET: Arborisation de la Capitale," August 1, 1952, FLC P2-2-9.

60 Le Corbusier, "Tableau de Synthese" [drawing by Samper], July 30, 1952, DVD #11 FLC 5283. With "Les Sept Voies de Circulation," or the Seven Vs, Le Corbusier classified the circulation system for Bogotà and Marseille Sud as well as for Chandigarh. These consist of arterial roads (V1); major boulevards (V2); sector definers (V3); shopping streets or bazaar streets (V4); neighborhood streets (V5); inner access lanes (V6); and pedestrian/bike paths (V7s). He subsequently added a V8-typology for pedestrian and slower movement in the larger parks.

61 Drew and Fry, "Chandigarh and Planning Development in India" (1955): 321.

62 Le Corbusier to Jane Drew, "*OBJET: Arborisation de la Capitale*" (1952), FLC P2-2-9.

63 Le Corbusier, "Arborisation des V4" [drawings by Samper], July 30, 1952, DVD #11 FLC 5284.

64 Le Corbusier to Jane Drew, "*OBJET: Arborisation de la Capitale*" (1952), FLC P2-2-9.

65 Drew and Fry, "Chandigarh and Planning Development in India" (1955): 320.

66 Le Corbusier, "Arborisation de Chandigarh" [drawings by Samper], July 31, 1952, FLC P2-2-10.

67 See Caroline Constant, "From the Virgilian Dream to Chandigarh: Le Corbusier and the Modern Landscape," *The Modern Architectural Landscape* (Minneapolis: University of Minnesota Press, 2012), 149–68; Maristella Casciato, "Chandigarh: Landscaping a New Capital," in *Le Corbusier: An Atlas of Modern Landscapes,* Jean-Louis Cohen, ed. (New York: Museum of Modern Art, 2013), 370–81.

68 Drew and Fry, "Chandigarh and Planning Development in India" (1955): 321.

69 Le Corbusier, Album Simla I, February 25, 1951, FLC W1-5-28.

70 Le Corbusier, "The Master Plan," *Marg Magazine* 15, no. 1 (December 1961): 5-19, here 8.

71 Le Corbusier, "Arborisation de Chandigarh" (1952), FLC P2-2-10.

72 *Le Corbusier Sketchbooks,* vol. 2 (1982), F24: 748. "La Main // par des massifs alternés de cyprès en couronnes // chambre d'ombre noir."

73 Le Corbusier, "Arborisation de Chandigarh" (1952), FLC P2-2-10.

74 *Le Corbusier Sketchbooks,* vol. 2 (1982), F26: 866. "Attention! Côté de la ville, il faut clore le Capitol par un glaçis continue en remblai horizontale / (cacher toute construction de la cite) ici glacis horizontal. . . ."

75 Ibid., E26: 753.

76 Le Corbusier Plans [drawing by Talati], January 6, 1956, DVD #11 FLC 31862.

77 Le Corbusier, "The Master Plan" (1961): 12.

78 See Daniel Siret, "Le Corbusier Plans. 1950 – Studies in Sunlight – Tower of Shadows (Chandigarh)," 2006, in *Le Corbusier Plans,* DVD #11 FLC.

79 *Le Corbusier Oeuvre Complète, Vol. 6: 1952–1957,* Willy Boesigner, ed. (Basel: Birkhäuser, 1995), 76.

80 Other cosmic elements that embody the relation with the sun are the enameled door, hyperbolic tower, and pinnacle of the Assembly building. These take the form of two parabolas depicting the summer and winter solar path with an upward-turning spiral derived from the sundial.

81 *Le Corbusier Sketchbooks,* vol. 2 (1982), F27: 915.

82 *Le Corbusier Oeuvre Complète,* vol. 6 (1995), 53.

83 Le Corbusier, "The Master Plan" (1961), 9.

84 Maxwell Fry, "Le Corbusier at Chandigarh," in *The Open Hand: Essays on Le Corbusier,* Russell Walden, ed. (Cambridge, MA: MIT Press, 1977), 350–63, here 363.

85 Mohinder Singh Randhawa, *Flowering Trees in India* (Calcutta: Indian Council of Agricultural Research, Sree Saraswaty Press Limited, 1957), 19.

86 *Le Corbusier Sketchbooks,* Vol. 2 (1982), F24: 707.

87 Le Corbusier understood bestiaries to be "figures in the direction of animal forms, vehicles of character, forces of the sign, algebraic capacity for entering into the relationship between themselves and thereby producing a poetic phenomenon." *Le Corbusier Sketchbooks,* vol. 2 (1982), F24: 707.

88 Le Corbusier to Jane Drew, "*OBJET: Arborisation de la Capitale*" (1952), FLC P2-2-9.

89 "Landscaping Chandigarh I" (1954), Randhawa archive, GMAG. This is the first of a series of unpagined notebooks entitled "Landscaping Chandigarh" that document the efforts of the Landscape Advisory Commission: Vol. 1, 1954; Vol. 2, 1955–1958; Vol. 3, 1959; and last volume, 1965–66. They are retained in Randhawa's archive at the Chandigarh's Government Museum and Art Gallery.

90 M. S. Randhawa, "A Care of Body and Spirit: Landscape and Gardening," *Marg Magazine* 15, no. 1 (December 1961): 48–52, here 51.

91 "Landscaping Chandigarh II" (1955–1958), Randhawa archive, GMAG.

92 Randhawa, *Flowering Trees in India* (1957), 114–129, here 117.

93 M. S. Randhawa, *Beautifying India* (Delhi: Rajkamal Publications, 1950), 9.

94 "Landscaping Chandigarh II" (1955-58), Randhawa archive, GMAG.

95 Randhawa, *Flowering Trees in India* (1957), 121.

96 "Landscaping Chandigarh II" (1955-58), Randhawa archive, GMAG.

97 Chhatar Singh, Rajnish Wattas, Harjit Singh Dhillon, and Surinder Mohan Dhami, *Trees of Chandigarh* (Delhi: B.R. Corporation, 2016), 53.

98 "Landscaping Chandigarh III" (1959), Randhawa archive, GMAG.

99 "Landscaping Chandigarh I" (1954), Randhawa archive, GMAG. Other species subsequently specified include sweet lime, pomegranate, fig, papaya, quince, mulberry, litchi, plums, guava, grape vine, sweet orange (Malta), orange (mandarin), English lemon, hill lemon, loquats, grafted mulberry, etc.

100 "Minutes of the Landscape Committee Meeting held at Chandigarh on the 13th December 1958," in "Landscaping Chandigarh II" (1955–1958), Randhawa archive, GMAG.

101 M. S. Randhawa, "Chandigarh: The Problems of a Growing City," *The Tribune* (Ambala: 1 November 1966), GMAG.

102 "Minutes of the Landscape Committee Meeting held at Chandigarh on the 13th December 1958," in "Landscaping Chandigarh II" (1955–1958), Randhawa, archive, GMAG.

103 Arjan Singh, Director of Agriculture, Punjab, to M. S. Randhawa, February 18, 1959, in "Landscaping Chandigarh III" (1959), Randhawa archive, GMAG.

104 The theme gardens are: The Bougainvillea Garden (Sector 3), The Flower Garden (Sector 10), The Rose Garden (Sector 16), The Shanti Kunj (Sector 16), The Canna Garden (Sector 23), The Hibiscus Garden (Sector 36), and The Garden of Rare Plants (Sector 36).

105 See FLC P2-2-12.

106 Singh et al, *Trees of Chandigarh* (2016), 41, 40.

107 Randhawa, *Flowering Trees in India* (1957), 126.

108 M. S. Randhawa to Shri R. L. Verma (Director of Publicity), December 18, 1958, "Landscaping Chandigarh II (1955–1958)," Randhawa archive, GMAG

109 Le Corbusier to Nehru (13 May 1960), cited in Ravi Kalia, *Chandigarh: The Making of an Indian City* (New York: Oxford University Press, 1999), 120.

110 *The Indian Express* (May 1, 2012).

111 Le Corbusier, *Modulor II* (Cambridge: Harvard University Press, 1958), 215.

112 *Le Corbusier, New World of Space* (1948), 9.

113 See Le Corbusier, *Towards a New Architecture,* Frederick Etchells, trans. (London: Architectural Press, 1946).

Sector 17, the city center

Sector 17, the city center

Sector 17, the city center

Chandigarh Central Bus Station

The Leisure Valley public park

Lake Sukhna promenade

Government housing, Sector 23, by Maxwell Fry

Government Housing (Peon's House), Sector 14, by Jane Drew

Government housing (Peon's House), Sector 22, by Pierre Jeanneret

rnment Housing (Peon's House), Sector 14, by Jane Drew

ernment housing, Sector 23, by Maxwell Fry

Capitol complex, view to Secretariat

ol complex, view to the Monument of the Open Hand

Capitol explanade, view to the Tower of Shadows and High Court building

r of Shadows

Capitol complex, view to the Assembly building

High Court building

Accompanying projects:

ORTEGA HOUSE AND GARDEN, 1943

THE GARDENS OF EL PEDREGAL RESIDENTIAL SUBDIVISION, 1947–1962

LAS ARBOLEDAS RESIDENTIAL SUBDIVISION, 1958–1961

LOS CLUBES RESIDENTIAL SUBDIVISION, 1963–1964

Luis Barragán: Architect and civil engineer
Mexico City, Mexico

Gardens of EL Pedregal

Known to intertwine landscape and architecture, Luis Barragàn created threshold areas—walled enclosures, courtyards, vegetated trellises, semi-covered terraces, water features, and patios—that expand the interior spaces of his Mexico City residential subdivisions into the outdoors and vice versa. These architectural elements filter the sunlight to provide broader spectrums of shade, humidify the dry air, cast shadows in various gradients and formats, increase thermal mass, offer shelter against the wind and sudden rain, and afford areas of retreat amid broad temperature differentials. While intensifying climatic scenarios, they also increase civic possibilities for resting, playing, interacting, or simply enjoying the vagaries of weather.

Gardens of El Pedregal subdivision
Plaza of the Fountains (destroyed)
Cráter (street)
Public park Luis Barragán (sunken "grotto")

Las Arboledas subdivision
Plaza and Fountain of the Trough

Los Clubes subdivision
Lovers' Fountain

Ortega House
The Four Gardens
Courtyard adjacent to the outdoor living-room
Interior courtyard

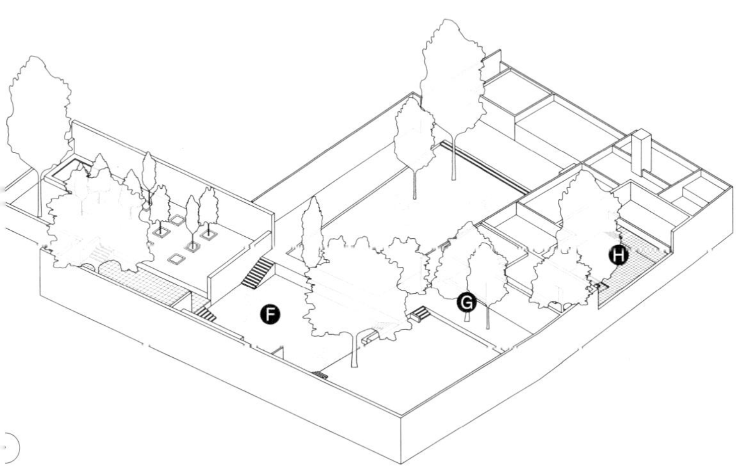

rtega House, gardens and courtyards

D In Las Arboledas
E In Los Clubes

Ⓐ Gardens of El Pedregal subdivision: Plaza of the Fountains (destroyed)

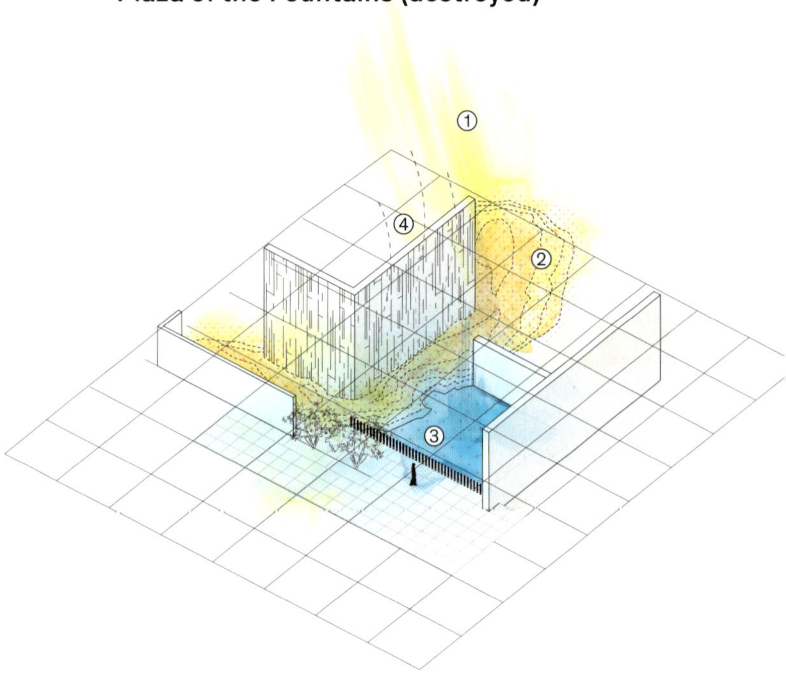

Thermodynamic performance:

① Solar radiation (exposed)
② Thermal mass / radiant heating: black volcanic rocks collect heat during the day and release it at night
③ Evaporative cooling / adiabatic evaporation: spray from water fountain
④ Free convection: rise of humid air accelerated by hot wall

Ⓑ Gardens of El Pedregal subdivision: Cráter (street)

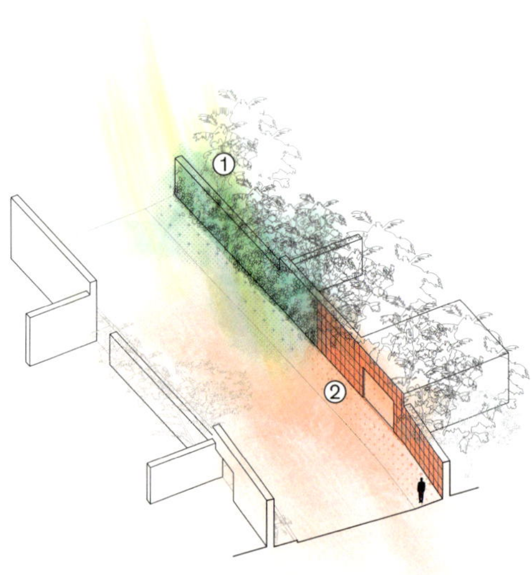

Thermodynamic performance:

① Evaporative cooling / isothermal evaporation: vegetation on walls
② Thermal mass / radiant heating: black stone walls collect heat during the day and release it at night

Ⓒ Gardens of El Pedregal subdivision: Public park Luis Barragán (sunken "grotto")

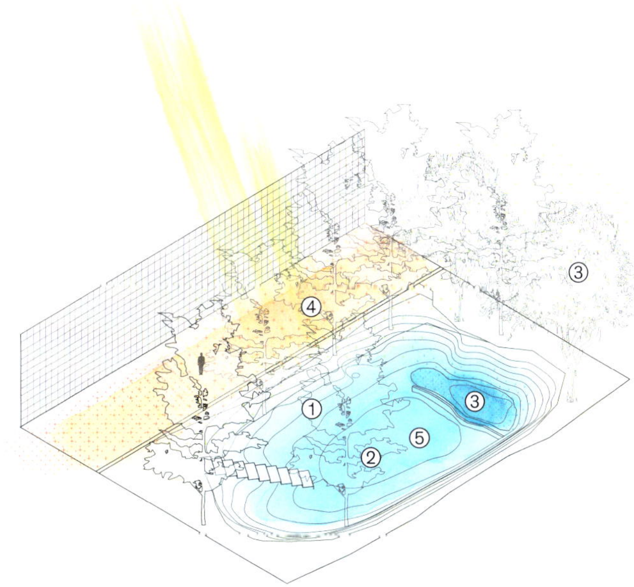

Thermodynamic performance:

1. Thermal mass / radiant cooling: shaded depression in ground stores cold (geothermal)
2. "Cold trap": cold stored by walls and shaded surfaces
3. Evaporative cooling / isothermal evaporation: vegetation and water surface
4. Solar radiation (exposed)
5. Solar radiation (reduced)

Ⓓ Las Arboledas subdivision: Plaza and Fountain of the Trough

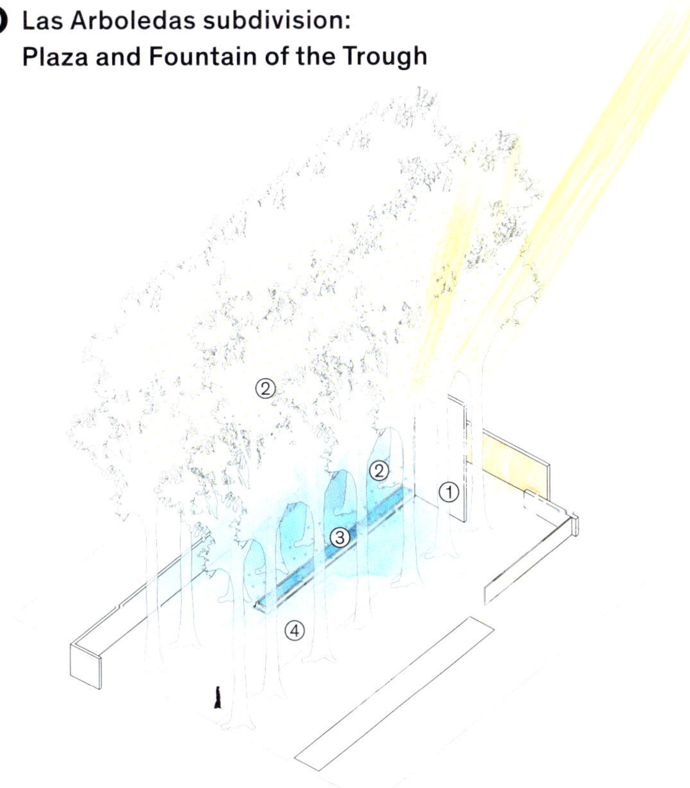

Thermodynamic performance:

1. Solar radiation (reduced): tree canopy with shadow projected on vertical wall
2. Evaporative cooling / isothermal evaporation: tree canopy and water surface
3. Reflective surface water on trough reflects dappled light and enhances perception of cooling
4. Radiant cooling: shaded ground, water surface, and tree leaves

E Los Clubes subdivision: Lovers' Fountain

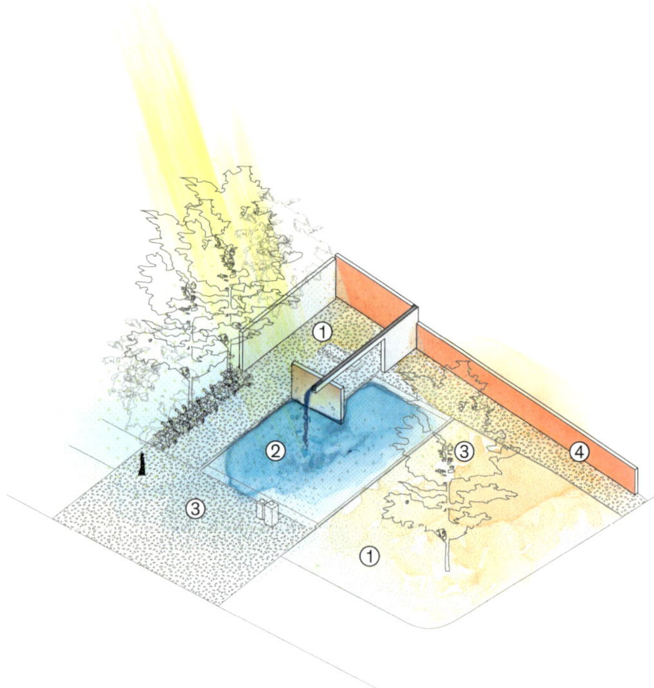

Thermodynamic performance:

1. Solar radiation (exposed and reduced)
2. Evaporative cooling / adiabatic evaporation: water spray from fountain and water splashing on coarse pebble ground (adiabatic effect amplified)
3. Evaporative cooling / isothermal evaporation: grassy surface and tree canopy
4. Radiant heating: exposed walls and ground

F Ortega House: The Four Gardens

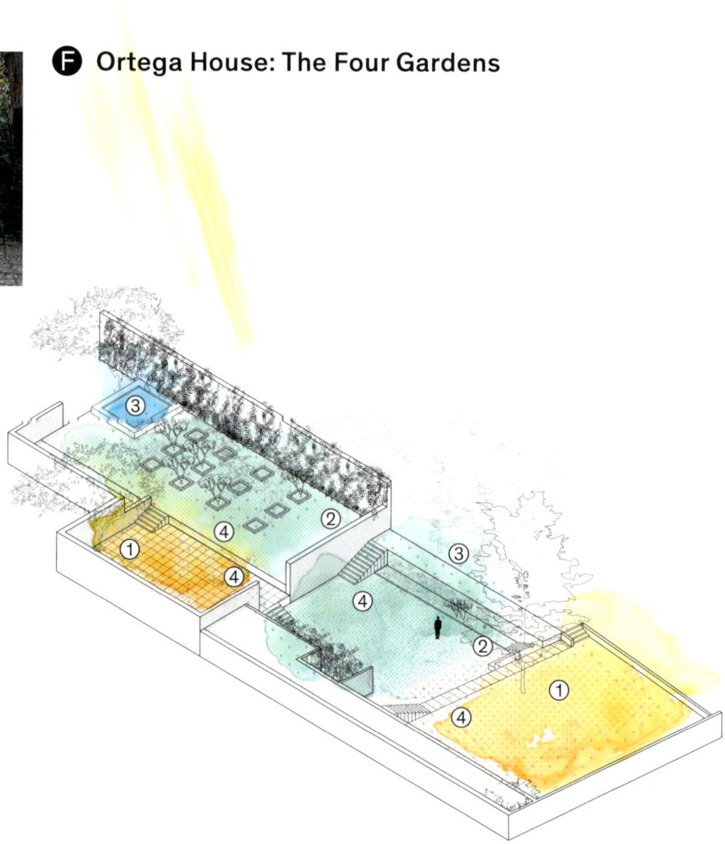

Thermodynamic performance:

1. Solar radiation (exposed)
2. Solar radiation (reduced)
3. Evaporative cooling / isothermal evaporation: vegetation and water surface (water tank)
4. Radiant cooling / radiant heating: sequence of thermal contrast (hot to cold, humid to dry)

G Ortega House: Courtyard adjacent to the outdoor living room

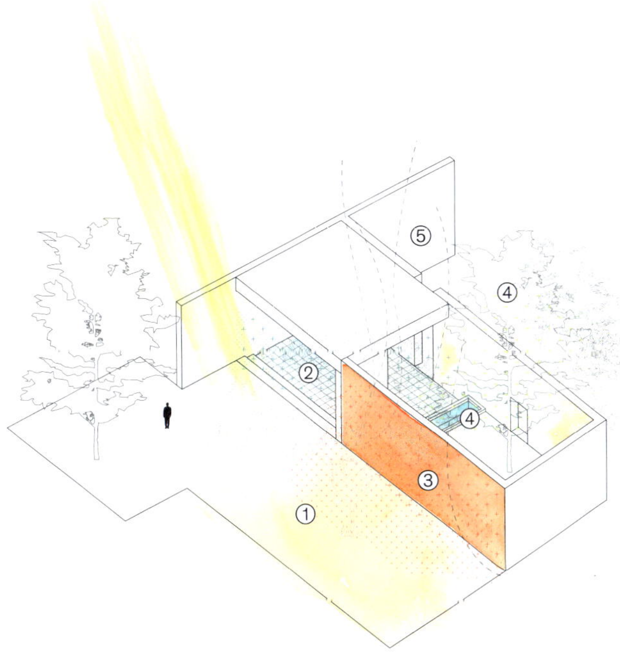

Thermodynamic performance:
1) Solar radiation (exposed)
2) Thermal mass / radiant cooling: sunken and shaded room stores cold
3) Thermal mass / radiant heating: exposed ground and walls store heat and release it at night
4) Evaporative cooling / isothermal evaporation: tree canopy and water on sunken surface
5) Free convection: hot air rises and drags cold air from shaded areas

H Ortega House: Interior courtyard

→ p. 339

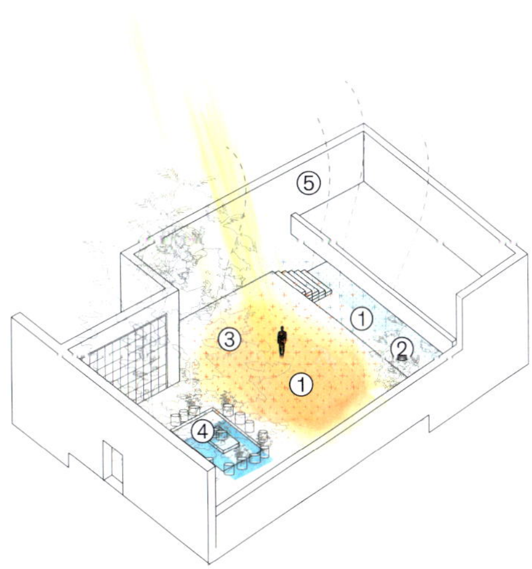

Thermodynamic performance:
1) Solar radiation (exposed and reduced)
2) Thermal mass / radiant cooling: sunken and shaded room stores cold
3) Thermal mass / radiant heating: exposed ground and walls store heat and release it at night
4) Evaporative cooling / isothermal evaporation: water on recessed surface and plants in ceramic pots
5) Free convection: hot and humid air rises and drags cold air from shaded surfaces

Public park Luis Barragán

Ortega House, the Four Gardens

Ortega House, interior courtyard

Las Arboledas subdivision, Plaza and Fountain of the Trough

Arboledas subdivsion, Plaza and Fountain of the Trough

Arboledas subdivision, Fountain of the Bell (deactivated)

Las Arboledas subdivision, Fountain of the Bell (deactivated)

Clubes subdivision, Lovers' Fountain

Atmosphere as

Program

PALEY PARK, 1967

Robert Zion & Harold Breen: Landscape architects
New York, United States

Accompanying project:

BAMBOO GARDEN, 1986–1989

Alexandre Chemetoff: Landscape architect,
Bureau des Paysages
Paris, France

Atmosphere as Program focuses on constructed microclimatic conditions—soothing, cooling, warming, or refreshing—as principal sources of delight. While foregrounding atmosphere as a condition conceived of and designed to affect psychophysiological sensations, this proposition does not necessarily refute more conventional programmatic means for activating the commons, such as spaces for sports, retail, or play. Instead, it claims that the formation of programs that lack specific form—such as ones based on atmospheric acclimatization—is central to the spatial experience and to the visitors' well-being. In other words, the natural processes of atmospheric exchanges constitute "programs" in their capacities to afford human nourishment. In such a proposition, space is a constructed environment that supports qualities of silence, rest, or contemplation. It is a place to recharge and to retreat in a comfortable and soothing environment through material exuberance—vegetal, aqueous, and earthbound. Such a place might offer opportunities to sit and cool down, to meander and pause, or to elicit introspection or engagement with the surrounding world in its temporal, haptic, and sensual dimensions. In such spaces, a unifying atmosphere composed with similar phenomena or meteorological matter might comprise different gradients of humidity, sunlight, or wind. Similar to acclimatized outdoor rooms, these spaces use different means to promote inhabitation, according to psychophysiological requirements.

The case of Paley Park in midtown New York City embodies this proposition. Imagined by the client William S. Paley to be a memorial space for his father, the park has a calming and welcoming essence in its simple effects: dappled light, aerated atmosphere, and tranquil ambiance. It is a pocket park—small and semi-enclosed—and its atmospheric qualities promote a sense of retreat and protection. Those seeking respite from the intensity of urban street life can find an antidote in the aesthetic of immersive slowness at Paley Park. Robert Zion wrote that Paley Park is "an outdoor room, human in scale, enclosed and protected, and sheltered from noise."[1] The restful sounds provided by the broad waterfall along its far end, the temperate environment created by the resulting humidity and buoyant air, and the protective serenity offered by the ivy-covered side walls and the grove of trees, all position the park's users—particularly those who seek a relaxing pause from their working hours—at the center of the experience.

Alexandre Chemetoff's concept for his Bamboo Garden was a "garden as a climate theater," reflecting on the practice of creating microclimates for horticultural purposes (to produce vegetable and fruits) and adapting this horticultural practice to a public garden.[2] In contrast to the aqueous and aerated environment of Paley Park, the Bamboo Garden offers an uncanny experience promoted by the vegetative exuberance of its overgrown mass of bamboo—an exotic plant in this locale—and by its varied atmospheres of cold followed by hot, humid followed by dry. Sunken six meters below the level of the surrounding Parc de La Villette in Paris, the garden is densely planted with various bamboo species, creating different textures, humidity levels, and light conditions experienced as one moves through the garden. Its overgrowth is stimulated by the amplified heat and humidity captured in the sunken space—sheltered against the wind and tempered by a thick, south-facing concrete wall. The effect is similar to a greenhouse where interior conditions are curated and constructed to operate distinctively from those of the park. The southern orientation of the Bamboo Garden wall enables it to collect heat during the day and radiate it back to the garden at night—a technique traditionally used for horticultural fruit walls. This heat wall works with the humidity created by the garden's multiple water channels and the wind reduction owing to its sunken configuration to form an augmented microclimate that nourishes the bamboo's over-growth. At the same time the bamboo's thick canopy nourishes the users during the day time with the corresponding radiant cooling afforded by the shaded areas of the ground, walls, water surfaces, and vegetation. A protective oasis, the Bamboo Park offers a memorable and refreshing experience for those seeking refuge from the excessive heat of the Parisian summer.

1 Robert L. Zion, "Parks Where the People Are—The Small Midtown Park," in Whitney North Seymour, Jr., *Small Urban Spaces: the Philosophy, Design, Sociology, and Politics of Vest-pocket Parks and Other Small Urban Open Spaces* (New York: New York University Press, 1969), 73–78, here 75.
2 Alexandre Chemetoff, *Le jardin des bambous au parc de la Villette* (Paris: Hazan, 1997), 8.

PALEY PARK, 1967

Robert Zion & Harold Breen: Landscape architects
New York, United States

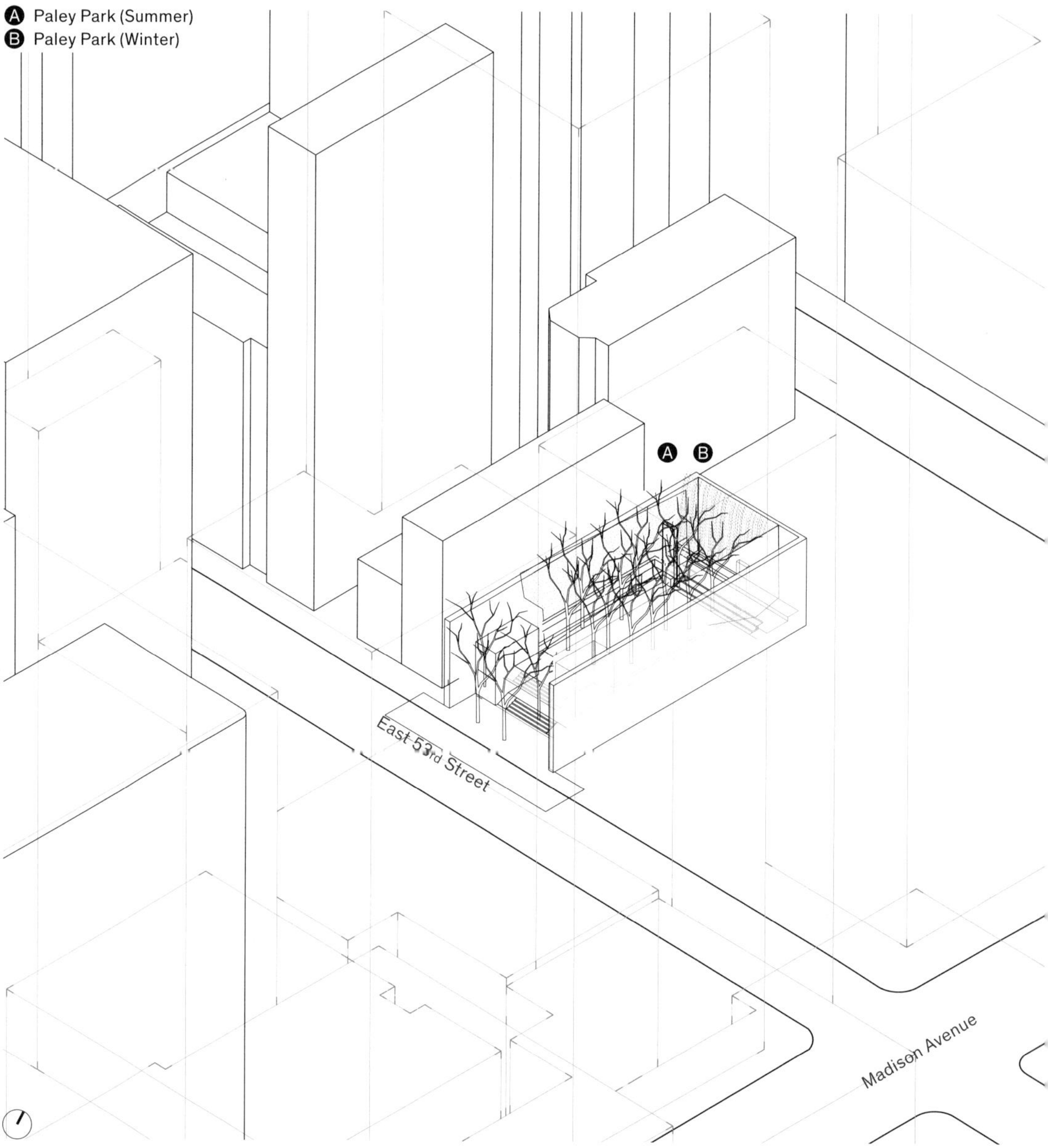

Paley Park: A Microenvironment for Well-being and Delight

Climate is one of the most compelling things in your life. It ranks in importance alongside nutrition, sleep, mental health.... Drastic weather changes actually alter your body's mechanism. Temperature changes are reflected in your metabolism—the rate at which you turn food into heat and energy. Blood pressure goes up and down with the thermometer. So isn't it obvious why climate affects your energy, your ambition, and your efficiency?
—Elizabeth Gordon, *House Beautiful* (1949)[1]

The tempering of environment for human well-being and delight is an enduring enterprise in design. Whereas the concept of well-being relates to ideas of comfort and health informed by quantitative analysis, that of delight evokes aesthetic and physiological experiences through spatial qualities. The role of atmosphere must accordingly be considered as the immediate envelope that provides the medium not only for breath but also for sensory acquisition. The German philosopher Gernot Böhme, in his essay "Atmosphere as the Fundamental Concept of a New Aesthetic," claims that the environment can be perceived through aesthetic engagement, and that it is the atmosphere and atmospherics, not indeterminate matter, that can be crafted.[2]

The interrelations between living systems and atmosphere may seem apparent, although these interrelationships are rarely acknowledged or formalized as a field of action within landscape design. The combination of land and water with air promises an opportunity to expand the disciplinary scope of landscape architecture as it reconciles human comfort with the ecological imperatives of the growing atmospheric disruption caused by rising air temperature and pollution.[3] This combination of natural elements is particularly revealing in the case of Paley Park (1967), a tiny, open space in New York City, created by the landscape architects Robert Zion and Harold Breen of Zion & Breen Associates. With their design for Paley Park, the partners conceived of atmosphere as a fundamental medium of landscape architecture for promoting well-being and delight in the built environment.

I. Situating Paley Park in the environmental movement of the 1960s

The development and construction of Paley Park took place amid the formation of a significant grass-roots environmental movement in the postwar United States and an associated design interest in the interrelations between human beings and the environment.[4] Mounting scientific evidence of deteriorating environmental conditions informed this heightened environmental awareness. In recognizing the poisoning of the air caused by the chemical revolution in agriculture, for example, Rachel Carson's bestselling book *Silent Spring* (1962) became a force for political action. As environmental historian Adam Rome points out, "Many Americans no longer could take for granted the healthfulness of their milk, because radioactive fallout from nuclear testing had contaminated dairy pastures."[5]

This new social consciousness called for new attitudes toward the built and natural environments. Urbanist Catherine Bauer Wurster, in her essay "Framework for an Urban Society," published in the Report of the President's Commission on National Goals (1960), presented the problem of vanishing open space in the cities and metropolitan regions. For Wurster, the loss of physical space was not the only urgent concern: "Clean air is an even more basic natural amenity than open space. It too is disappearing in many urban areas."[6] Episodes of excessive air pollution had become frequent in New York City. Repeated incidents of "smaze"—a "blend of smoke and haze"—in 1953, 1962, and 1966 prompted a series of health alerts, as *The New York Times* reported: "Air drawn from the street and pumped through trapping fluid quickly turned the fluid red because of its high sulphur dioxide."[7] Environmental activist Stewart L. Udall, President John F. Kennedy's secretary of the interior, proclaimed in his book *The Quiet Crisis* (1963) the need to improve both air quality and open spaces as determinant factors for a better quality of life:

> The Olmsted ideas are still applicable, and even today most American cities have unrecognized opportunities, both within their corporate limits and on their fringes, to save large and small Central Parks for the future. Every well-conceived urban redevelopment project offers an opportunity to create green spaces in the central city and avenues of action are open to conservationist city leaders and citizen groups.... They should invite the Olmsteds of our time to participate in the re-designing of our cities.[8]

The concept of Paley Park was thus imagined and constructed in the context of a community outcry for improved quality of life—for more open spaces, cleaner air—and of public support for addressing environmental deterioration.[9] In the same year that *The Quiet Crisis* was published, landscape architects Zion and Breen prepared an exhibition for the Park Association of New York, held at the Architectural League. In their exhibit "New

Parks for New York," the partners proposed to replace parking lots and underutilized small urban spaces with "tiny parks" or "parklets" to ameliorate the city's congested and polluted environment. These small parks, Zion and Breen maintained, "should not be looked upon as mere amenities of City Life; they have become necessities.... Their presence must be felt everywhere." The model of Central Park, as a fundamental space forged within the rapid urbanization of the nineteenth century, could not be used as a strategy for the congested, polluted, and consolidated urban context of the twentieth century. Indeed, one of the main intentions of the exhibition was the dissolution of the singular "large park" concept while testing the partners' new urban park idea. In the exhibition booklet, Zion and Breen maintained: "A myth, without justification, has arisen among some park administrators that 3 acres is the minimum feasible size for an urban park. Such acquisition ... in highly developed areas is clearly impossible. Few [such] parks have been acquired."[10]

II. The microenvironment of Paley Park

A year before the Architectural League exhibition, Zion had suggested the idea of a park network in an article in the *AIA Journal*. There he proposed a series of amenities that "would add to the pleasure of life in New York or any other city." These amenities would include indoor gallerias, tree-filled squares, "zoolets," water squares, and prototypical "parklets" throughout the city.[11] Zion and Breen would develop this concept of a "parklet" in both their subsequent exhibition and their design for Paley Park, realized on a narrow infill site on East 53rd Street between Fifth and Madison Avenues. Fundamental to the Paley Park design are the concepts of scale, replicability, and purpose. While the idea of utilizing atmosphere as an operational medium for small-scale urban projects expanded the scope of landscape architecture practice, these ideas also challenged the municipal authority's park policies, which were based on large-scale interventions and extensive programming.

Paley Park, Zion explained, is "an outdoor room, human in scale, enclosed and protected, and sheltered from noise." It is a model that should "be felt everywhere ... on the way to work, on the way home, as well as during the lunch hour."[12] The characteristically small and replicable concept, close to people and away from traffic, fit neither the policies of New York City's Department of Parks nor the goals of its commissioner, Robert Moses, who considered these tiny parks to be "impractical." In response to Mayor John Lindsay's plan to implement such parks in the city, Moses declared, "These tiny parks will not bring light and air to the neighborhoods where they are built and will in the end prove to be neighborhood nuisances."[13] In a rebuttal supporting Mayor Lindsay's intentions and countering existing municipal park policies, *The New York Times* reported that "the myth that three acres is the minimum feasible size for an urban park has blotted out a lot of green in New York's canyons of concrete, steel and glass.... The Park Association and the Architectural League of New York dispelled the myth."[14]

William S. Paley, chairman of CBS, was a crucial advocate for the implementation of the tiny-park concept in the dense and busy core of midtown Manhattan. Paley, who had been invited by President Harry Truman to chair the federal Materials Policy Commission in the 1950s, had a personal interest in the country's conservation of natural resources and improvement of environmental quality.[15] As the owner of a small parcel of land at 3 East 53rd Street, Paley saw Zion and Breen's "parklet" concept as the ideal opportunity "to try a new experiment for the enjoyment of the out-of-doors in the heart of the city ... where the population of residents, commercial employees and visitors is most concentrated."[16] His parcel of land fit Zion and Breen's idea of a parklet—small and quiet, inviting and comfortable, with minimal distractions. These attributes aligned not only with his political endeavors to improve environmental quality but also with his personal motivation to create a memorial to his recently deceased father.

Paley Park sits amid three tall buildings and receives southwest light. Composed of minimal elements—trees, waterfall, ivy-covered walls, and movable seating—the park is a bounded parcel of land, less than one-tenth of an acre in size (roughly 42 feet by 100 feet), and sited slightly above 53rd Street, yet visible from and connected to the street by a few broad steps. Ideas of quantity are thus replaced by quality in Paley Park. Visitors such as the office worker and the shopper can recover from their daily activities in a comfortable and soothing environment. City-dwellers seeking respite from the speed of the postwar urban lifestyle, dominated by motorized infrastructure such as expressways, highways, mechanized stairs, and elevators, can find an aesthetic antidote in the park's immersive slowness. As Zion declared, small parks were necessary urban places for loitering, lingering, and doing nothing beyond pausing and releasing the tensions of an increasingly frantic daily life.[17] Like a spa, Paley Park operates as an inviting pocket for physiological and mental delight. The restful sounds, temperate environment, and visual smoothness reposition the visitor amid an effective envelope in which shade, water, and air form a total landscape. As Park Association President Whitney North Seymour noted: "Above all, the important consideration is people."[18]

The full length and height of the park's side and rear walls are covered with material designed to mitigate street sounds, cool the air temperature in summer, and provide shelter in the winter. English ivy (*Hedera helix*) covers the side walls, and the twenty-foot-high waterfall extends the full width and height of the back wall. The rugged texture of the ivy cushions the sound of traffic emanating from the street and reduces the glare, while

Paley Park from East 53rd Street

Movable park seating by Harry Bertoia

moderating the radiant heat from the adjacent walls. The dark green ivy leaves also offer a tactile sensation and a soothing visual effect. The evaporative cooling resulting from the walls' vegetation, the waterfall's splashing water on the granite pavers, and the site's exposure to the predominant summer breezes, work together to create a cool retreat from the surrounding streets during the hot summers. The waterfall also generates a continuously restful soundscape away from the harsh street noise. In winter the waterfall is heated by a steam turbine (except in January, when it is turned off for annual maintenance), and the droplets of heated water combine with the cold air to fill the space with a warm, thick vapor.[19] → p. 178 Ⓐ Ⓑ
Patches of moss that form between the park's four-inch granite pavers create a kind of spongy carpet to register visitors' footprints on its shaded and humid surface, signaling another microenvironment. The movable wire-mesh chairs by Harry Bertoia ("Bird Chair," 1950–1952) afford the potential for an individualized experience, as visitors can choose the most appropriate place to sit and rest, whether it be moist or warm, shaded or lit, loud or quiet, near the waterfall or closer to the sidewalk. Seventeen honey locust trees (*Gleditsia triacanthos*), positioned in a twelve-foot quincunx grid, orchestrate the middle ground by providing a sense of spatial depth where light and moisture are revealed against the enveloping walls. The spacing of the trees adds the potential for meandering and synesthetic engagement. The textured canopy makes a dappled light that

Ⓐ Paley Park (Summer)

→ p. 340

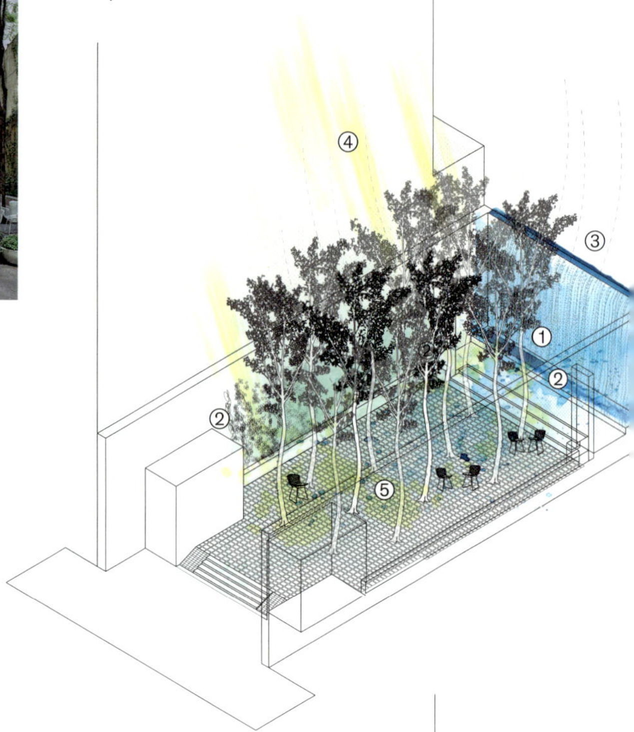

Thermodynamic performance:

① Evaporative cooling / adiabatic evaporation: spray from water fountain
② Evaporative cooling / isothermal evaporation: water surface from fountain, tree canopy, and vines on walls
③ Free convection: humid air rises
④ Forced convection: forced down draft from adjacent building
⑤ Solar radiation (reduced): tree canopy creates dappled light condition; vines on walls exposed to sunlight reduce thermal loads and the effects of radiant heating

Ⓑ Paley Park (Winter)

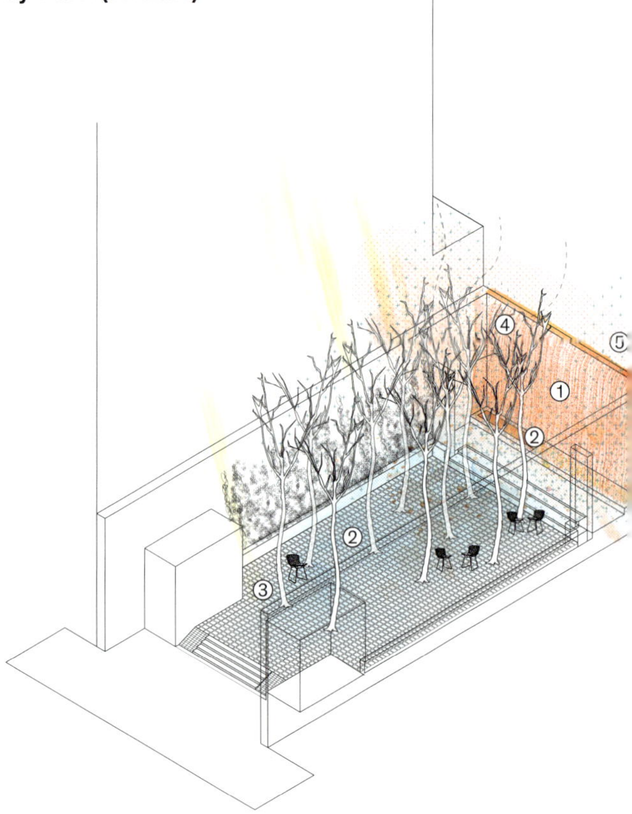

Thermodynamic performance:

① Evaporative cooling / isothermal evaporation: water surface from fountain
② Radiant heating: heated water fountain and exposed ground stores heat and releases it at night
③ Low albedo: dark cobblestone stores heat from sun radiation (non-reflective material)
④ Convective vapor transfer: transformation of hot water from liquid to vapor increases heat
⑤ Free convection: humid air rises

partially obstructs the surrounding skyscrapers; as an incomplete ceiling, the canopy emphasizes the sense of enclosure without shutting out the light and breezes.

Instead of investing in extensive programming or striking effects, Paley Park is "notable for what it does not do.... It is not colourful. It is not playful or decorative. It is not 'fun.' It is instead something finer and more appropriate, a marvel of restraint, sophistication, and urbanity," as architect Stanley Abercrombie has observed.[20] The park's spatial, atmospheric, and climatic qualities derive from the tactical combination of design elements—ivy, water, trees, stone, moss—and their cumulative effects. The American psychologist James J. Gibson, in his book *The Senses Considered as Perceptual Systems* (1966), introduced the term "affordance" to describe the physical and affective possibilities emanating from the constructed environment relative to the host.[21] In this sense Paley Park combines the various "affordances" of the different landscape elements to create a comfortable and pleasing atmosphere, through the designers' skillful curation of meteorological subjects, such as air, temperature, light, humidity, and sound. The consideration of atmosphere as a space that is not only malleable via climatic design but also accessible via the senses makes Paley Park a memorable and salutary urban experience.

III. Air, climate, and weather

The constructed atmosphere in Paley Park fits neatly into a topic of emerging significance during the postwar years in the United States: the correlation between human health and the climate or weather. Climatology and the conditioning of air for greater comfort and well-being were shared interests of various social groups in the beginning of the 1950s, from professionals (physicians, psychologists, public health officials, architects) to families. In 1949 the popular lifestyle magazine *House Beautiful* launched a program, entitled the "Climate Control Project," to examine the climatic environments in selected American cities. Over twenty-two months, *House Beautiful* published studies and articles about the relationships of human health to built form and climate. The opening page of the first issue devoted to this initiative foregrounds human influence on the climate's capacity to influence human health and well-being: "Man is submerged in a sea of climatic elements: wind, humidity, temperature, sun rays, grass, trees, lakes, dew, snow. But man-made factors also enter into climate—paving of streets, the materials of our homes, factory smoke, the windy canyons of tall buildings, the parched hot soil of our eroded farms, even the color of our own roofs. All of these are subject to endless manipulations—for better, for worse."[22]

A primary goal of the Climate Control Project was to translate complex Weather Bureau data into a set of comprehensible guidelines and

View from East 53rd Street

View toward East 53rd Street

visualizations for all readers. This translation included basic climatic analysis of temperature, humidity, solar radiation, and precipitation, as well as information about "all things that touch on our five senses," like sound, sun, rain, wind, snow, and sanitation. Techniques for planning the suburban garden, such as adding months to the pleasant outdoor season, choosing the best land according to optimized sun and wind exposure, or mastering the indoor climate, were fully illustrated and explained for the lay reader. As the editors of *House Beautiful* proposed, it is possible, to "make your own climate" with simple affordable manipulations, indoors and outdoors. The director of the Climate Control Project, architect James Marston Fitch, proclaimed, "Climate Control is no substitute for good architecture and good engineering, but it is the most significant supplement to them made during the Twentieth Century."[23]

Almost two decades later, the minimal design elements deployed in Paley Park's outdoor environment would expand seasonal use to maximum effect, while accommodating the visitor's physiological and psychological needs. Responding to the environmental awareness of its era, Zion and Breen implemented techniques that address the societal aspiration for a higher quality of urban life. The recognition of atmosphere within design is articulated in the slogan that *House Beautiful* championed: "Better Living and Better Health."[24] The experimental design of atmosphere and atmospheric "conditioning" of Paley Park, as Anne Spirn observes, integrates "the most basic principles of climatic comfort—a fact that contributes to [its] overwhelming social success."[25]

The design of Paley Park's temperate and pleasant environment was immediately replicated in the large-scale plans envisioned by the New York City administration of Mayor Lindsay. The use of climatic strategies at the city level, it was thought, could counter the detrimental consequences of existing environmental conditions on human health and, importantly, transform the congested, polluted city into an attractive destination for economic investment. In 1967, the year of Paley Park's completion, Lindsay invited landscape architect Lawrence Halprin to prepare a set of recommendations to increase the quality of open spaces in the city's housing and urban-renewal areas.

Mayor Lindsay and the Housing and Development Administration were most likely aware of Sea Ranch, the popular coastal development of vacation homes in northern California, established in 1963 and planned by Halprin and Associates. Sea Ranch is an experiment in the innovative techniques of bioclimatic design for outdoor environments, in which, as Halprin asserted, "man could plan development *with* nature rather than ignore her!"[26] Working with cultural geographer Richard Reynolds and micro-meteorologist Franklin Raney, Halprin and his team made use of pioneering climatic studies in Victor Olgyay's *Design with Climate: Bioclimatic Approach to Architectural Regionalism* (1963).[27] There Olgyay argued that physical and psychological reactions are dependent upon the climatic and environmental elements of solar radiation, air temperature, humidity, and air movement. According to Halprin, the Sea Ranch project could claim the idea of a total landscape in which atmosphere, lithosphere, and hydrosphere operate as interdependent scopes, as he elaborated: "A year of careful ecological studies revealed a great deal about land which was not apparent at the start. It was found by precise meteorological and wind studies along the shore that the wind, which is strong, could be controlled by particular types of architectural design."[28] This heightened awareness of the landscape as a whole—sea and topography, sky and wind, vegetation and light—and its skillful manipulation for the residents' comfort and immersive delight continue to define the experiential identity of Sea Ranch.

The final report, *New York, New York: A study of the quality, character, and meaning of open space in urban design,* which Halprin and his team delivered to Mayor Lindsay in 1968 followed the same bioclimatic approach that Halprin's firm had tested at Sea Ranch. The report examines the ecological interrelations between city-dwellers and their contiguous environments—"sun, light, climatology, air and wind movements, radiation impact, and the optimum condition for these in relation to building masses and open spaces and their effects on microclimate"—to conclude: "It was in the area of human and psychological interaction with the environment that we discovered a vast vacuum."[29]

Moreover, the report is directed to reducing the environmental stress exerted by the existing urban form upon human comfort and well-being. Its bioclimatic recommendations are based on simple microclimatological principles of air movement and solar paths: tree plantings along the north-south summer breeze lines to increase evaporation and reduce solar radiation on the ground; north–south openings in solid urban blocks to reduce overheating in the inner courtyards; windbreaks and plantings to relieve the climatic stress of wide, open spaces during winter storms; seasonal and temporary structures to ameliorate weather extremes; and south–north orientation of future buildings, rather than north–south, for increased shade and sheltering.[30]

Conclusion

Being in the landscape means being immersed in the "weather-world."[31] Just as architecture actively envelops space *against* meteorological elements, so landscape architecture actively engages and sculpts *with* these same meteorological elements. This physical and psychological engagement implies haptic contact with the material visual elements as well as with the immaterial meteorological elements, such as wind, sun radiation, and humidity. Through atmosphere, Gernot Böhme observes, "aesthetics opens up as a completely different field if it is approached from ecology.... The new resulting aesthetics is concerned with the relation between environmental qualities and human states."[32]

Acknowledging atmosphere as design medium enables new readings and tools for the discipline of landscape architecture. For example, such acknowledgment implies a genealogical expansion of landscape into the realm of "airscape," where the human body—both individual and collective—is positioned at the center of the disciplinary inquiry. As Zion declared, "American cities have 'designed' pleasure right out of their lives by using efficiency and economy as their sole design criteria."[33] By fulfilling fundamental bioclimatic concepts of comfort, delight, and well-being, Paley Park expands the life-affirming values of landscape and urban design as it contributes a sustainable, nurturing space to a city responding to environmental decline.

An earlier version of this essay was published in *Urban Landscape: Critical Concepts in Built Environment,* Vol. 3, Anita Berrizbeitia, ed. (London: Routledge, 2015), 233–41.

1 Elizabeth Gordon, "What Climate Does to YOU and What You Can Do to the CLIMATE," *House Beautiful* 91, no. 10 (October 1949): 131.

2 Gernot Böhme, "Atmosphere as the Fundamental Concept of a New Aesthetics," David Roberts, trans., *Thesis Eleven* 36 (1993): 113–126, here 121.

3 Other challenges include expansion of season lengths, faster evaporation rates, and increased droughts. For more, visit EPA-United States Environmental Protection Agency at https://www.epa.gov.

4 See Samuel P. Hays, *Beauty, Health, and Permanence: Environmental Politics in the United States, 1955–1985* (New York: Cambridge University Press, 1987).

5 See Adam Rome, "'Give Earth a Chance': The Environmental Movement and the Sixties," *Journal of American History* 90 (September 2003): 525–54.

6 Catherine Bauer Wurster, "Framework for an Urban Society," in *Goals for Americans: Program for Action in the Sixties* (Englewood Cliffs, New Jersey: Prentice-Hall, Inc., 1960), 241.

7 "Smog Is Really Smaze: Rain May Rout It Tonight," *New York Times* (21 November 1953): 1.

8 Stewart L. Udall, *The Quiet Crisis* (New York: Holt, Rinehart and Winston, 1963), 176–77.

9 The Clean Air Act of 1963 granted the federal government authority to regulate pollution emission standards, reduce air pollution, and invest in sulfur-cleaning technologies.

10 Robert L. Zion and Harold Breen, *New Parks for New York* [catalogue of exhibition held at the Architectural League of New York, May 1963], (New York: Park Association of New York, 1963), 5.

11 Robert L. Zion, "Some Impractical Ideas for the Improvement of Cities," *American Institute of Architects. Journal* 37, no. 2 (Feb. 1962): 25–29, here 25, 27, 26.

12 Robert L. Zion, "Parks Where the People Are—The Small Midtown Park," in Whitney North Seymour, Jr., *Small Urban Spaces: The Philosophy, Design, Sociology, and Politics of Vest-Pocket Parks and Other Small Urban Open Spaces* (New York: New York University Press, 1969), 73–78, here 75, 74.

13 "Tiny Parks Draw Attack by Moses." *New York Times* (11 May 1966): 50.

14 "Those Vest-Pocket Parks," *New York Times* (16 May 1966): 1.

15 The Material Policies Commission also endorsed the establishment of an independent organization to analyze the country's natural resources and environmental issues, leading to the creation of the non-profit "Resource for the Future," which conducts research focused on environmental, energy, and natural resource issues, primarily via economics and other social sciences.

16 "Big Little Memorial," *AIA Journal* 45, no. 3 (March 1966): 82.

17 See Zion, "Parks Where the People Are" (1969), 73–78.

18 Whitney North Seymour, Jr., "Introduction," in Zion and Breen, *New Parks for New York* (1963), 1.

19 See Jerold S. Kayden, *Privately Owned Public Space: The New York City Experience* (New York: J. Wiley, 2000), 157.

20 Stanley Abercrombie, "Evaluation: A Prototype Left Unreplicated: Paley Park, New York, Zion & Breen." *Architecture: The AIA Journal* 74, no. 12 (December 1985): 54–55.

21 See James J. Gibson, "The Theory of Affordances," in *Perceiving, Acting, and Knowing: Toward an Ecological Psychology*, Robert Shaw and John Bransford, eds. (New York: Wiley, 1977); James J. Gibson, *The Ecological Approach to Visual Perception* (Boston: Houghton Mifflin, 1979).

22 Gordon, "What Climate Does to YOU and What You Can Do to the CLIMATE" (1949): 130.

23 "551.5: Climate Control Project." *Weatherwise* 2, no. 6 (1949): 139 ff., here 139, 143.

24 Ibid., 131.

25 Anne Whiston Spirn, *The Granite Garden: Urban Nature and Human Design* (New York: Basic Books, 1984), 63.

26 Lawrence Halprin, *The RSVP Cycles: Creative Processes in the Human Environment* (New York: G. Brazill-er, 1969), 117.

27 See Kathleen John-Alder, "A Field Guide to Form: Lawrence Halprin's Ecological Engagement with the Sea Ranch," *Landscape Journal* 31, no. 1–2 (2012): 53–75.

28 Halprin, *The RSVP Cycles* (1969), 118.

29 Lawrence Halprin & Associates, *New York, New York: A Study of the Quality, Character, and Meaning of Open Space in Urban Design* (San Francisco: Chapman Press, 1968), 1.

30 Ibid., 88.

31 See Tim Ingold, "Landscape or Weather-World," *Being Alive: Essays on Movement, Knowledge and Description* (London: Routledge, 2011), 126–35.

32 Böhme, "Atmosphere as the Fundamental Concept of a New Aesthetics" (1993), 113–126, here 114.

33 Zion, "Some Impractical Ideas for the Improvement of Cities" (1962): 25.

Waterfall and movable seating by Harry Bertoia

View from East 53rd Street

rfall and movable seating by Harry Bertoia

Vine-covered side walls and waterfall

rfall

Accompanying project:

BAMBOO GARDEN, 1986–1989

Alexandre Chemetoff: Landscape architect, Bureau des Paysages

Paris, France

- **A** South-facing retaining wall
- **B** Path above water channel through thick bamboo canopy
- **C** Pathway through thick bamboo canopy
- **D** Aerial walkways atop sprinkler system
- **E** Acoustical Chamber ("Le Cylindre Sonore")

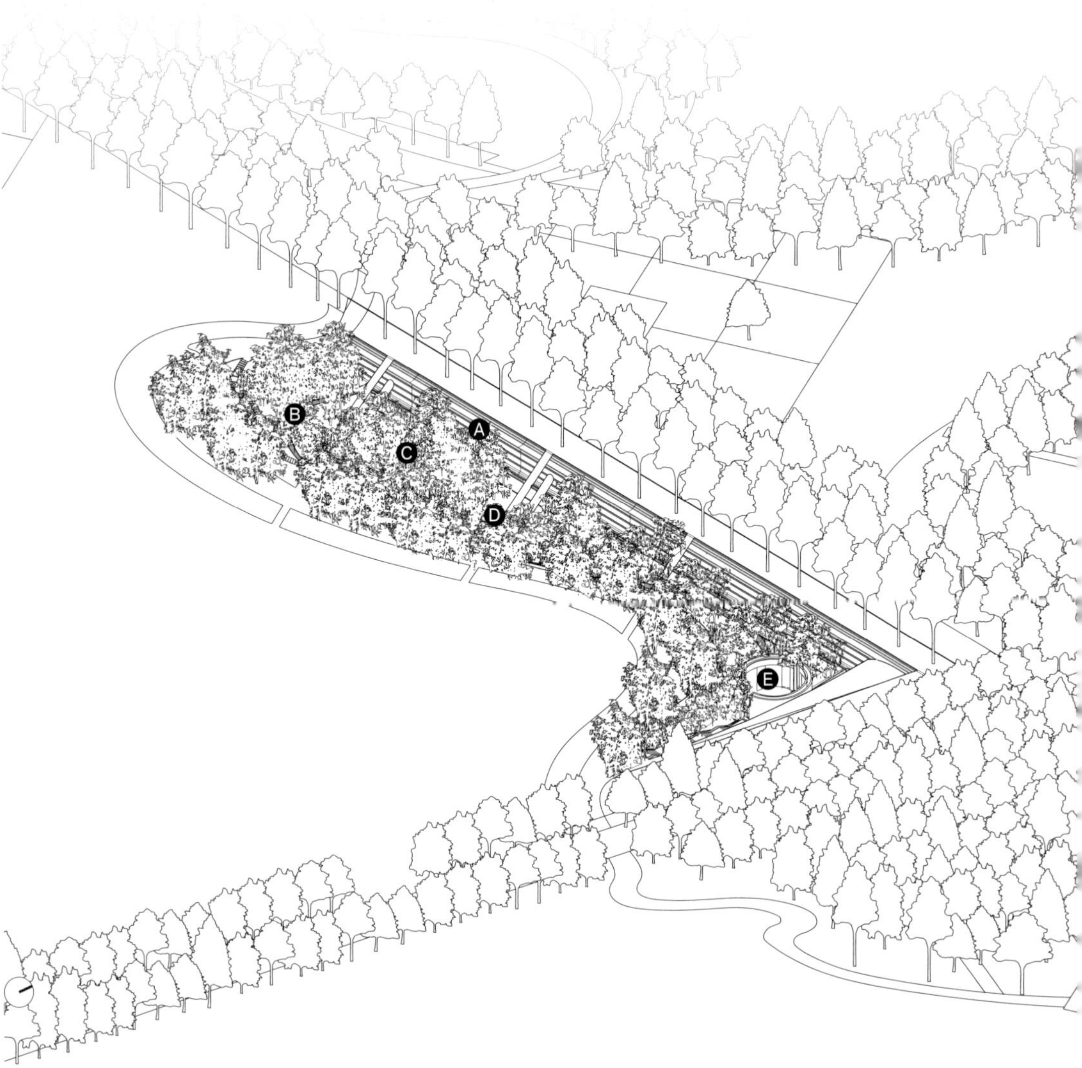

To endow his Bamboo Garden with thermal conditioning, landscape architect Alexandre Chemetoff depressed his design six meters below the level of the surrounding Parc de la Villette. This topographical configuration provides shelter against the chilling winds as well as the potential for geothermal cooling and warming from the enveloping soil. Drawing upon the traditional horticultural practices of creating microclimates to host and nurture plants from other environments, Chemetoff took advantage of the thermal mass and radiant heating effects of the garden's south-facing retaining wall, which stores heat during the daytime and slowly releases it back to the garden at night, preventing frost by creating a warmer microclimate. A protective oasis and a world of its own, the Bamboo Garden offers a vigorous microclimate for growing various bamboo species in the rather cold climate of northern France, offering the visitor uncanny experiences of its memorable cooling (daytime) and warming (night-time) properties.

Ⓐ South-facing retaining wall

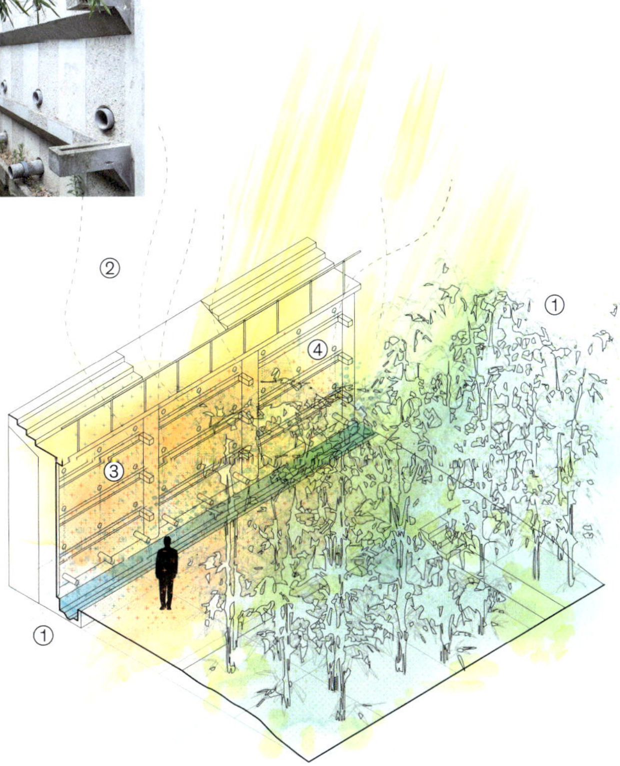

Thermodynamic performance:
) Evaporative cooling / isothermal evaporation: bamboo canopy and water surface in channels
) Free convection: humid air rises, induced by heated wall
) Thermal mass: south-facing wall (thermal collector) with high thermal inertia
) Radiant heating: wall releases stored solar energy at night

e south-facing concrete wall operates a retaining wall for the garden, which is meters below the Park de la Villette

Ⓑ Path above water channel through thick bamboo canopy

→ p. 341

Thermodynamic performance:

① Evaporative cooling / isothermal evaporation: thick mass of bamboo
② Evaporative cooling / adiabatic evaporation: splashes from running water in canal (sound enhances perception of cooling)
③ Radiant cooling: shaded ground, water surface, and tree leaves

Ⓒ Path through thick bamboo canopy

Thermodynamic performance:

① Evaporative cooling / isothermal evaporation: thick mass of bamboo
② Solar radiation (reduced): thick bamboo canopy
③ Radiant cooling: shaded ground and tree leaves

D Aerial walkways atop sprinkler system

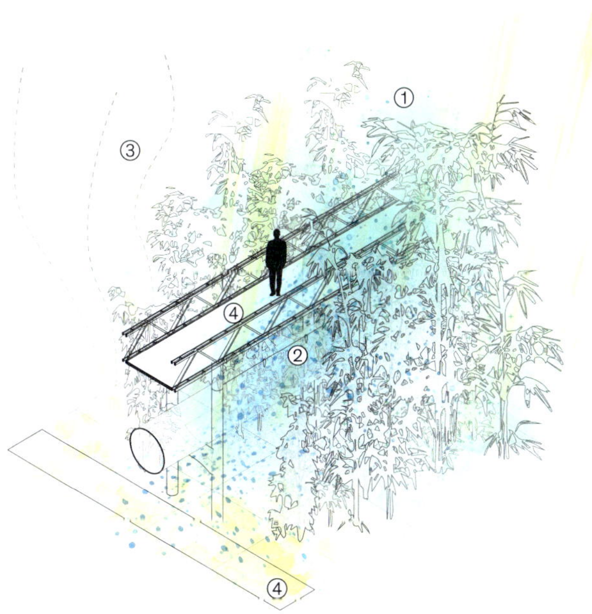

Thermodynamic performance:

- Evaporative cooling / isothermal evaporation: thick mass of bamboo
- Evaporative cooling / adiabatic evaporation: sprinklers under aerial walkway
- Free convection: humid air rises as droplets of water from sprinklers evaporate upon touching the warm ground
- Solar radiation (exposed)

E Acoustical Chamber ("Le Cylindre Sonore")

Thermodynamic performance:

- Thermal mass / radiant heating: exposed walls collect heat from solar energy and release it back during the night
- Free convection: humid air rises as droplets of water evaporate upon touching the warm ground
- "Cold trap": cold air (denser than warm air) gets trapped in early morning and at night
- "Heat trap": semi-enclosed surface (and exposed to sunlight) reduces convective heat transfer to the air
- Cylindrical reflective walls amplify sound from water moving through the space, increasing perception of cooling
- Evaporative cooling / adiabatic evaporation: water splashes as it falls from upper openings into channel

Walkway with paving pattern by artist Daniel Buren

View to aerial walkway

View from Parc de la Villette aerial walkway

Water channels at stair to Acoustical Chamber ("Le Cylindre Sonore")

from Bamboo Garden to Parc de la Villette

Acoustical Chamber ("Le Cylindre Sonore")

Pathway and water channel at base of south-facing wall

Stair from Bamboo Garden to Parc de la Villette

View from Parc de la Villette to the Bamboo Garden

from Parc de la Villette to aerial walkway

Atmosphere as Shared Situ

ion

SESC (SOCIAL SERVICE OF COMMERCE) POMPÉIA COMMUNITY CENTER, 1977–1986

Lina Bo Bardi: Architect
São Paulo, Brazil

Accompanying project:

UNIVERSITY CITY OF CARACAS, 1944–1969

Carlos Raúl Villanueva: Architect
Caracas, Venezuela

The proposition of *Atmosphere as Shared Situation* examines the civic nature of meteorological phenomena and thermodynamic events in their capacity to elicit delight and promote gathering in the community realm. By facilitating the recognition of weather as a shared domain, these projects foreground the political dimension of both the individual and the collective body in a manner reminiscent of ancestral traditions of celebrating innate biological and psychophysiological interactions with the larger cosmos. Similar to atmosphere as thermal threshold, this proposition acknowledges the disciplinary intersection of architecture and landscape architecture in constructing the mediation with weather and its thermodynamic exchanges and natural cycles. Whereas in the former proposition, such mediation for civic interaction was accomplished by thickening the wall, in this proposition a series of climatic situations supporting varied communal activities are distributed throughout the building complexes. These moments comprise a network of furnishing-like artifacts that operate at the scale of infrastructure that is capable of supporting public retreat, circulation, educational activities, rest, play, and, ultimately, awe. These “constructions” are recognizable and iconic in themselves insofar as they operate as meeting points and ceremonial moments within the overall projects.

The SESC Pompéia—a community center in the heart of São Paulo’s dense urban fabric—embodies Lina Bo Bardi’s civic commitment to creating a place for the community to gather and play amid the happenstances of weather. in her design for this nurturing space, Bo Bardi elaborated upon architecture’s social responsibility by constructing spatial situations for life to occur amid its enveloping air, light, and nature—the “subtle substances,” as she termed them, that are sensed by all. These collective situations are supported by what she playfully named “little things”: the hearth, the beach, the open shower, the cave, the waterfall (*cachoeira*), the aerial walkways, and the river. Through their bioclimatic and symbolic affordances, these “little things” reflect the disciplinary intersection of architecture and landscape architecture. Whether at the scale of furnishings or equipment or at the scale of open areas for gathering and play, Bo Bardi’s “little things” engage atmospheric events to amplify awareness of humanity’s relationship with the larger cosmos in its cultural, psycho-physiological, and anthropological dimensions.

Whereas the SESC Pompéia exemplifies the proposition of atmosphere as shared situation in a distributed assembly of bioclimatic and symbolic moments, the University City of Caracas showcases a continuous bioclimatic infrastructural system in support of activities at a range of scales. Conceived in support of a pedagogical institution located in a tropical environment that is mostly sunny, albeit with frequent rain patterns, this infrastructure provides essential features for ameliorating the local climate. It shelters circulation among buildings and open spaces, cools spaces for learning, and provides restful instances throughout the campus to support social interaction and community-building in a comfortable and revitalizing manner. It is composed of a continuous network of covered walkways and plazas, ample corridors and atrium spaces bounded by latticed screen-walls, light wells, bosques, and interior gardens, all interwoven in the built form of the campus. While typologically simple, this infrastructural network comprises a conglomeration of formal configurations and material assemblies. Its integrated vegetation and strategic orientation relative to wind and solar exposure enables it to operate as a system of bioclimatic "engines" in prompting community gathering and pedagogical activities. These moments constitute a response to the psychophysiological challenges associated with the extremes of the tropical climate and the need to form retreats with poetic, and sometimes unexpected, richness. For instance, under the covered walkways, classes take place in the open air amid continual cross ventilation, while market vendors assemble under the shade to serve the student community; by the light wells that perforate the building masses, students gather away from the bustling campus life to enjoy the punctual aeration and cooling effects of the buoyant air and indirect light; and under the covered plaza, groups assemble informally on the ground, savoring the combination of sensations produced by the radiant cooling of the shaded concrete and the cross ventilation.

SESC (SOCIAL SERVICE OF COMMERCE) POMPÉIA COMMUNITY CENTER, 1977–1986

Lina Bo Bardi: Architect
São Paulo, Brazil

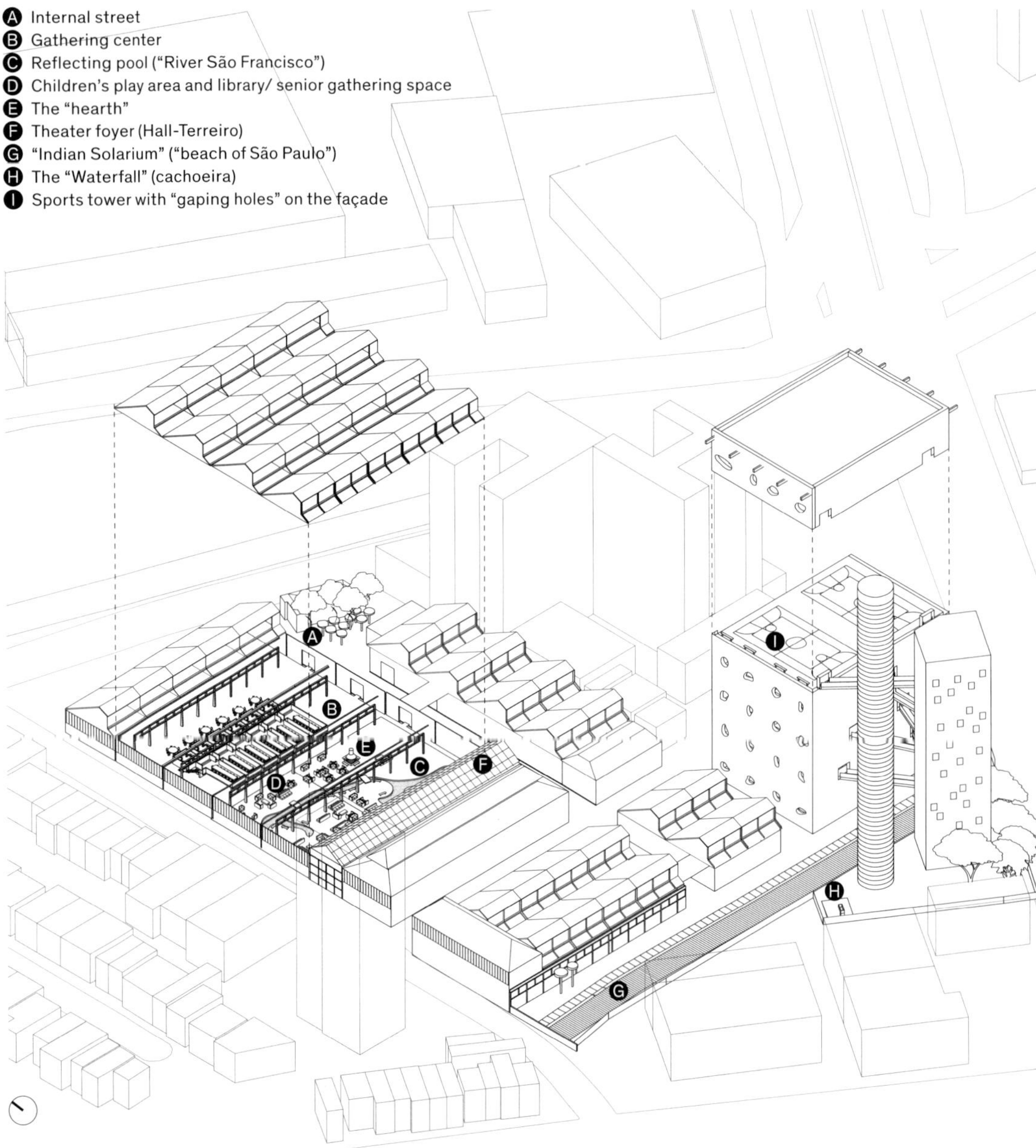

Making Weather Apparent: Curating Situations for *Life* to Occur in the SESC Pompéia Community Center

> *So what does organic, natural architecture mean? We understand it is not to be limited a priori, but an "open" architecture which accepts nature, that makes itself comfortable and seeks to mimic it like a living organism, an architecture that manages to assume almost mimetic forms at times, like a lizard on sun-baked rocks.*
>
> —Lina Bo Bardi, 1958[1]

In Lina Bo Bardi's work, the idea of an "open" architecture suggests a profuse spatial entanglement with weather as a design medium. Like "a lizard on sun-baked rocks," space is a homeostatic entity in continuous interaction with meteorological elements and conditions: rainfall, solar radiation, wind, humidity; cold, hot, dry, wet. Consequently, the recognition of architecture as a "living organism," subject to the imponderable, assumes two dimensions in her work: it forefronts the connection between meteorological forces and the organism's well-being, or, in architectural terms, the causal relationship between atmospheric conditions and bodily comfort; and it proclaims architecture's social responsibility to form a nurturing collective realm contingent upon the integration of what she termed, the "subtle substances" of air, light, and nature.[2] These aims are particularly germane to Bo Bardi's Social Service of Commerce Community Center, or SESC Pompéia, a cultural and leisure center built in São Paulo between 1977 and 1986, which remains of vital relevance to the local community. With Bo Bardi's intervention in and additions to the former Pompéia factory complex, the atmospheric conditions of space assume physiological, symbolic, and emotional prominence by reconnecting the human body with its biological constitution and with cosmic reality. Thus, weather emerges as metonym with subversive power to recall primitive, forgotten types of knowledge through the body's constant interaction with its environment. Embracing weather enabled Bo Bardi to promote the "total freedom of the body, [and a] deinstitutionalized way of living" and to resist the status quo, the normalized, and the functional qualities she associated with the Western conditions of consumption and technological development as catalyzed by the Congrès Internationaux d'Architecture Moderne (CIAM) and the so-called Modern Movement in Europe.

The integration of landscape, including its bio-climatic affordances and meteorological phenomena, was of increasing relevance for Bo Bardi as she developed a mounting commitment to forming an architecture of social and collective significance. In recognizing the necessity for a *human*-centric space in the context of Brazil's economic pressures, social inequality, and loss of cultural references, how did Bo Bardi apprehend the idea of a "living organism"? How did she materialize the idea of weather's "subtle substances" in her architecture? This essay probes the design techniques at various scales that Bo Bardi developed at São Paulo's SESC Pompéia in which weather appears as a significant design medium. It explores Bo Bardi's materialization of collective situations through what she called "little things"—sometimes as furnishings, sometimes as uncanny spatial juxtapositions—in which she embraced atmospheric events to catalyze the innate, but often elapsed, bonds between human life and nature.[3]

I. Cultural and political contexts

When Bo Bardi moved from Italy to Brazil in 1946 with her husband, the journalist and art dealer Pietro Maria Bardi, she saw the country as "a new place for utopias" and a "privileged place for artistic creation."[4] Inspired by her initial entry into the harbor of Rio de Janeiro, Bo Bardi composed a tribute to the Ministry of Education and Health building designed by a group of young Brazilian architects under the guidance of Le Corbusier: "the building advanced like a great white and blue ship against the sky.... I felt myself in an unimaginable country where everything was possible."[5] She was moved not only by the potential of modern architecture as reflected in this building but also by the vitality of everyday life that she encountered in the streets of Rio de Janeiro. A watercolor drawing, made a few days after her arrival, captures the vibrancy of the Cinelândia theater district, marked by contrasts and coexistences: formal and spontaneous, static and fluid. Framed by large trees to one side and large billboards to the other, her drawing renders a space of freedom amid a light rainfall. In the foreground, two men sit atop a colorful truck selling vegetables, while in the background crowds of people cross the street under umbrellas, all of whom coexist with the meteorological happenstance. In this scene, people and nature interact in a deinstitutionalized and unrestricted manner that is both provisional and hedonistic, without the limitations associated with social hierarchies or official cultural codes. There is an overall sense of joy and celebration amid the drizzling rain. Weather is part of the collectively sensed situation—fluid and ephemeral—that will find root in the spatial expression of Bo Bardi's architectural philosophy. In her search, landscape and meteorological phenomena would become sovereign.

Bo Bardi's intellectual repertoire reflects the revisionary debates concerning Italy's postwar reconstruction that focused on anchoring societal welfare with the idea of the "house"—not as a collection of styles but as a place to nurture lived experiences. "While bombs mercilessly demolished human works," she wrote, "we understood a house must exist for human 'life'; it must serve and comfort." She declared that reconstruction efforts could replace the myth of monumentality and aim for an architecture to live in that is necessarily "simple, clear, and modest."[6] With such aspirations, Bo Bardi set the tone for her lifelong disciplinary quest: to make architectural space capable of hosting, serving, and nurturing human life—in particular, that in underprivileged communities. Her early collaborations with architect and critic Bruno Zevi (1918–2000) and exposure to the Marxist writings of Antonio Gramsci (1891–1937) were primary influences in this pursuit. Just as Zevi's premise of "organic architecture" precipitated her interest in forging a deeper connection between architecture and nature, so Gramsci's interest in the social value of vernacular modes of expression inspired her to explore this disregarded aspect of daily life and culture.[7] In the work of both these authors, Lina Bo found conceptual tools to probe architecture's social potential while working within constraints. She would later describe the spatial results of this pursuit as *arquitetura pobre,* or "poor architecture," in its use of limited resources to affect a modest but harmonious fusion of architecture and nature.[8]

Lina Bo admired rural architecture for achieving such a fusion: for its integration with nature, including the weather. In her article entitled "Architettura e natura: La casa nel paesaggio" (Architecture and nature: The house in the landscape) of 1943, she wrote: "A more realistic approach will restore the relationship between architecture and LAND–CLIMATE–ENVIRONMENT–LIFE, thus destroying any form of superficiality, prejudice, and decorativism." In support of her interest in vernacular typologies, she remarked on photos of examples that reflect "a deep connection to the landscape and the life of the surroundings ... achieving a harmonious fusion rather than the total 'separation' between house and nature." For example, of a house near Abiquiú, New Mexico, she wrote: "The outer walls are a delicate pink, similar enough in tone to the surrounding rockface for the house to melt into the background.... The fireplaces provide enough heat for the whole house." Of a cabin in the park, she noted, "Its siting allows it to take advantage of the fresh southern breezes in summer while providing some insulation against the freezing winds in winter.... [A] row of trees planted along the north face acts as a windbreak in winter."[9]

The intersection of architecture, landscape, and weather is further evidenced in two examples of Lina Bo's early design thinking published in Gio Ponti's *Domus* magazine: a seaside house and a garden in Sicily—both developed in collaboration with architect Carlo Pagani. Both are conjectural designs in support of a hedonistic lifestyle amid the Mediterranean environs. In introducing the "House by the Sea," Bo and Pagani cited the importance of the site's atmosphere as a primary design element. "Sicilian soil is sacred," they claimed, "Magna Graecia is everywhere living; in the atmosphere, in the landscape, in the memory. We do not want architecture to be absent from this mythical, surprising, fascinating climate." In their proposal, a simple white house stands on a promontory, exposed to the sea and the winds. In an elaboration of the idea of a *hortus conclusus,* it is surrounded by white walls that would afford a simultaneous sense of seclusion and protection against the "hot winds of the South."[10] The compound is at the center of the site, surrounded by open meadows that are interrupted in a festive way by smaller gardens or landscape "situations," cultivated with local plants: agaves, olive trees, myrtle bushes, and cacti. Opposite the villa is an "Exotic Garden," also enclosed within walls; this lightly wooded enclosure has a small brook running through it and a twig hut at its center, recalling the primitive hut in Marc-Antoine Laugier's *Essai sur L'Architecture* (1753). Just as the house's cubic design—based on the Mediterranean domestic typology of patios, verandas, and thick walls—embodies modern seaside living, so its "Exotic Garden" symbolizes the essential conditions for supporting such a lifestyle: an oasis where architecture and landscape cooperate in acclimatizing and sheltering human life. Bo and Pagani expanded upon this idea in their second study: a further elaboration of the garden typology. In introducing this project, Ponti oriented the reader: "Entering the garden you can see the entrance patio that joins the house to an enclosure, where the seasonal flowers are cultivated in irregular flowerbeds; all around the house is lawn, bushes, and trees. Small streets lead to pleasant corners of the pond, the fountain, the outdoor living room with the small fireplace."[11] As Ponti suggested, the garden is composed of landscape "situations" where the residents and visitors would gather or meander throughout its diverse environments, in different seasons and temperatures: from colder to warmer, dryer to wetter, lit to shaded. The aggregation of plants and small-scale elements comprises a series of seven acclimatized moments, which Bo developed individually. These consist of the pond (*lo stagno*), the wild garden with a thatched hut (*il giardinetto selvaggio*), the fountain (*la fontana*), the flower garden (*il giardino fiorito*), the outdoor living room (*il soggiorno all'aperto*), the outdoor play space (*il gioco all'aperto*), and the entrance patio (*il patio d'ingresso*). Converging to form a space for sensing and living are such architectural elements as thick walls, fireplaces, large umbrellas, canopies, huts, and covered passageways among the garden's hedges, flowerbeds, fountains, and lakes. As Bo Bardi would later claim, "Architecture depends not only on the idea of 'interior space' but equally on its 'inhabitable' circumstance."[12] With her development of the SESC Pompéia, this idea of "inhabitable circumstance" would emerge, along with her assimilation of landscape's bio-climatic affordances.

This impetus to curate situations for "life to occur" recalls Gramsci's ethical objective to foreground popular culture. If a significant purpose of design is to curate situations for living, then what would comprise a spatial reflection of this concept? Bo Bardi was committed to finding a manner of expression capable of serving humankind as a new form of humanism, in other words, as a *sensible* mediation between human life and the environment: "The spaces of an architectural work condition the human being," she insisted, "and not the other way around."[13] It was during the late 1950s and early 1960s, during her time in Salvador da Bahia, that Bo Bardi would find the appropriate cultural milieu in which her design ethos would mature.

II. In Northeast Brazil, Salvador da Bahia

Bo Bardi's intellectual affiliations with Zevi and with Gramsci's writings came to fruition during her period of curatorial and administrative work at the Museum of Art in São Paulo (MASP) from 1948 to 1951 and during her subsequent years in Salvador da Bahia (1958–1963). While directing the MASP, Bo Bardi co-founded the magazine *Habitat* (1950) with her husband and began traveling to remote areas in northeastern Brazil in connection with the MASP's exhibition programs. In letters to Zevi, she captured her impressions of the area's small rural towns in lush landscapes, the local artisanal craftwork, and the inhabitants' daily struggles in their demanding environment. The focus of design, she highlighted, should be on "the extreme simple and fresh ways of building, the taste for clear and clean solutions of primitive constructions, the complete absence of rhetoric and a human modesty united with a festive sense of life."[14] It is here, according to Zevi, that Bo Bardi had the "encounter with the authentic Brazil"—the underprivileged communities, their inventiveness, and technical simplicity.[15] The significance of this "encounter" is reflected in Bo Bardi's numerous contributions to *Habitat,* which are dedicated to the region's everyday objects, including clothing, ceramics, and furniture as well as landscapes and architecture. For example, she alluded to the hammocks of the cargo/passenger boats along the São Francisco River as *sensible* mediators between the body and weather. They allow the body, while resting, to be immersed in the comforting, flowing breezes for continual cooling.[16] Bo Bardi understood that the most important dimensions of such examples resulted from human creativity when confronted with a combination of limited resources and the challenges imposed by the area's environmental conditions. She felt that modern architecture had not yet found the spatial language to exemplify the same ethos.

Bo Bardi opened the second issue *of Habitat* with a reflection on Brazilian modern architecture and its disregard of such vernacular knowledge and impetuses. Entitled "*Bela Criança*" (Beautiful Child), it highlights the young age of Brazil's modernism, which she felt was beautiful, although she found its spatial motivation to be unripe and disengaged from its local roots. As she elaborated, "Contemporary Brazilian architecture was not born out of the Jesuit architecture, but from the '*pau a pique*' [wattle and daub] shelter of the solitary man, who works solely with the branches of the forest, it comes from the '*seringueiro'* house [of the rubber-tapper], with its wooden floor and thatch roof."[17] She was accordingly critical of the 1943 international exhibition "Brazil Builds" at the Museum of Modern Art in New York City, which introduced Brazil's modern architecture, including the works of Oscar Niemeyer, Lucio Costa, Roberto Burle Marx, Afonso Reidy, Gregori Warchavchik, Flavio de Carvalho, and Lino Levi, to a North American audience. This event featured four centuries of Brazilian architecture, including a selection of colonial examples from the seventeenth and eighteenth centuries—forts, monasteries, churches, chapels, "*fazendas*" (farm-houses), and palaces. To Bo Bardi, this exhibition reflected a disciplinary breach in the historical review of Brazil's architectural repertoire because the "authentic" Brazil—the underrepresented popular culture of the fundamentally Afro-Brazilian, "*caipira*" (rural) inhabitants of the country's remote interior—were simply omitted. She believed that architects should voice their concerns, particularly with respect to the neglected and the underprivileged. As Zevi had expounded when he and Bo were formulating the editorial stance for their periodical, *A*, launched in 1945: "ACCUSATION must be our major motivation."[18]

Bo Bardi became further embedded in the social and cultural contexts of the underprivileged populace of northeastern Brazil during her period living in Salvador da Bahia. After accepting the commission to renovate and direct the Museum of Modern Art of Bahia, she established connections with a group of left-leaning intellectuals at the University of Bahia who were also interested in the "national–popular" aspects of culture as sanctioned by Gramsci.[19] In favoring the local vernacular culture over European or North American models, she embodied Gramsci's view of the *active* intellectual: one who inquiries into the cultural life of oppressed groups so as to identify mechanisms for social emancipation in the modern world. In architectural terms, this meant three things: the refusal of dogmatic stylistic classifications; the espousal of the innate human entanglement with the natural cycles; and the discovery of the unauthored beauty contained in vernacular modes of expression, including buildings, everyday objects, and social practices.

From the beginning of her contact with Salvador da Bahia, Bo Bardi's architectural language shifted in that the meteorological elements of rainfall and sunlight became active design mediums with both psychobiological and symbolic importance. For example, while her earlier Glass House

(1950) in São Paulo can be described as a modern volume bounded by wide windows overlooking the landscape, the Chame-Chame House (1958–1964) in Salvador reflects a turn to the opaque (versus the transparent), the immersed (versus the distanced), the rough (versus the polished), and the organic (versus the rectilinear).[20] In the Glass House, nature and weather are welcomed through the transparency of the windows and such elements as the channels that collect and direct the rainwater into oval basins. The inhabitants, however, are *sheltered* from these external phenomena, as Bo Bardi explained: "The idea was to have a house that gave physical protection from the wind and rain."[21] In contrast, the Chame-Chame House—designed symbolically and literally around an existing jackfruit tree and with façades covered with ferns and bromeliads as if "blended into the plant world"—appears to grow from the ground.[22] Bo Bardi integrated these as well as other local materials and environmental elements in her design to promote physical and spiritual soothing. The jackfruit tree provides shade, and waterspouts direct the rainfall to collecting basins, while a roof garden, although unrealized, was to afford further protection against excess solar radiation. The plant– and pebble–encrusted façades are like a spotted animal in constant thermal interaction with the environment to keep the inside cool. A hearth at the center of the house has physiological as well as symbolic and social importance; it provides warmth for comfort and represents collective living and tranquility.

In 1958, when Bo Bardi was completing the final version of the Chame-Chame House, she delivered a lecture at the Federal University of Bahia where she queried: "What does organic, natural architecture mean?" In response, she claimed, as cited in the epigraph, that it is not an architecture "to be limited a priori, but an 'open' architecture which accepts nature, that makes itself comfortable and seeks to mimic it like a living organism, an architecture that manages to assume almost mimetic forms at times, like a lizard on sun-baked rocks." Like "sun-baked rocks," architectural space is a bio-climatic construct that simultaneously mediates the forces of weather and provides well-being and delight for its residents. The Chame-Chame House represents Bo Bardi's first attempt to build architecture as an "organism suitable for life" that is open to the imponderability of weather. Henceforth she would continue her design explorations on bio-climatic effects supported by elements such as ponds, waterfalls, fountains, enlarged gutters, aromatic gardens, trellised shutters, fireplaces, and vertical plant walls—typological assemblies she would further refine and amplify with her cultural and leisure center for the community of Pompéia in São Paulo.

III. SESC Pompéia: A "citadel" for people's pleasure

Founded in 1946, the SESC Pompéia is a nonprofit organization in Brazil funded by a coalition of business and trade concerns to provide facilities for community education, culture, recreation, and health programs as a right for all social classes. The concept for its network of cultural and leisure centers originated with the publication of the "Carta da Paz Social" (Charter for Social Peace) in response to a number of factors: the worldwide post-war reconstruction and the fall of Getúlio Vargas's dictatorship; the establishment of a democratic constitution with an associated increase in individual freedom; the country's rampant industrialization; and the necessity to simultaneously legitimize the business and working classes to ensure stable economic growth. As noted in the Charter: "The capital must not be considered solely as a vector for profit, but primarily as a means for economic expansion and collective well-being."[23]

In agreement with the Charter's promotion of community empowerment and of collective well-being, Bo Bardi responded enthusiastically to the invitation of the SESC directors to design a new complex at the core of Pompéia's working-class community in São Paulo. The SESC Pompéia was built in two phases: the renovation of a preexisting building complex; a steel-drum factory built in 1938 for the German company Mauser & Cia Ltd., carried out in 1978–1982; and the construction of new buildings for the organization's sports program in 1982–1986. The site, of approximately 1600 square meters, included a series of industrial sheds aligned east–west, with an internal street, running north–south, that divides the repetitive sheds into two principal sections. In an organization that begins from the main entrance on Rua Cléclia, Bo Bardi located service functions, including maintenance rooms, staff areas, an outdoor eating area, and an industrial kitchen, in the smaller block of sheds to the north, while placing the public functions in the bigger block to the south. These cultural, recreational, and educational facilities include a gathering center (with a library, reading room, children's play area, and exhibition spaces), a 760-seat theater, and workshops. In the open area to the southwest she developed a broad wooden boardwalk above an existing rainwater channel, which leads to three massive new concrete towers that constitute the sports facilities: a large swimming pool beneath four stacked playing courts; gymnastics and changing rooms; and a water tower. In the spirit of the cosmological alignment of the *cardo* and the *decumanus* found in ancient Roman cities, Bo Bardi recognized the value of solar and wind orientation for the complex's various functions and their principal linkages: the internal street and the wooden boardwalk. Each of these connectors has a distinct climatic identity; the internal street running through the sheds is aerated and shaded, while the boardwalk at the southern end of the complex is hot and humid.

The first concept that Bo Bardi presented to the SESC regional director, sociologist Renato Requixá, involved limiting costs through adaptive reuse, thereby affirming the administration's search for an alternative to a tabula rasa approach to planning for the site's development. The idea garnered immediate support.[24] Requixá had just returned from the United States where he visited Ghirardelli Square, a converted chocolate factory in San Francisco designed by landscape architect Lawrence Halprin and architects Wurster, Bernardi & Emmons.[25] Halprin used the term "recycle" to describe his design approach in which he augmented accessibility, integrated the complex with the adjacent communities, and increased the network of public walkways connecting the existing factory pavilions. Ghirardelli Square embodied certain principles that Requixá considered relevant for the development of the SESC Pompéia: open access, reuse of existing structures, and a welcoming setting achieved through cost-saving measures. The reuse of the old factory sheds for the new SESC Pompéia was thus a "political operation" for Bo Bardi.[26] Such a project, developed in a context of economic deprivation and limited leisure options, would, in a Gramscian sense, serve the oppressed by promoting social emancipation through culture, education, sports, and recreation. Architecture would accordingly be empowered to improve human life, glorify the site's labor history, and enhance communal well-being in a growing city of declining social opportunities. But what spatial attributes might distinguish such an architecture of communal well-being?

The construction of the SESC Pompéia parallels Bo Bardi's growing interest in understanding the potential for architectural space to operate at multiple dimensions: anthropological, biological, and psychological. In early 1976, immediately prior to receiving the invitation to submit a proposal to the SESC, Bo Bardi published an article titled "Planning the Environment: 'Design' at an Impasse." Here, she cautioned against the cooptation of planning by technocrats who, in response to avid capitalism, would replace emotion and poetic allusions with overtly rational and abstract models. She pointed to Brazil's rampant industrialization during the 1950s, implemented as part of President Vargas's development plan, which, owing to pressures from the real estate market and the widespread adoption of extraneous Western-style architectural references, was detrimental to the local vernacular culture. This process, she reasoned, would eventually result in architecture's loss of meaning for Brazilian communities as well as human detachment from the natural cycles and simple pleasures of life in contact with the seasons, plant growth, and weather. "We must develop a collective consciousness," she urged; "any diversion at this time is tantamount to a crime, in view of the erosion of our culture." Toward this end, she viewed nurturing the public's recognition of the value of the local culture to be crucial. In the same article, she elaborated on her notion of the "environment, which covered everything from urbanism to architecture to industrial design and other cultural manifestations."[27] In Bo Bardi's design trajectory, the idea of environment would grow in both ecological and psychobiological terms.

Twenty years earlier, in her theory of architectural practice, *Propaedeutic Contribution to the Teaching of Theory of Architecture* (1957), Bo Bardi had asserted the need to plan the human habitat "with a view to creating a connection with nature, not only by designing green areas, but by reconstituting entire forest strips in areas where there is extensive deforestation." She added, "It is crucial that we listen to the warning, which is profoundly important and necessary for the physical and spiritual survival of [humankind]."[28] The accompanying illustrations include photos and drawings in which nature "colonizes" old monuments: examples, she explained, of a possible "harmonic fusion" among architecture, landscape, and weather.[29] Bo Bardi felt that this fusion would reconnect humankind with its biological rhythms and with the larger cosmos, promote social life, and forge a deeper awareness of primordial human instincts. Living with and among the natural cycles—in an immersive rather than a distanced manner—would prompt awareness of one's limitations and indulgences. This recognition would eventually trigger emotions, promote individual freedom, and galvanize collective life of the sort that Bo Bardi had enthusiastically embraced in the streets of the Cinelândia theater district upon her arrival in Rio. "Until man enters the building, climbs steps, and takes possession of the space in a 'human adventure' which develops over time," she maintained, "architecture does not exist; it is a non-humane diagram."[30] The SESC Pompéia would reify this notion of "human adventure" as a sensorial journey through space, consistent with her view of architectural space as contingent upon the activation of the senses. Just as the "possession" of space invokes the individual body as a sensor, so it comprises a bigger sense of belonging to a vast world. Thus, to *possess* space is to *sense* it. Adopting the declarative stance of a manifesto, Bo Bardi proclaimed the SESC complex to be a "*cidadela,*" meaning "not just a 'citadel' but also a goal."[31] She imagined the SESC to be a welcoming and nurturing living environment: a sanctuary for the community to gather and play in a space where the fusion of architecture, landscape, and weather is given expressive force.

4. Making weather apparent at the SESC

Characterized by subtropical weather patterns, São Paulo experiences dry and hot air during the day, and its atmospheric conditions can change dramatically with sudden bursts of rainfall. The impressions Bo Bardi registered during her first visits to the former Mauser Brothers steel-drum factory not only showcase her commitment to the anthropological, biological, and psychological affordances of space but also establish the climatological premises for the project's development. Recognizing the value of the existing complex as an instance of the community's industrial history as well as its potential for the joyful celebration of the site's atmospheric happenstances, she eulogized:

> When I first entered the abandoned Pompéia Drum Works in 1976, what piqued my curiosity—in terms of its potential for transformation into a leisure center—were the large factory sheds arranged rationally, ... [and] the elegant and innovative concrete structure. Remembering fondly the pioneer Hennebique, I then thought about the need to preserve the work.... The second time I visited ... the elegant Hennebique structure no longer felt solitary: there was a happy crowd of infants, mothers, fathers, older people passing from one pavilion to another. The rain was dripping through the cracked roofs, children were running around, and boys were playing soccer, laughing as they kicked the ball through the puddles.... I thought: all of this should continue like this, with all this happiness.... This is where the story of the design for the SESC Pompéia Cultural Center begins.[32]

In describing the place through its historical relevance and the potential for daily life to flourish amid its meteorological contingencies, Bo Bardi conceived of weather and the human interaction with it as found "situations." Just as keeping the old factory can be understood as an antidote to the loss of cultural reference driven by the fast pace of modernization, so maintaining a spirit of joyfulness amid inclement weather conditions is a way of supporting the "possession of space"—the "human adventure," as she described it.[33] Maintaining the old factory would celebrate the local history of labor, while amplifying the atmospheric situations would enhance communal life. Thus, the integration of weather, its atmospheric happenstances and elements—rainfall, humidity, heat, and wind—would play a significant role in Bo Bardi's interest in imparting collective life in her spatial definition of the SESC Pompéia. As she elaborated following its completion: "In an overcrowded, distressed city, a ray of light may suddenly shine, a freshening breeze, can suddenly arise... [T]he continuing joy of the broken-roofed factory: a little joy in a sad city."[34] Just as the elements of weather are capable of promoting joyfulness due to their imponderability, so they also activate the connection to nature by eliciting the most original, ancestral, and visceral psychophysiological sensations: the delight of coldness on a warm day or of warmth on a frigid night; or, simply, the thrill of observing the "rain dripping through the cracked roofs" or watching the children laughing as they kick a ball through the puddles.

In "Nature and Architecture," Bo Bardi maintained: "nature pacifies, and for this very reason the study of nature should be the primary source for the study of architecture—the product and creation of man."[35] Borrowing a concept from the nineteenth-century art critic John Ruskin, namely that "All judgment of Art is founded on the knowledge of Nature," she incorporated this idea in her architecture.[36] The reference to Ruskin is worth highlighting, as he saw the power of atmospheric phenomena—in this case the uncanny atmosphere of London's sky tinted by the emerging airborne pollution from the Victorian-era industrialization—as the catalyst for a new sensibility. In support of his argument, Ruskin praised the Romantic painter William Turner's work in making this "new" nature perceptible, contrary to the established representations in medieval paintings:

> Out of perfect light and motionless air, we find ourselves on a sudden brought under somber skies, and into drifting wind; and, with fickle sunbeams flashing in our face, or utterly drenched with sweep of rain, we are reduced to track the changes of the shadows on the grass or watch the rents of twilight through angry clouds. And we find that whereas all the pleasure of the medieval was in *stability, definiteness and luminousness,* we are expected to rejoice in darkness, and triumph in mutability; to lay the foundation of happiness in things which momentarily change or fade; and to expect the utmost satisfaction and instruction from what is impossible to arrest, and difficult to comprehend.[37]

Bo Bardi's initial description of the old factory—a meteorological scene in which the community rejoices triumphantly in the mutability of weather—belies a similar romantic impulse. But, how did this impetus lead to a design strategy attentive to meteorological performance?

From the outset of the design process Bo Bardi recognized the favorable attributes of the existing complex for climatic amelioration owing to the orientation of the factory buildings and their internal street relative to solar and wind exposure. The east–west alignment of the sheds had offered thermal relief to the factory workers, while the north–south orientation of the internal street funneled the dominant southeastern winds through the complex. Furthermore, the north-facing sides of the shed roofs, clad in brick rooftiles, would block direct solar radiation (which originates from the north in the southern hemisphere) from penetrating the interiors and thus reduce thermal loads, whereas the large operable clerestory windows on their southern sides would allow the dominant breezes to penetrate the sheds for continual cross ventilation—all in support of the workers' demanding physical activities. By leveraging the site's bioclimatic performances, Bo Bardi demonstrated her basic pledge to avoid mechanical systems for climatic control, in accordance with her "aversion to air conditioning."[38]

Bo Bardi titled her first sketch for the SESC complex "Landscape" to reflect her commitment to landscape's bio-climatic affordances for collective well-being. The drawing depicts a section within the larger blocks of sheds, flooded with intense sunlight, that would evolve into the gathering center.[39] Two levels connected by serpentine ramps invite people to meander fluidly amid a plethora of overgrown plants set beneath a glass roof. Due to potential heat gains and the need to limit construction costs,

Bo Bardi ultimately abandoned the idea of converting this agglomeration of sheds into a tropically lush, warm, and humid greenhouse.[40] In a subsequent plan drawing for the same space, she dissolved the existing dividing walls to welcome the movement of wind, the meandering of visitors, and the potential growth of the plants. Planted strips, large gardens, and bodies of water within this block of sheds are conveyed in this drawing with expressive strength. In sketches for other spaces in the complex, Bo Bardi continued to explore this idea of colonizing space with exuberant plant life amid meteorological events. Boundaries between built structures, planted areas, and bodies of water are similarly dissolved, reflecting Bo Bardi's idea of "harmonic fusion" between people and nature, architecture and landscape, community life and meteorological rhythms. Referencing the Brazilian landscape architect Roberto Burle Marx, she maintained that "tropical flora" should be used "to bring the natural landscape back within the confines of the modern city."[41] In articles she published in *Habitat,* Bo Bardi frequently paid tribute to the work of Burle Marx, including several of his projects in Rio de Janeiro, Petrópolis, and São Salvador in which he combined tropical vegetation with decorative ceramic tile walls and masses of water and rocks. Highlighting his sensibility to botanical life, she asserted, "It is necessary to feel the forests, to become friends with these multiple worlds of flora."[42] Positioning Burle Marx's design practice as a precedent for the "continuous and irreplaceable relationship between construction and nature," she added, with bio-climatic sensibility:

> That is why we have repeatedly protested against … the fact that cities are reduced to mountains of concrete—particularly the tropical cities. These cities don't need architecture that accumulates heat. Instead they need an architecture that facilitates the life of their inhabitants. A tropical city should be a city in the midst of plants, a city harmoniously thought out, systematized and built in the midst of trees, foliage, flowers.[43]

This spatial sensibility in Burle Marx's work found its expression in Bo Bardi's initial sketches for the SESC Pompéia—metonyms for meteorological scenes colonized by lush plantings, rainfall, sunlight, air movement, and people.

Bo Bardi imagined the entrance to the SESC at the via Rua Clélia as a threshold between the bustling city and the service center complex. Just inside the entrance, in a space currently used for outdoor seating, she proposed a dense garden of medicinal and aromatic plants for use by the local community.[44] In her drawing entitled "*paisagismo*" (landscaping), she cited approximately forty-five different plant species to be included in this garden and throughout the complex, indicating her curative and nurturing intent. Although her idea of a medicinal garden at the entrance remained unrealized, the built work incorporates numerous examples of such a recourse to natural phenomena. As the visitor proceeds along the internal street, for example, she encounters the dominant wind and the wide pebbled channels that border the walkway. These receive the rainfall that drops in gutters from the old factory roofs and is carried in large drainpipes to a subterranean stream—the Águas Pretas riverbed—which occupies an open strip of land near the southern edge of the parcel. As the water falls energetically into the gutters, it also splashes on the ground, creating a living symbol of water's power in the cycles of life. Bo Bardi anticipated that the splashes would stimulate the growth of small weeds in the cobblestoned pedestrian street, and she called them "*plantinhas espontaneas*" (spontaneous little plants).[45] This plant "colonization" would reduce heat accumulation and humidify the walkway throughout the day. → p. 230 Ⓐ

In her design for the public areas in the sheds to the right of the entry, Bo Bardi deployed a modified version of this idea of an aerated, planted, and liquid-like environment, as reflected in her initial sketches and manifested in the character of the internal street. In addition to the programmatic elements of the gathering center, cited earlier, she inserted a curvaceous, amoeba-like reflecting pool that meanders through the space, about which she claimed: "Architecture does not need to be romantic in a petty, domestic, expressive sense, but it can be poetic. I think that my stream, which is a reflecting pool, is a sort of River São Francisco."[46] This water feature conflates her various design impetuses: environmental and social, symbolic and climatic. Naming the pool "River São Francisco" is Bo Bardi's most conspicuous homage to the people of northeastern Brazil, whom she described as "poor, but rich in fantasy and invention." She had been exposed to the environmental and social challenges of the São Francisco River valley in the context of a community resettlement scheme, the Camurupim Community Project, which she undertook in 1975, one year before she began work on the SESC Pompéia. This experience made her aware of the hardship of living in sites of economic and geographical deprivation that were under pressure for development. Eulogizing the region's "hardship and poetry," she imported stones from the river's headwaters in the Canastra mountains to place at the bottom of the SESC water feature, which meanders organically under the gathering center's truss-and-beam ceiling to impart a sense of playfulness and fluidity to the space.[47] By including an exuberant collection of indigenous aquatic plants in the waterbed, she increased the humidity and vitality of the volume, collapsing architecture and landscape with tropical extravagance. Although these plantings have not survived, perception of the water is heightened by the sound of a few delicate water jets dispersed over the course of the "River" and the resulting diaphanous reflection of sunlight, which make the shallow pool a memorable bioclimatic feature. While young visitors interact with the "River" by crossing its small bridges, the shaded water surface and its occasional water jets cool the area through evaporation. The stratification of the atmosphere that results from the colder air rising from the shaded surfaces of water and ground in combination with the heat collected on the brick-tiled roofs above encourages continuous air buoyancy. Cross ventilation, enabled by the perforated masonry walls and operable clerestory windows, increases the cooling effects in this dynamic building volume. → p. 230 Ⓑ, → p. 231 Ⓒ

For the nearby children's play and learning area, Bo Bardi devised concrete volumes that she cantilevered from the second-floor library so that they hover above a cave-like environment. The resulting cooling effects afford an opportunity for children to interact and learn while sheltered against thermal loads. In the library volumes above, seniors are reading the newspaper and playing board games. This intergenerational coexistence in a space of varied thermal gradients is essential to Bo Bardi's social concept in which such activities as "eating, sitting, talking, walking, sitting, taking a little sun" are encouraged, as she elaborated, "Architecture is not only a utopia, but a means to achieve certain collective results.... People of all ages, elderly and children, all getting along well."[48] → p. 231 Ⓓ

Adjacent to her "River" and the children's area is another climatic moment—the "hearth."[49] Located just inside the main entry to the gathering space, it offers visitors a collective sense of the fire's radiating heat on cold nights. Beyond its bioclimatic affordances, fire also has symbolic significance, particularly among members of South America's Indian and African communities. As the central focus of many collective situations, fire is synonymous with survival, nourishment, celebration, and comfort. By including a hearth in the gathering hall, Bo Bardi brought water, wind, and heat together. → p. 234 Ⓔ

The next climatic moment in the SESC Pompéia complex is the theater immediately south of the gathering center. Access is through a grand foyer a narrow preexisting shed covered with a roof of glass tiles that extends from the SESC's internal street to the Rua Barão do Bananal. This allows the sunlight to enter, evoking a bright public square protected against the rain, as Bo Bardi recognized in calling this foyer the "*Hall-Terreiro*" (Hall–Public Square).[50] This space recalls the informal urban squares made from compacted earth found in medieval European cities as well as Brazilian villages, where popular events and activities such as markets, exhibitions, shows, and religious celebrations would take place, including the "*candomblé* ritual"—a religious practice associated with the Afro-Brazilian communities.[51] Operable floor-to-ceiling wooden lattice partitions at the ends of the foyer allow the sounds of city life to percolate inside the complex, while enabling the dominant southeastern winds to permeate the space without obstruction. The thermal mass of the floor and the walls heats the air, creating a significant sensation of warmth. The foyer thus operates as an augmented atmospheric stage, immersing visitors in an intensified interplay with nat-

Ⓐ Internal Street

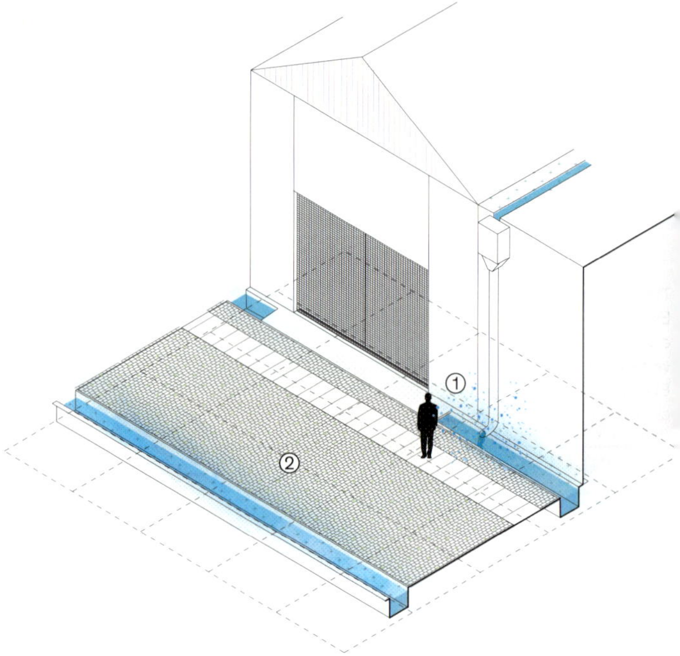

Thermodynamic performance:

① Evaporative cooling / adiabatic evaporation: rainfall splashing on pebble-stone gutter amplifies adiabatic effect (sound enhances perception of cooling)

② Evaporative cooling / isothermal evaporation: vegetation growing between cobblestones

Ⓑ Gathering center

→ p. 342

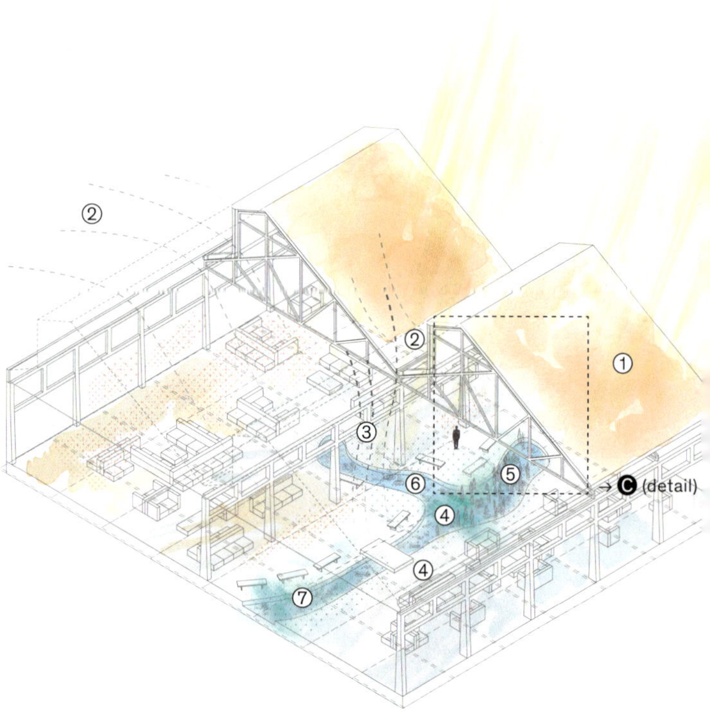

Thermodynamic performance:

① Solar radiation (blocked): brick roof oriented to the north and windows to the south

② Forced convection / cross ventilation: operable windows open to prevailing winds

③ Free convection / chimney effect: hot air rises resulting in temperature stratification (colder air at bottom, hotter at top)

④ Radiant cooling: shaded water surface and ground

⑤ Evaporative cooling / isothermal evaporation: water surface and aquatic vegetation

⑥ Evaporative cooling / adiabatic evaporation: small water jets (sound enhances perception of cooling)

⑦ Reflective water surface enhances perception of cooling

C Reflecting pool ("River São Francisco")

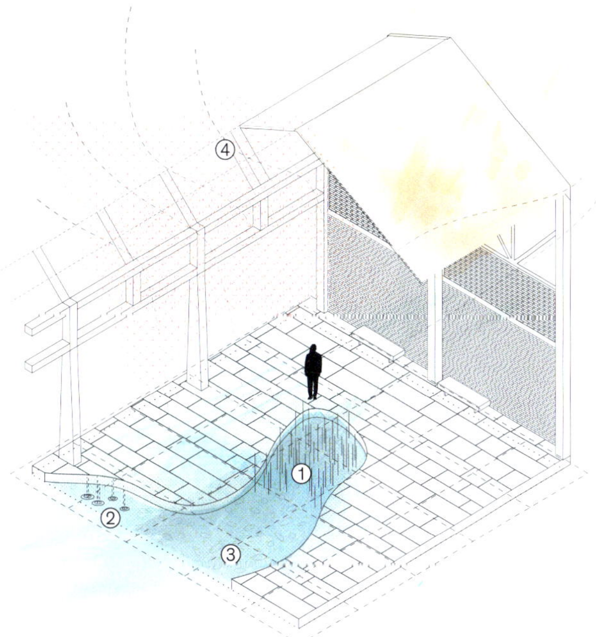

Thermodynamic performance:
Evaporative cooling / Isothermal evaporation: water surface and aquatic vegetation
Evaporative cooling / adiabatic evaporation: small water jets (sound enhances perception of cooling)
Reflective water surface enhances perception of cooling
Free convection / chimney effect: hot air rises, resulting in temperature stratification (colder air at bottom, hotter at top)

D Children's play area and library/ senior gathering space

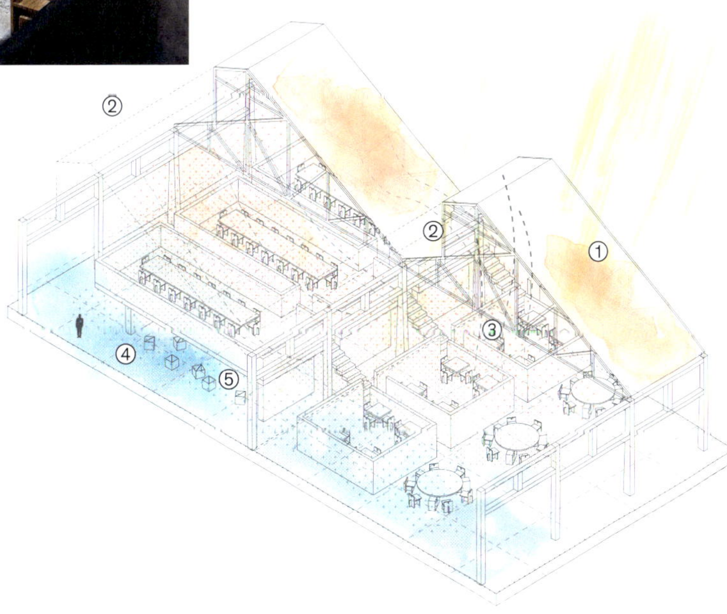

Thermodynamic performance:
Solar radiation (blocked): brick roof oriented to the north and windows to the south
Forced convection / cross ventilation: operable windows open to prevailing winds
Free convection / chimney effect: hot air rises, resulting in temperature stratification (colder air at bottom, hotter at top)
Solar radiation (reduced): slabs above space reduce the diffuse light
Radiant cooling: shaded ground and walls

ural elements and the physiological effects of its cooling breezes and warming sunlight. → p. 234 F

This immersive experience continues inside the theater volume. Bo Bardi described its wooden seats, which lack cushions, as "exposed to the elements," in contrast to theaters made for the "comfort of the Consumer Society." As she elaborated: "The wooden seating at Pompéia is a simple attempt to restore to the theater its quality of 'distancing and involving,' rather than mere seating."[52] By situating the body in unanticipated and less comfortable conditions, she intensified the effect of spatial immersion. Just as the foyer could become a hothouse on days with diminished wind, so sitting through a theater play could cause discomfort, augmenting awareness of the body's physical vulnerability.

At the end of the internal street a similar thermal sensibility occurs with the wooden deck that Bo Bardi referred to as the "Indian Solarium," which leads in turn to her new sports block. Whereas the Indian Solarium provides an opportunity for the community to sun bathe, the sports block that terminates the sequence—composed of two tall concrete structures and a water tower—hosts a series of stacked spaces for indoor sports activities. The strip of land occupied by these new elements presented a series of design challenges, as Bo Bardi explained: "The presence of a subterranean 'rainwater' channel' (actually the famous Águas Pretas riverbed) made almost all of the grounds destined for the sports zone a 'no-build' area." She imagined two distinct ways of straddling between the existing factory structures and the new athletic towers and between the towers themselves. The first, on the ground, is the Indian Solarium, a linear platform of wooden decking built over the rainwater channel, to celebrate the presence of the water and take advantage of its humidifying capabilities; this leads from the factory complex to her new structures. The second, which she termed the "aerial solution," consists of a series of elevated passageways that connect the two sports towers, which themselves straddle the channel.[53]

Just as the term *solarium* evokes an embracing of solar radiation and heat, so the Indian Solarium is oriented to the rising and setting sun. Locally known as the beach of São Paulo, it is one of the most popular features in the SESC complex. Throughout the day members of the community sit, lie, and sunbathe on the boardwalk, experiencing its combination of warming and cooling effects. Through conduction and radiation, the deck provides heat to those lying on its dark wooden planks, while the exposed water in the channel below evaporates and rises through the gaps in the wooden decking to provide a cooling sensation. The air buoyancy promoted by this localized effect cools down the heated bodies, resulting in an uncanny, but thrilling, contrast. → p. 235 G

To amplify the cooling opportunities of the Indian Solarium, Bo Bardi distributed two large water features along its length: an "open-air com-

munal shower" and a "waterfall" (*cachoeira*).[54] As Olivia de Oliveira notes, these elements have symbolic significance in their evocation of *candomblé* rituals that involve water in motion as significant components.[55] Aware of the *candomblé* deity Oxumaré—servant to Father Xangô and symbol of life's multiplicity through water collection and retention—Bo Bardi alluded to the curative powers of water in both its physiological and spiritual aspects. She endowed her complex with the power to collect and direct the rainfall by integrating the oversize drainage channels of the factory complex with the newly exposed subterranean river channel and its waterfall and collective shower. In her coeval project for the historic center of Salvador da Bahia (1986), Bo Bardi also proposed waterfalls, which she named respectively "Father Xangô's waterfall" (*Cachoeira de Pai Xangô*) and the "Water Wheel for hot days" (*Roda de Água para os dias de calor*).
→ p. 235 H

If the Indian Solarium celebrates sunlight and water in motion, then the "aerial" solution, a series of skywalks of pre-stressed concrete that connect the two sports towers, exposes the visitor to São Paulo's sky, its rain, and its breezes. This pair of monumentally scaled concrete buildings at the eastern end of the Indian Solarium reflect Bo Bardi's desire to convey the complex's presence on São Paulo's skyline. Echoing earlier reflections on monuments colonized by landscape and weather, she wrote: "I thought about the marvelous architecture of the military 'fortresses' dotted along the Brazilian coast or hidden throughout the interior—in cities, in forests, in the margins of deserts and in arid backlands." To address the city's climatic variability, Bo Bardi extended oversize waterspouts from the roof of the larger sports tower. As the rainfall gushes from these spouts, a spectacular collection of cascades reminds the visitor of architecture's capacity to celebrate the forces of nature. Referring to the amoeba-like openings in the southeast and northwest façades of this building, Bo Bardi elaborated: "those gaping 'holes' like the openings in prehistoric cave dwellings, with no glass... allow for continual cross-ventilation."[56] Covering these openings are wooden screens in square frames that slide on horizontal tracks to admit constantly changing amounts of sunlight and fresh air while contributing to cave-like interiors that are chilled by the continual breezes and their shaded walls. → p. 236 I

To register the evocative power of the seasonal cycles, Bo Bardi specified a distinct color scheme for each of the four stacked sports levels to reflect the colors of a certain time of year. "That way," she explained, "people who go to play basketball, for example, ... they'll say they'll be in Spring."[57] Beneath these sports levels is the grade-level indoor swimming pool, for which Bo Bardi made a series of watercolor drawings in which she used color to celebrate the diurnal and nocturnal cycles of meteorological rhythms—an idea that was unfortunately never implemented. These

E The "hearth"

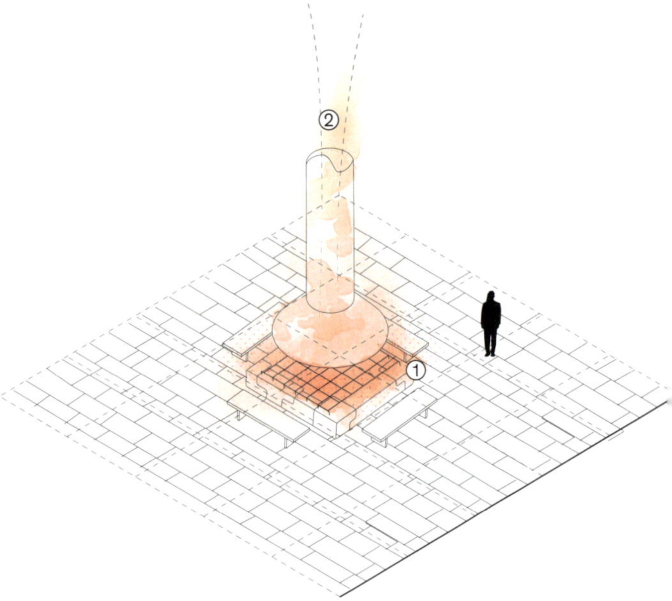

Thermodynamic performance:
① Radiant heating: fireplace
② Free convection: hot air rises and drags colder air with it

F Theater foyer (Hall-Terreiro)

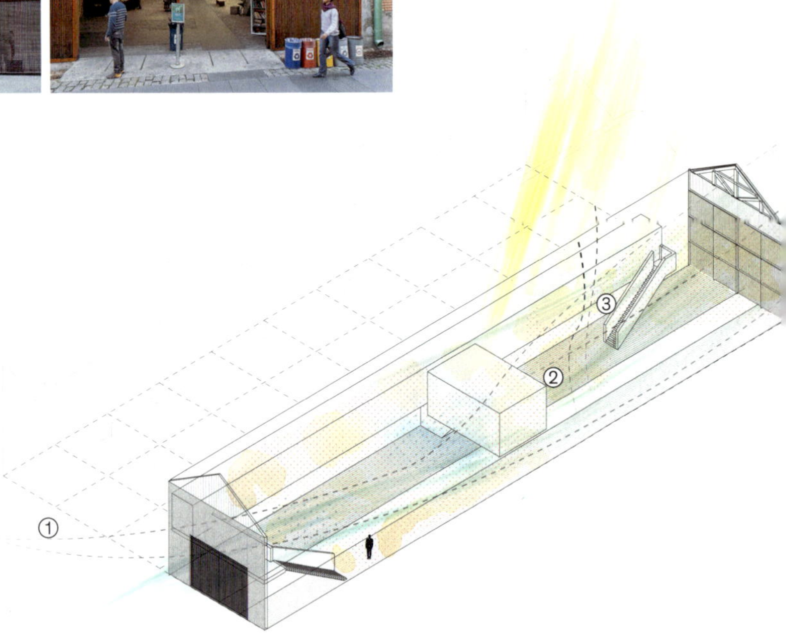

Thermodynamic performance:
① Forced convection / cross-ventilation: wooden lattice at both ends promotes breezes
② Solar radiation (exposed): glass-tile roof exposes interior space to sunlight and collects heat
③ Free convection: hot air rises and drags colder air

G "Indian Solarium" ("Beach of São Paulo")

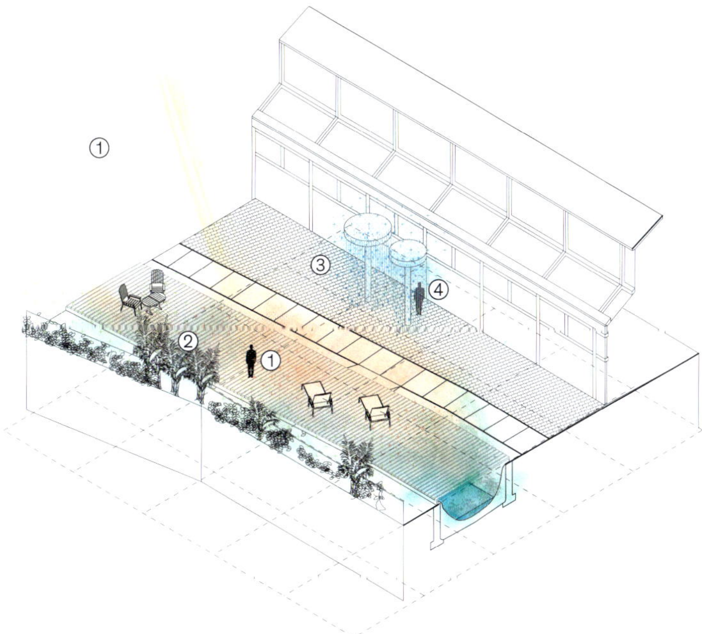

Thermodynamic performance:

- Collection of solar radiation and heat transfer by conduction (warming): dark wooden deck
- Evaporative cooling / isothermal evaporation: vegetation and creek heated by warm deck above
- Evaporative cooling / adiabatic evaporation: open-air shower
- Heat transfer by conduction (cooling): cold shower

H The "Waterfall" (cachoeira)

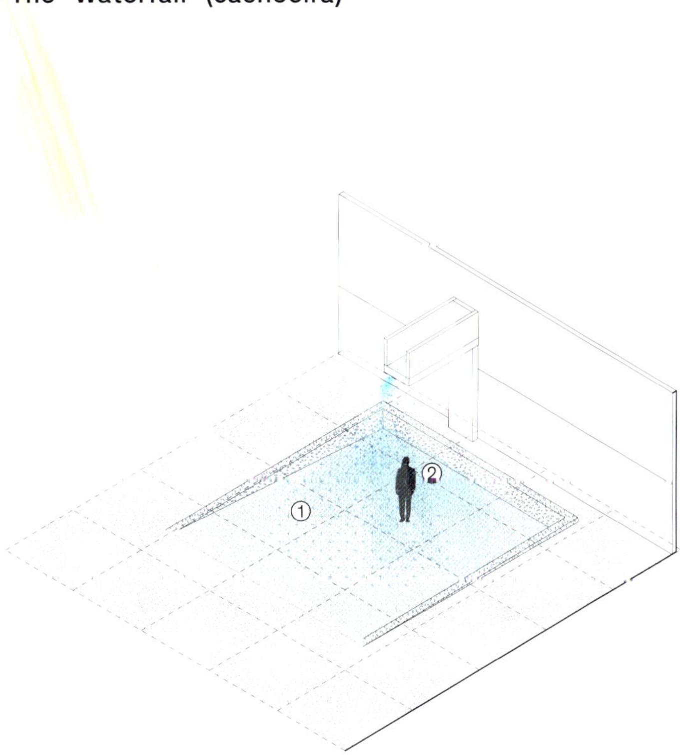

Thermodynamic performance:

- Evaporative cooling / adiabatic evaporation: water falling and splashing on pebble-stone ground amplifies adiabatic effect (sound enhances perception of cooling)
- Heat transfer by conduction (cooling): cold shower

❶ Sports tower with “gaping holes” on the façade

Thermodynamic performance:

① Forced convection / cross ventilation: holes open to prevailing winds

② Radiant cooling: shaded ground and walls

③ Solar radiation (reduced): small openings and wooden screens reduce direct and diffuse sunlight

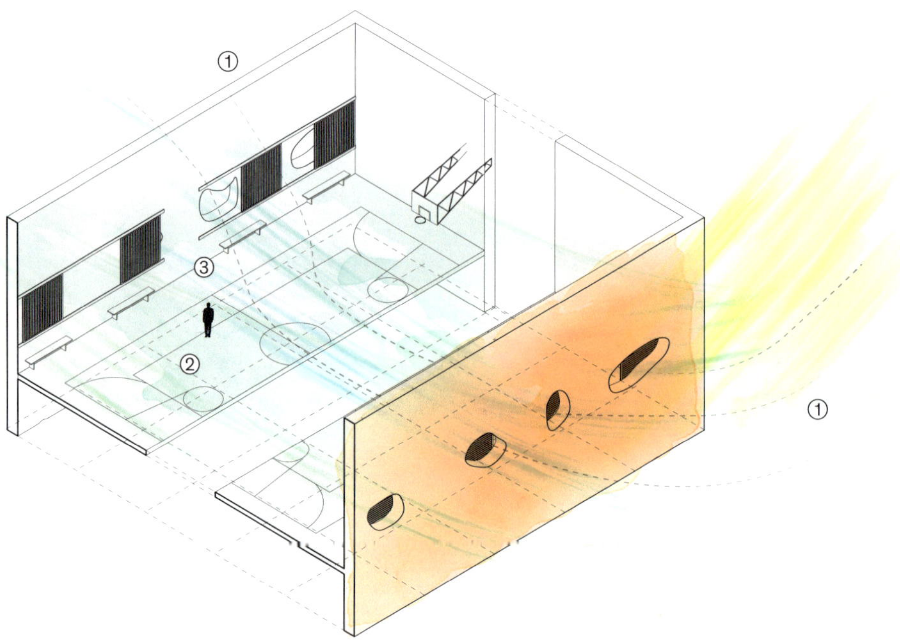

drawings capture São Paulo's climatic tones: the "*noite*" (night) with a uniform dark blue; the "*alvorada*" (dawn) with a scheme of blurred blues; the "*chuva*" (rain) with different gray intensities; and the "*nuvens*" (clouds) with expressive clumps of white and gray.

Symbolizing energy reverberating in space, this evocation of weather and atmospheres is reminiscent of the work of French conceptual artist Yves Klein. Bo Bardi was familiar with his *Air Architecture* (1957–1962)—a speculative project focused on reconnecting people with the meteorological elements, as he explained: "My walls of fire, my walls of water, like the roofs of air, are the materials for the construction of a new architecture. With these three classical elements, fire, air and water, the city of tomorrow will be constructed, flexible at last, spiritual and immaterial."[58] Bo Bardi showed a catalog of Klein's work to the SESC representatives at a meeting on the sports center design. Reflecting upon Klein's affinity for endowing the immaterial with presence, she formed an idea of making environments palpable and immediate through what she described as "inhabitable circumstances" for collective life to occur in its physiological and symbolic dimensions. Despite the multiple scales of her interventions at SESC Pompéia, Bo Bardi summarized her work with modesty and with a bioclimatic sensibility: "We added just a few little things," she explained, "a little bit of water, a hearth."[59]

Conclusion

In referring to the SESC Pompéia as the "*citadela*," Bo Bardi envisioned a protected space in the city dedicated to collective freedom and contingent upon an interplay with meteorological elements and phenomena—a sanctuary where "a ray of light may suddenly shine, a freshening breeze can suddenly arise." Expanding on this concept, she envisioned a place that would "condition the human being." Because the conditioning of humankind implies the acknowledgment of physiological, symbolic, and emotional needs, this objective resulted in the creation of a *living* architecture in homeostatic relation to São Paulo's climate. While celebrating the larger cosmic cycles—the seasonal, diurnal, and nocturnal sequences—she synchronized the community's natural life with a meteorological sensibility and associated sensations. Her interventions remind visitors that, owing to their biological vulnerabilities and the causal pleasures arising from their exposure to the happenstances of weather, they are also part of nature. Bo Bardi's accounts frequently reflect this affiliation with weather as related to people's pleasure and emotions, such as her description of the Cinelândia theater district upon her arrival in Rio de Janeiro or her first impressions of the old factory's dripping rain through the cracked roofs and the laughing boys playing soccer amid the puddles. Bo Bardi's objective was to find the language for an architecture that would sustain this joy and promote delight: a "little joy in a sad city," with its collected rain, mitigated sunlight, available warmth, aromatic flowers, and cooling breezes.[60] Symbolically and bio-climatically, Bo Bardi's "little things"—the hearth, the beach, the cave, the river, the open shower, and the waterfall, as well as the vertical gardens, enlarged gutters, aerial skywalks, and pebbled surfaces—remind visitors that they can come together and celebrate, that they belong to a larger cosmos where natural phenomena can alleviate the struggles of everyday life. She imparted symbolic relevance to certain of her interventions through the names she gave them, reminding the community of other places and geographies: the "River of São Francisco" and the "Indian Solarium." Bo Bardi's architectural philosophy of a human-centric space depends on the power of space to reconnect humankind with primordial and visceral sensations, to bind the visitors with their biological and spiritual selves, reminding them of their relevant presence on the earth.

1 Lina Bo Bardi, "Arquitetura e Natureza ou Natureza e Arquitetura" [handwritten lecture notes], Salvador, September 27, 1958, Instituto Lina Bo Bardi and Pietro Maria Bardi Archive, *São Paulo* [ILBPMB]. All translations are by the author, unless otherwise noted. Lina Bo changed her name to Lina Bo Bardi in 1946, when she married the Italian art critic and journalist Pietro Maria Bardi. Because this essay elaborates on her work developed before and after this event, her name is cited accordingly.
2 Lina Bo and Carlo Pagani, "Sensibilità dei material," *Domus* no. 201 (September 1944): 314–319, here 316.
3 Lina Bo Bardi, "The Architectural Project" [1986], *Stones Against Diamonds,* Anthony Doyle and Pamela Johnston, trans. (London: AA Publications, 2013), 97–102, here 100, 98. First published as *Cidadela da Liberdade,* Giancarlo Latorraca, ed. (São Paulo: SESC, 1986).
4 "Lina Bo Bardi" [video interview], 1994, ILBPMB.
5 Lina Bo Bardi, "Currículo Literário," in *Lina Bo Bardi,* Marcelo Carvalho Ferraz, ed. (São Paulo: Lina Bo & P. M. Bardi Institute, 1993), 9–12, here 12; based on "Na Europa a casa do Homem ruiu," *Rio* no. 92 (February 1947): 53–55. Also in Lina Bo Bardi, "Pequena carta ao Artigas" [handwritten note], c. 1984, ILBPMB. The local architects responsible for the Ministry of Education and Health in Rio consisted of Oscar Niemeyer, Affonso Reidy, Carlos Leão, Jorge Moreira, and Ernani Vasconcelos.
6 Ibid., 10, 11.
7 Bruno Zevi was the founder of Associazione per l'architettura organica (APAO, Association for Organic Architecture) and author of *Verso un'architettura organica* (1945). Antonio Gramsci was a prolific writer and a member of the Communist Party in Italy who was imprisoned during Benito Mussolini's fascist regime.
8 Lina Bo Bardi, "Museu de Arte de São Paulo," in *Lina Bo Bardi,* Ferraz, ed. (1993), 100–115, here 100.
9 Lina Bo Bardi, "Architecture and Nature: A House in the Landscape," *Stones Against Diamonds* (2013), 21–26, here 21, 22, 23 [emphasis in original]. Originally published as "Architettura e Natura. La casa nel paesaggio," *Domus* no. 191 (November 1943): 464–71. Under the leadership of Giuseppe Pagano, the 1936 Milan Triennale placed rural architecture at the core of the exhibition. Rural building techniques were positioned as the authentic tradition to be considered for modernization. That same year Lina Bo planned to dedicate an issue of the journal *Quadrante* to the rural house, but the activities of the journal were interrupted before her proposal could be carried out.
10 Lina Bo and Carlo Pagani, "Casa Sul Mare di Sicilia," *Domus* no. 152 (August 1940): 30–35, here 30.
11 Lina Bo and Carlo Pagani, "Un Giardino disegnato da Bo e Pagani," *Domus* no. 156 (December 1940): 42–43, here 42.
12 Lina Bo Bardi, "Lecture notes, School of Fine Arts, University of Bahia" (April 1958), 1, ILBPMB.
13 Bo Bardi, "The Architectural Project" (2013), 101.
14 Lina Bo Bardi to Bruno Zevi (c. 1955), ILBPMA.
15 Bruno Zevi, "Incontro con Lina Bo Bardi, un supervisore con mitra e speroni," *L'Espresso* (Rome, May 27, 1973).
16 See Lina Bo Bardi, "Amazonas: O povo arquiteto," *Habitat* no. 1 (October-December 1950): 68–71.
17 Lina Bo Bardi, "Bela Criança," *Habitat* no. 2 (January-March 1951): 3.
18 Bruno Zevi, "Idee per A" and "Per Bardi e Pagani" [typed notes], c. October 1945, Fondazione Bruno Zevi, Rome. In 1945 Bo contacted Zevi suggesting that they develop a magazine, titled "A," which she envisioned as showcasing architecture that could be accessible to everyone. In response, Zevi added that the magazine should be a vehicle for social emancipation focused on issues such as reconstruction and democracy. The first issue was released in February 1946; the following year it was renamed *A: Cultura della vita.* See Zeuler R. M. de A. Lima, *Lina Bo Bardi* (New Haven: Yale University Press, 2013).
19 See Zeuler R. M. de A. Lima, *Verso Un'architettura Semplice* (Roma: Fondazione Bruno Zevi, 2007).
20 Dates for the Chame-Chame house are approximate because the building process was interrupted some time prior to 1961 before resuming in 1962–64.
21 Lina Bo Bardi, cited by Flavio Motta, "SUMÁRIO: Uma nota de Interiors," *Habitat* no. 12 (September 1953): 5.
22 Olivia de Oliveira, *Subtle Substances: The Architecture of Lina Bo Bardi* (Barcelona: Gustavo Gili, 2007), 87.

23 *Carta da Paz Social* [Janeiro 1946], (Rio de Janeiro: Serviço Social do Comércio, February 2012), 12.
24 Architect Julio Neves's earlier proposal for the SESC Pompéia project, which involved leveling the factory and replacing it with new buildings, was abandoned due to prohibitive costs.
25 Lima, *Lina Bo Bardi* (2013), 158.
26 Lina Bo Bardi, "Planning the Environment: 'Design' at an Impasse" [1976], *Stones against Diamonds* (2013), 86-90, here 90. Originally published as "Planejamento Ambiental: 'Desenho' ni Impasse," *Revista Malasartes 2* (December-February 1976): 4–7.
27 Ibid., 88, 89.
28 Lina Bo Bardi, "Propaedeutic Contribution to the Teaching of Architecture Theory: Nature and Architecture" [1957], in Cathrine Veikos, *Lina Bo Bardi: The Theory of Architectural Practice* (Routledge, 2014), 67. Originally published as *Contribuição Propedêutica ao Ensino da Teoria da Arquitetura* (São Paulo: Habitat, Ltd., 1957).
29 Bo Bardi, "Architecture and Nature" (2013), 22.
30 Lina Bo Bardi, "Arquitetura como movimento. Nota sobre sintese das artes," manuscript from the Conference on Dance and Architecture, Salvador, 1958, cited in Oliveira, *Subtle Substances* (2007), 298.
31 Bo Bardi, "The Architectural Project" (2013), 100.
32 Bo Bardi, "The Architectural Project" (2013), 97. The French engineer and builder François Hennebique (1842-1921) was a pioneer of reinforced concrete construction. He developed the unified component of beams and columns as a single monolithic structural system used in the barrel factory: possibly the only example realized in Brazil.
33 Bo Bardi, "Arquitetura como movimento," cited in Oliveira, *Subtle Substances* (2007), 298.
34 Bo Bardi, "The Architectural Project" (2014), 98.
35 Bo Bardi, "Propaedeutic Contributions" (2014), 67.
36 John Ruskin, *The Works of John Ruskin*, Edward Tyas Cook and Alexander D. O. Wedderburn, eds. (London: George Allen and New York: Longmans, Green, and Co., 1903-1912), 645.
37 John Ruskin, "Of Modern Landscape," in *Modern Painters: Of Many Things*, part 4 (New York: Wiley & Halsted, 1859), 245 [emphasis in original].
38 Lina Bo Bardi, "The Architectural Project" (1986), 98.
39 Bo Bardi drawing, June 10, 1977.
40 Bo Bardi's idea of building a greenhouse is also reflected in her initial sketches from 1957 for the São Paulo Museum of Art (MASP) where the idea was similarly abandoned.
41 Lina Bo Bardi, "Lettera dal Brasile," *L'Architettura: cronache e storia* (July 1956): 185, cited by Esther da Costa Meyer, "After the Flood," *Harvard Design Magazine* 16 (Winter/ Spring 2002): 5–13, here 7.
42 Lina Bo Bardi, "Os jardins de Burle Marx," *Habitat* no. 3 (April–June 1951): 7–15, here 7.
43 Lina Bo Bardi, "Arquitetura e Arquitetura de jardins," *Habitat* no. 13 (December 1953): 52–53, here 52.
44 Further examples of aromatic and medicinal gardens in Bo Bardi's work include those she designed for the Museum of Modern Art of Bahia (1963) and the Benin House (1987).
45 Lina Bo Bardi, "Area do Deck e muros" [drawing, April 6, 1980] in André Vainer and Marcelo Ferraz, *Cidadela Da Liberdade: Lina Bo Bardi e o SESC Pompéia* (São Paulo: Edições Pompéia, 2013), 65.
46 Lina Bo Bardi, cited by Casimiro Xavier de Mendonça, "A oficina da criação," *Veja* no. 14 (April 1982): 126-29, here 128.
47 Lina Bo Bardi, "Intensive Therapy" [1988], *Stones against Diamonds* (2013), 103–104, here 103–104, here 104. First published as "Terapia Intensiva," *AU – Arquitetura e Urbanismo* 18 (June–July 1988), 37.
48 Lina Bo Bardi, in "SESC Pompéia" Leaflet History, SESC Pompéia São Paulo (2006), 14, https://issuu.com/sescsp/docs/folhetohistorico_ing.
49 The hearth reflects Bo Bardi's admiration for Frank Loyd Wright's "organic" domestic architecture in which the hearth occupies a central position.
50 Lina Bo Bardi, "Hall-Terreiro," cited by Lima, *Lina Bo Bardi* (2013), 167
51 For *candomblé*, see Raul Lody, *Espaço-Orixa-Sociedade: Arquitetura e Liturgia do candomblé* (Salvador: Ianamá, 1988).
52 Bo Bardi, "The Architectural Project" (2013), 99, 100.
53 Ibid., 98.
54 Ibid., 100.
55 See Oliveira, *Subtle Substances* (2007), 161.
56 Bo Bardi, "The Architectural Project" (2013), 100, 98, 100.
57 Lina Bo Bardi, "Novo Marco da Cidade," *Isto é* 30, no. 4 (1986): 4–6, here 5.
58 Yves Klein, cited in *Air Architecture: Yves Klein*, Peter Noever and Francois Perrin, eds. (Hatje Cantz, 2004), 11.
59 Bo Bardi, "The Architectural Project" (2013), 98.
60 Ibid., 100, 101, 98.

From the industrial sheds to the sports complex

From Avenue Pompéia to sports towers' elevated passageways

the “Indian Solarium” to the sports complex

Elevated passageways

Gymnastics tower corridor and stair

nastics room

Sports tower court with "gaping holes"

Library and seniors' reading room

eforma propõe venda de
sinas e aumento de tarifa

Gathering center with hearth and reflecting pool ("River São Francisco")

Accompanying project:

UNIVERSITY CITY OF CARACAS, 1944–1969

Carlos Raúl Villanueva: Architect

Caracas, Venezuela

- A Northern campus covered walkway
- B Covered walkway (teaching area)
- C Central campus covered walkway
- D Covered plaza: light well and vegetation bed (north side)
- E Covered plaza: reflecting pool (western edge)
- F Covered plaza: light well and vegetation bed (south side)
- G Covered plaza: light well and vegetation bed (eastern edge)
- H Bosque of palm trees
- I Interior garden and ventilation wells

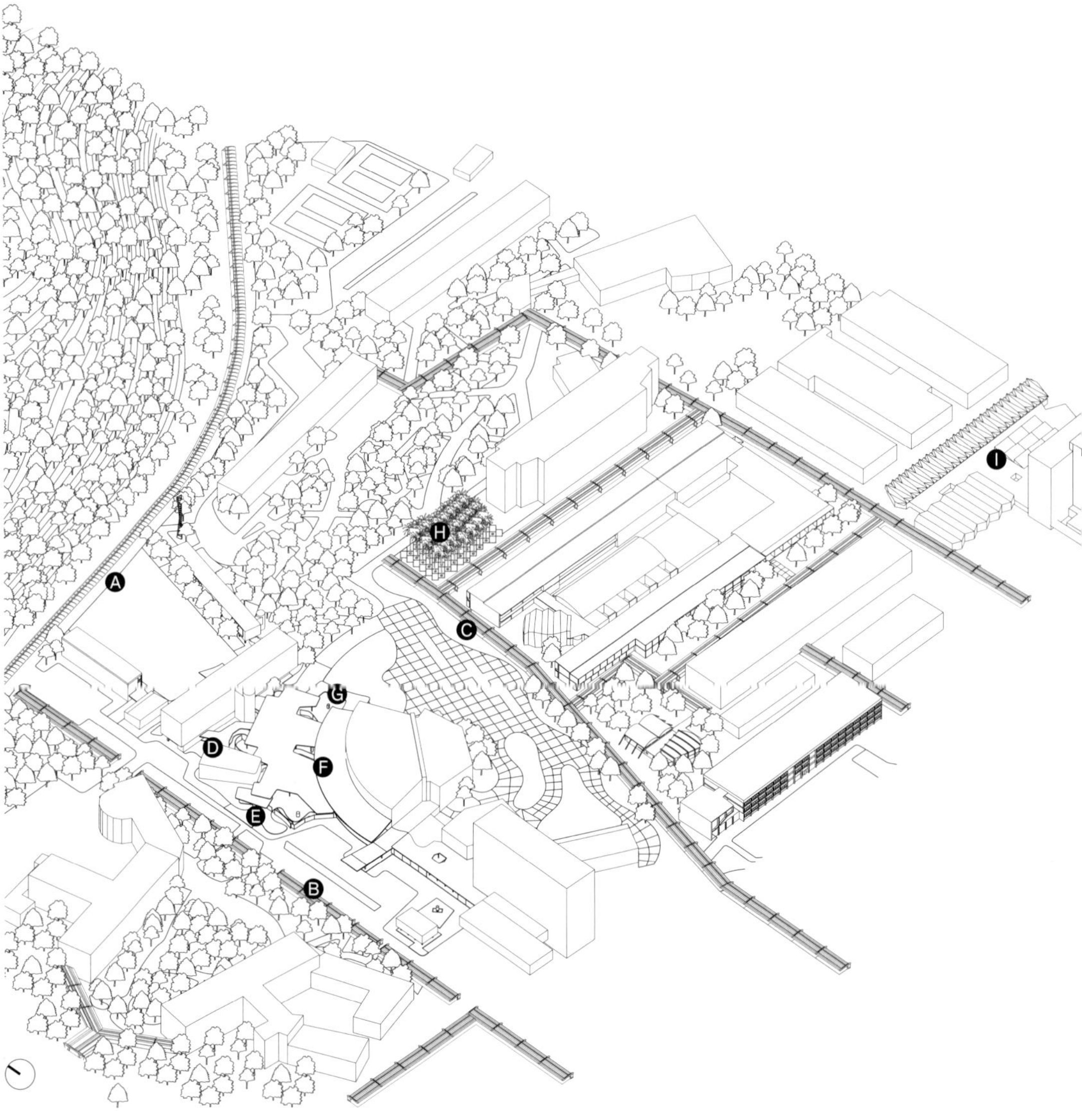

For this educational complex set in a tropical environment, architect Carlos Raúl Villanueva developed multiple acclimatized zones to foster learning and interaction among members of the university community. Priorities included providing shelter against the heavy rain and blazing sunlight and promoting cross ventilation amid a network of covered walkways and plazas. The complex features ample corridors and atriums bounded by latticed screen walls, light wells, bosques, and interior gardens that contribute to microclimatic and poetic moments throughout the campus.

Ⓐ Northern campus covered walkway

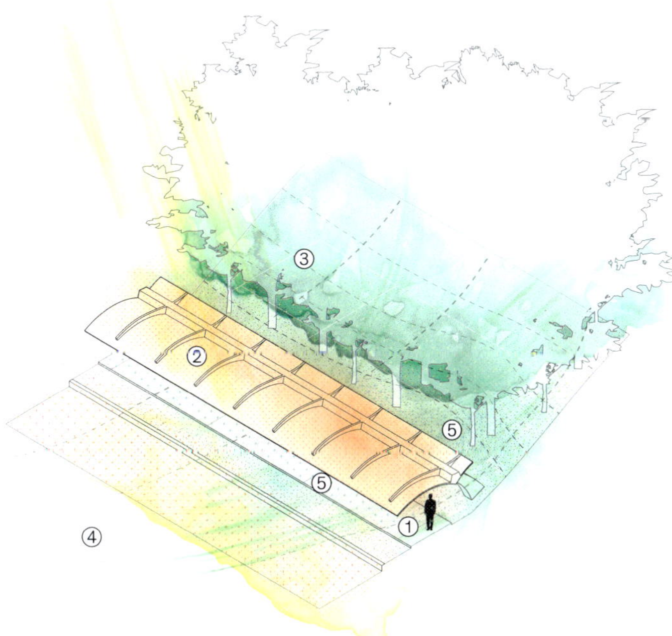

Thermodynamic performance:

- Solar radiation (reduced): covered walkway
- Rain shelter: covered walkway
- Evaporative cooling / isothermal evaporation: forest
- Free convection / katabatic flow: cold mass of air falls down slope in the evening and during the night
- Radiant cooling: shaded surfaces

B Covered walkway (teaching area)

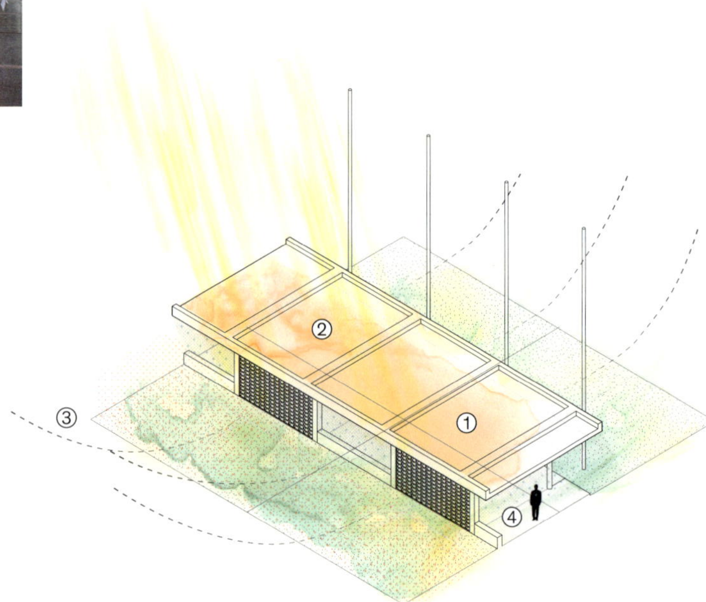

Thermodynamic performance:

① Solar radiation (reduced): covered walkway and lattice screen walls
② Rain shelter: covered walkway
③ Free convection: humid air rises from adjacent grassy surfaces
④ Radiant cooling: shaded surfaces

C Central campus covered walkway

→ p. 343

Thermodynamic performance:

① Solar radiation (reduced): covered walkway
② Rain shelter: covered walkway
③ Free convection: humid air rises from adjacent grassy surfaces
④ Radiant cooling: shaded surfaces
⑤ Evaporative cooling / isothermal evaporation: grassy surfaces and tree canopy

D Covered plaza: Light well and vegetation bed (north side)

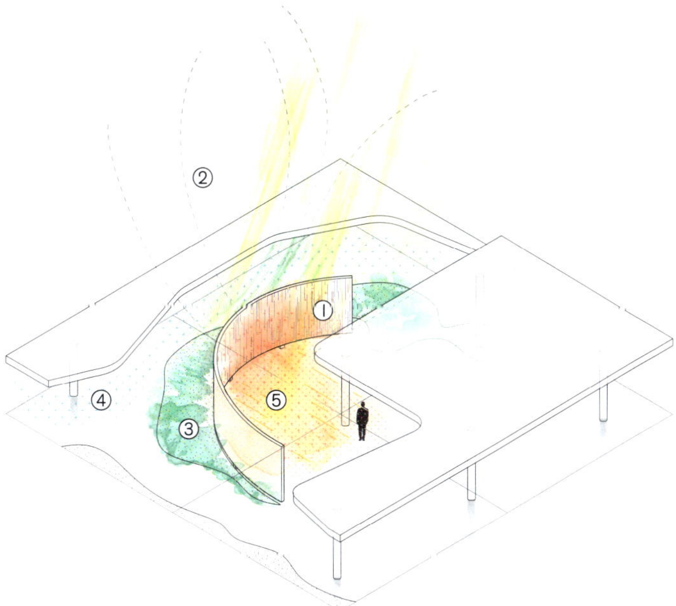

Thermodynamic performance:
Reflective wall: vertical tile surface reflects sunlight onto shaded polished concrete ground plane, enhancing perception of cooling
Free convection / chimney effect: air heated by warm walls and ground rises through opening in plaza roof
Evaporative cooling / isothermal evaporation: grassy surface
Radiant cooling: shaded ground
Solar radiation (exposed)

E Covered plaza: Reflecting pool (western edge)

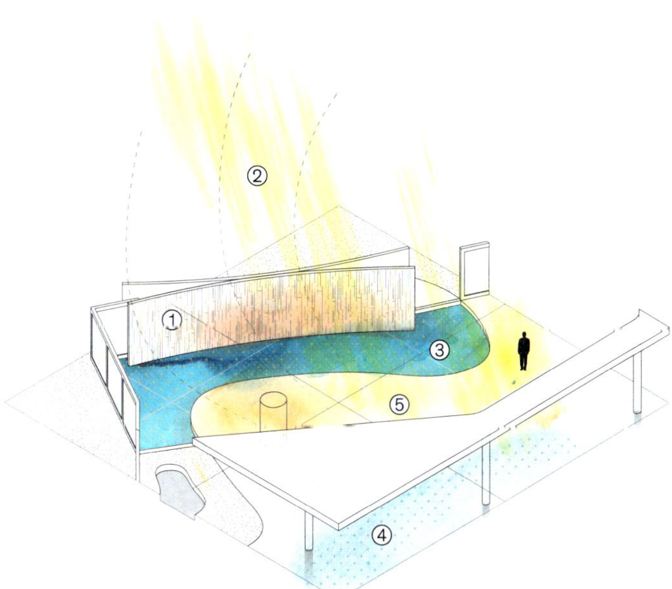

Thermodynamic performance:
Reflective wall: vertical tile surface reflects sunlight onto shaded polished concrete ground plane, enhancing perception of cooling
Free convection / chimney effect: air heated by warm walls and ground rises through opening in plaza roof
Evaporative cooling / isothermal evaporation: water surface
Radiant cooling: shaded ground
Solar radiation (exposed)

Ⓕ Covered plaza: Light well and vegetation bed (south side)

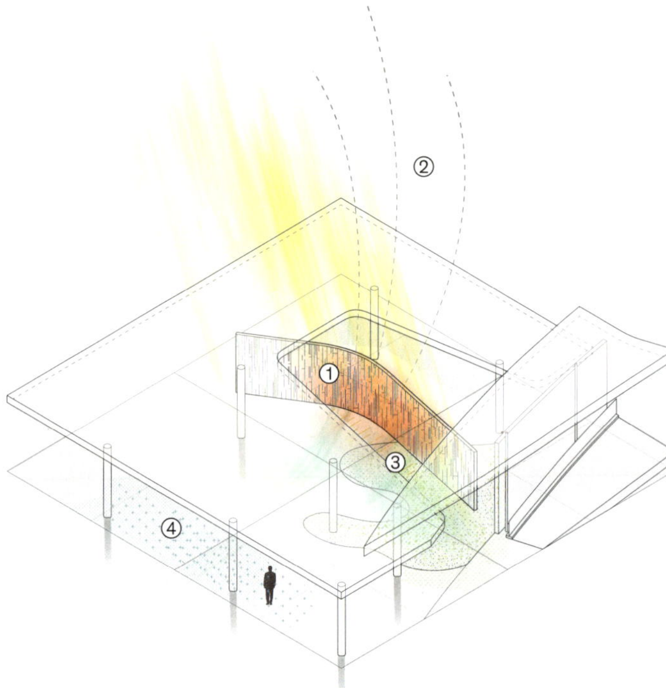

Thermodynamic performance:

① Reflective wall: vertical tile surface reflects sunlight onto shaded polished concrete ground plane, enhancing perception of cooling
② Free convection / chimney effect: air heated by warm walls and ground rises through opening in plaza roof
③ Evaporative cooling / isothermal evaporation: grassy surface
④ Radiant cooling: shaded ground

Ⓖ Covered plaza with light well and vegetation bed (eastern edge)

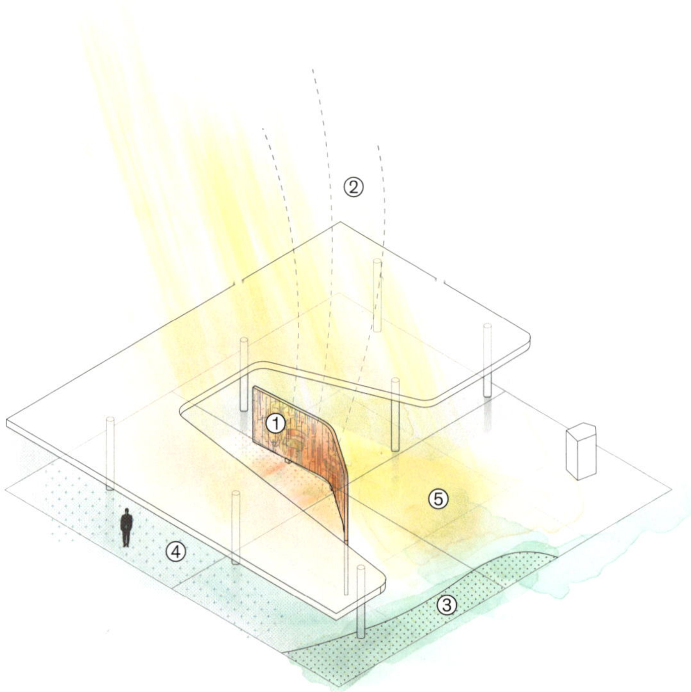

Thermodynamic performance:

① Reflective wall: vertical tile surface reflects sunlight onto shaded polished concrete ground plane, enhancing perception of cooling
② Free convection / chimney effect: air heated by warm walls and ground rises through opening in plaza roof
③ Evaporative cooling / isothermal evaporation: grassy surface
④ Radiant cooling: shaded ground
⑤ Solar radiation (exposed)

H Bosque of palm trees

Thermodynamic performance:
- Evaporative cooling / isothermal evaporation: tree canopy
- Solar radiation (reduced): tree canopy
- Radiant cooling: shaded ground

I Interior garden and ventilation wells

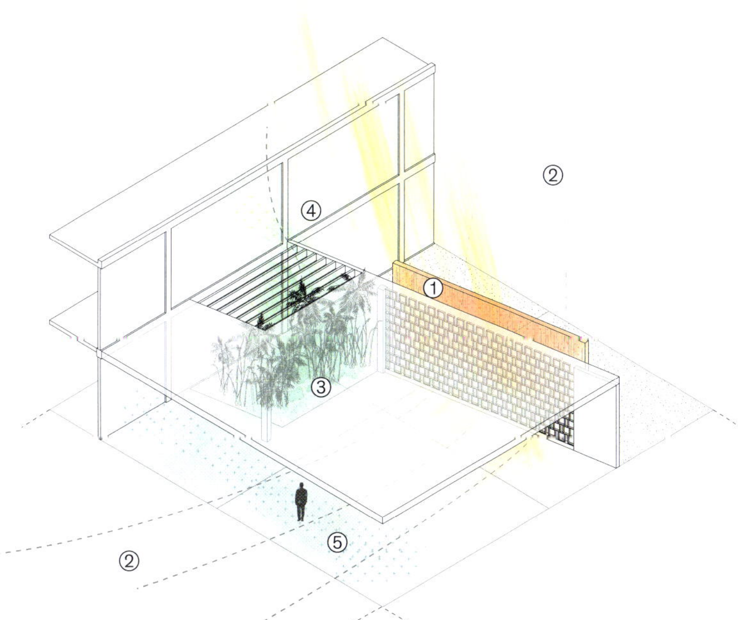

Thermodynamic performance:
- Reflective wall: vertical tile surface reflects sunlight onto shaded polished concrete ground plane, enhancing perception of cooling
- Forced convection / cross ventilation: breeze through perforated wall
- Evaporative cooling / isothermal evaporation: interior garden
- Free convection: humid air rises
- Radiant cooling: shaded ground and walls

Central campus covered walkway and bosque of palm trees

Northern campus covered walkway along internal street

Eating areas

Covered walkway and teaching area

ered plaza and access to Aula Magna

Covered plaza and access to Aula Magna

Atmosphere as Thermal Con

ast

GEOMETRIC HOT SPRINGS, 2009

Germán del Sol: Architect
Villarrica National Park, Pucón, Chile

Accompanying project:

SEA RANCH, c. 1963–1966

Lawrence Halprin: Landscape architect
With associated architects Moore, Lyndon, Turnbull, Whitaker, and Joseph Esherick & Associates
Sonoma County, California, United States

Atmosphere as Thermal Contrast recognizes the juxtaposition of disparate environmental conditions as a primary means of eliciting acute psycho-physiological responses. While the most recognized sensory domains play a prominent role in sustaining a sense of discomfort or delight, the body's ability to detect temperature contributes equally to such aims. Sensing coldness or warmth depends upon the temperature of the immediate environment in relation to the exposure or sheltering provided by heat, humidity, or wind, for example. Contrasting thermal conditions can provoke stimulating and challenging experiences that might be riveting and invigorating as well as memorable. Comfort is considered to occur within certain thresholds, descending from the generally accepted core body temperature, or normothermia, of about 36.8°C (98°F) to as little as 15°C (59°F) and rising to as much as 45°C (113°F).[1] The proposition of atmosphere as thermal contrast considers the body in these more radical and less normative thermal ranges by including discomfort, sublimity, and surprise as integral aspects of the spatial experience. Here, the body's deliberate exposure to dramatic thermal disparities prompts the realization of human limits and vulnerabilities relative to climatic thresholds.

Designed by the architect Germán del Sol, the Geometric Hot Springs, located in a narrow gorge adjoining the Villarrica National Park in Pucón, Chile, embodies this proposition of atmosphere as thermal contrast, owing to the spring water that emerges from deep within the earth at a uniform temperature of 80°C/176°F. The climate is characterized by high degrees of humidity and relatively low temperatures that range from 23°C (73°F) in January to 6°C (43°F) in July, often accompanied by cold rain or prolonged snowfall. Del Sol capitalized upon the thermal contrasts afforded by the site's differing water temperatures, vapor densities, relatively cold climate, and sunlight exposure, as well as the gorge's lush vegetation. He created seventeen hot-water pools amid the frigid cascades and stream that emanate from the snow-capped mountains to afford the visitor contrasting atmospheric experiences. Above a cold-water stream that originates in natural cascade at the upper end of the site, del Sol created a bright red wooden walkway that threads through lush vegetation to connect the series of hot-water pools and basins set against the gorge's pebbly hillsides. An open channel directly under the walkway feeds the pools with hot water, which emerges at different points in the complex and cools gradually, so that the temperature in the pools ranges from 45°C/114°F to 30°C/86°F. The walkway threads in various directions from the entrance to a restaurant and open plaza, as well as to the various pools, cascades, steam basins, and changing pavilions, encouraging visitors to explore the facility as they immerse themselves in the contrasting conditions of bright sunlight and deep shadow, rain and fire (in the restaurant's open hearth), cold and heat, snow and fog, and the smell of earth versus the sulfurous odor of water, which the local populace associates with curative powers. The wide gaps between the walkway's planks enable rainwater to pass through and steam to rise from the hot water channel directly below. The warm walkway melts the snow and protects the bathers from the cold air as they meander barefoot among the pools. As the hot water fills the pools, it spills over into the cold stream below, producing thick clouds of vapor. These vaporous clouds filter the sunlight as it penetrates the gorge's dense vegetation and engulf the visitors to render them almost invisible. With warm feet and icy torsos, the bathers move through the sequence of pools. After luxuriating in comfort, they become enveloped in the site's environmental contrasts.

The premise of atmosphere as thermal contrast can also entail different scales of intervention. Such a range of scales is found at Sea Ranch, a five-thousand-acre second-home community in the coastal landscape of Sonoma County, laid out according to a master plan by Lawrence Halprin and Associates. Halprin envisioned Sea Ranch as a "place where wild nature and human habitation could interact."[2] This interaction involves human contact with the site's climatic profile: cold and damp, with gusty and chilly winds and abrupt masses of fog coming from the sea. Relevant questions posed in the design process included how to take advantage of the site's diverse climate characteristics and how to curate human contact with the site's natural weather instabilities while also affording possible moments of retreat and delight.

Elaborating on this duality of exposure and retreat, Halprin's firm developed a set of design principles to address the site's climatic profile: cold and damp, with gusty and chilly winds and abrupt masses of fog coming from the sea. Topographic formations, vegetation, and building envelopes were devised to interact with wind flow—to shelter residents and increase their comfort as well as to expose them to the site's more hostile climatic conditions. Large swaths of land were left as common meadows, open to the sea winds and sprays, where the weather fluctuations envelop the visitors. Cypress hedgerows flanking these meadows break the wind to create warm and sheltered microclimates. Earthen berms and new plantings bound the site's public amenities and deflect its wind patterns to form additional pockets of shelter. At a smaller scale, wind-baffling fences around private decks and gardens create zones of reduced turbulence for residents to sit in the open sunshine and take in uninterrupted views of the ocean and the sky, where weather lives.

1 Other variables determining this thermal threshold include age, health fitness, gender, physiological metabolism, and level of physical activity.
2 Lawrence Halprin, *The Sea Ranch... Diary of an Idea* (Berkeley: Spacemaker Press, 2002), 25.

GEOMETRIC HOT SPRINGS, 2009

Germán del Sol: Architect

Villarrica National Park, Pucón, Chile

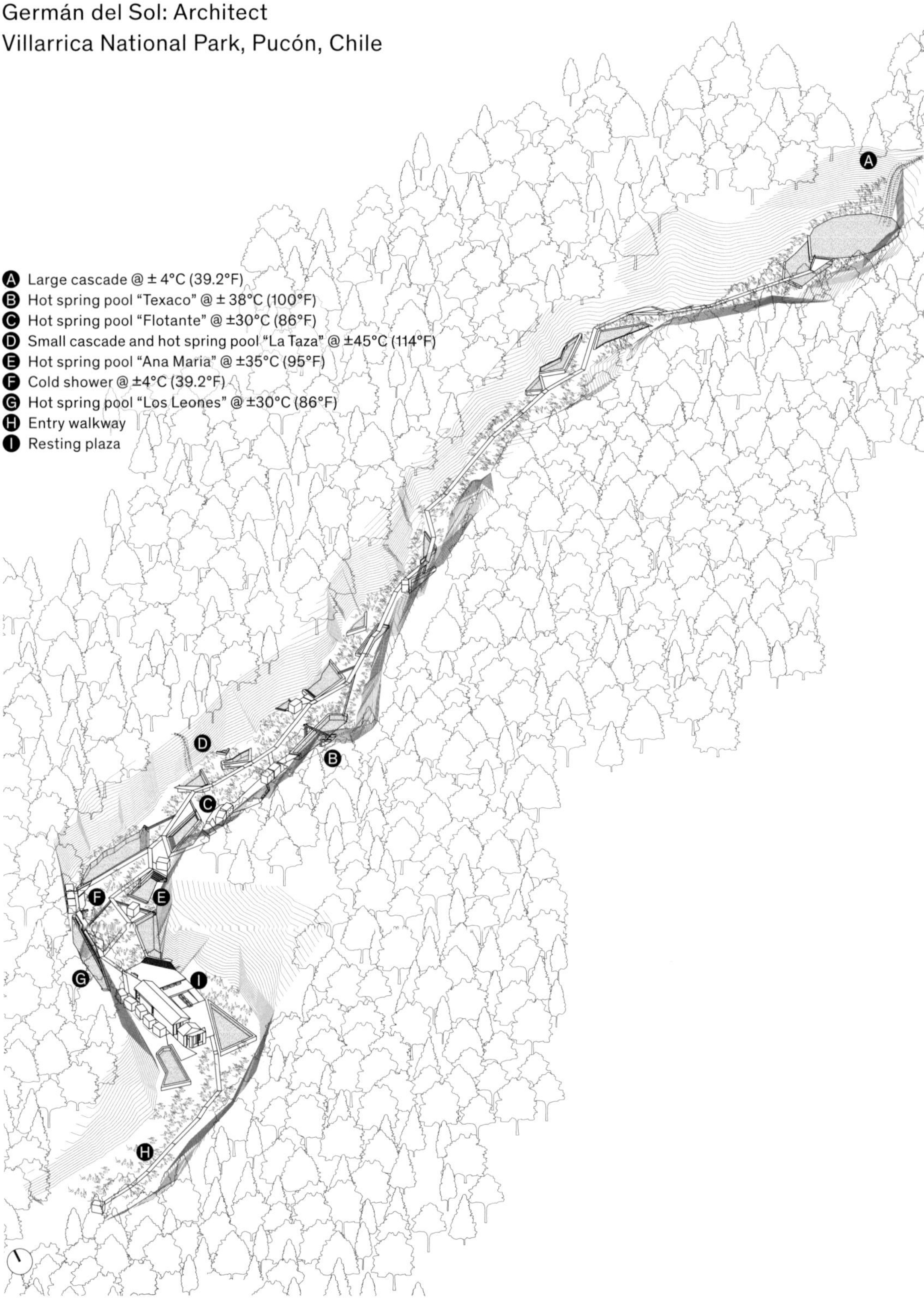

- **A** Large cascade @ ± 4°C (39.2°F)
- **B** Hot spring pool “Texaco” @ ± 38°C (100°F)
- **C** Hot spring pool “Flotante” @ ±30°C (86°F)
- **D** Small cascade and hot spring pool “La Taza” @ ±45°C (114°F)
- **E** Hot spring pool “Ana Maria” @ ±35°C (95°F)
- **F** Cold shower @ ±4°C (39.2°F)
- **G** Hot spring pool “Los Leones” @ ±30°C (86°F)
- **H** Entry walkway
- **I** Resting plaza

On Atmosphere and Space: Silvia Benedito in Conversation with Architect Germán del Sol

Silvia Benedito:

I just visited your Geometric Hot Springs in the Villarrica National Park in Chile. The physical and immaterial qualities of this landscape and its atmospheres are so powerful. You have crafted the presence of nature by synthesizing many disciplines—architecture, landscape architecture, anthropology, and biometeorology. Can you tell me more about your approach to the landscape?

Germán del Sol:

In Spanish-speaking cultures, landscape architecture is known as *paisajismo*. The Spanish word *paisaje* for landscape comes from *país* meaning country. Instead of saying landscape, we say something like "país-scape," which is closer to the concept of territory and culture. Landscape is not just nature; landscape is the relation between people and nature.

SB: Landscape, or *paisaje,* is an interrelational entity—one that brings closer together the countryside and the city, the natural and the artificial, the people and the built environment, with their visible and qualitative characteristics.

GS: Yes. The idea of a larger common country is important for the Andean states because we share the same origin, the Inca Empire. The pre-Columbian people on the southern tip of South America had a great culture—very refined and abstract. They were very good at focusing on things that were important, while excluding the unimportant.

SB: Does that refinement derive from the importance of craft?

GS: Yes, because it takes time to do things well. When conditions are so demanding, you have to look beyond, to transcend—not in religious terms, but in spiritual or poetic terms. For instance, the llamas' corrals throughout the region have a very fine "lace" wall. It took months to "weave" these structures, which contain a cultural meaning beyond their practical use.

SB: You worked with the same kind of devotion and care to make the Geometric Hot Springs. How long did it take for you to develop this project?

GS: Oh, a long time—but we completed it! You know, in pre-Columbian cultures, you could work on a piece of a wall all your life and never see it finished. Work was a task to which you dedicated time. There was a focus on the act of doing, rather than on the final outcome.

SB: How did you discover the site?

GS: Someone told me about a farm for sale on the southern side of the Villarrica Volcano, close to Coñaripe, with hot springs. Since ancient times the Mapuche people had talked about these waters. They called this region the *Cajón Negro,* or black chest, as they believed that gold was hidden in black chests and buried like treasure. Later, I realized that the "gold" was indeed the water of the hot springs.

SB: In the Mapuche culture, hot springs were places of ritual. Their fluctuating states—vapor, ice, the sulfur scent, the thermal gradients between very hot and very cold, the sound of the water—were associated with a sense of well-being and healing (physical and spiritual). How do these extreme external conditions affect the body's physiological self-regulating responses?

GS: Bathing in hot springs makes your heart beat very fast. Doctors say that it is equivalent to slow running. And it has other kinds of healing powers related to rheumatism. But the power is mostly spiritual! You place your attention and actions outside of yourself. In this sense, I see raw nature as a way of being in contact with the unknown. In cities, we try to build a calculated world, where everything seems to be under control. In nature, you realize that you are exposed to the unknown.

SB: One of the techniques that you use to trigger physical and spiritual healing is the orchestration of spatial contrasts or the coexistence of contrasting atmospheres made of light intensities and temperatures, air thickness and scent, sound and silence, compression and openness. These "substances" intensify the moment of contact with nature and its multiple states, while acknowledging the physical and spiritual presence of one's own body.

GS: Yes—I never thought about it in those terms. In the project, you are more in touch with chaos than you are normally. And that makes the experience unforgettable.

SB: There is no separation between the project and the world-space that contains it; there is neither inside nor outside.

GS: This contact with the world is common in all the pre-Columbian cultures, at least in the south. The Mapuche are people of the land; their tradition is one of being in touch with the whole territory, not with a small house or town. They live outside rather than inside. Not because they weren't able to build houses—open spaces are just more important than enclosures. So, direct contact with surrounding nature became very important for the Geometric Hot Springs.

SB: In the project, there is a striking overlap between methodical design decisions and serendipitous events. The design is an armature that enables and curates the appearance of the atmospheric elements and their diaphanous qualities. These become simultaneously matter and condition. How do you account for serendipity and chance?

GS: Chance played an important role in this project. We were lucky; we were able to find the necessary hot water to make it work. I didn't want to build more than necessary, in a material and poetic sense. I wanted to create a microclimate with available resources—spring water, gravity, forest, light, and rock—without any other means.

SB: You believe in the importance of stories—some true, some evocative. How did stories influence the design process?

GS: The farm had a ravine with a large waterfall and a few hot spring sources. The owners had invented a story about a monster that lived in a very deep cave behind the waterfall. All the workers were afraid of that place. The owners told the story because they didn't want the workers relaxing in the hot waters instead of working. Over the years, and because of this story, all the organic debris from the farm was thrown in the ravine. We almost cried when we saw it. Later, we had to remove it all to access the springs, being careful not to destroy the rock walls—otherwise, we could lose the hot water. This was a very soft rock, and we had to keep its integrity.

SB: It sounds like a (geo) archeological enterprise. Could you use machines in the excavation process?

GS: No—machines would have destroyed the rocks. We had to dig with shovels and brooms to the deepest point without touching the sidewalls where the hot springs could be. Then, to find the hot spots, we had to take the temperature of the ravine bed and the sidewalls with a special thermometer. I imagined this water running through the sidewalls as if through little veins. And, whenever we could read an increase of temperature, we knew we had found a source. Then, we had to temporarily separate the stream from the bottom of the ravine. So we built a wooden canal—a temporary riverbed elevated in the air—to channelize the running water in order to dry the base and work underneath. This allowed us to clean the bottom and to find more hot springs

SB: I'm trying to imagine this in vertical section. Are you saying that you actually elevated the riverbed so you could work underneath?

GS: Yes—we lifted the riverbed in order to find the hot springs. These locations are where we now capture and contain the very hot water for distribution. Protected and not accessible, these collecting pools spill into a wooden "black canal" that, through gravity, feeds the seventeen bathing pools, covering 17,000 square feet, downslope along the ravine.

SB: The black canal is an important infrastructural element and an enabler of many spatial conditions in the project. Can you explain its various roles and effects?

GS: It carries the hot water for distribution under the wooden pathway that connects every pool and platform. It is open in order to produce the microclimate—allowing the heat and steam to emerge through the pathway. The higher temperature and humidity levels make the whole ravine lusher with native plants and warmer in winter. Also, the heat that comes from the black canal melts the ice and snow on the pathway so people can comfortably walk barefoot.

Ⓐ Large cascade @ ± 4°C (39.2°F)

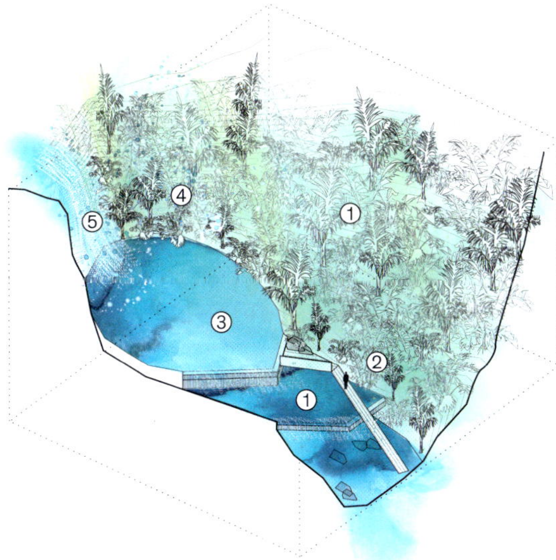

Thermodynamic performance:

1) Thermal mass / radiant cooling: shaded hillsides (geothermal) and stream stores cold
2) Solar radiation (reduced)
3) “Cold trap” cold storage from the gorge’s hillsides and cold stream surface
4) Evaporative cooling / isothermal evaporation: thick mass of vegetation
5) Evaporative cooling / adiabatic evaporation: cold water cascade (water sound enhances perception of cooling)

Ⓑ Hot spring pool “Texaco” @ ± 38°C (100°F)

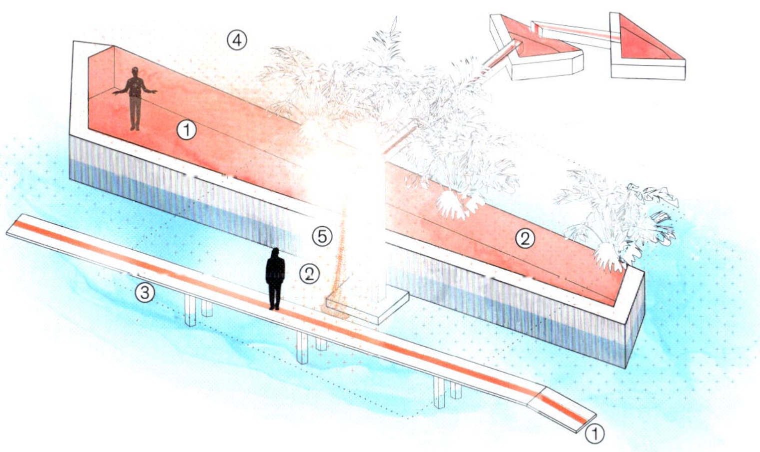

Thermodynamic performance:

1) Heat transfer by conduction (direct touch): hot pools and wooden channel containing hot spring water under walkway
2) Radiant heating: hot surfaces (hot water, walls, and walkway)
3) Radiant cooling: cold stream
4) Convective vapor transfer: hot water evaporates, vapor mixes with the air and rises
5) Evaporative cooling / adiabatic evaporation: hot shower

Ⓒ Hot spring pool "Flotante" @ ±30°C (86°F)

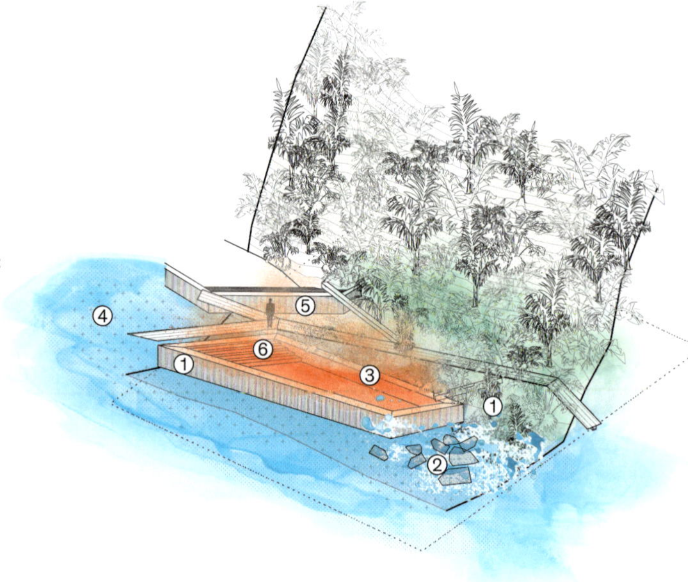

Thermodynamic performance:

① Evaporative cooling / isothermal evaporation: thick mass of vegetation and humidity from cold water touching on hot walls
② Evaporative cooling / adiabatic evaporation: water from stream splashing as it hits rocks (sound enhances perception of cooling)
③ Radiant heating: hot surfaces (hot water, walls, and walkway)
④ Radiant cooling: cold stream
⑤ Convective vapor transfer: hot water evaporates, vapor mixes with the air and rises
⑥ Heat transfer by conduction (direct touch): hot pools and channel containing hot spring water under walkway

Ⓓ Small cascade and hot spring pool "La Taza" @ ±45°C (114°F)

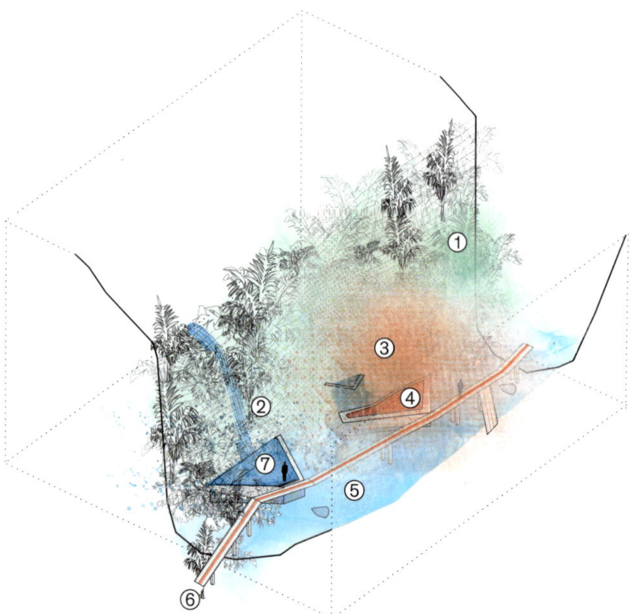

Thermodynamic performance:

① Evaporative cooling / isothermal evaporation: thick mass of vegetation
② Evaporative cooling / adiabatic evaporation: cold cascade (water sound enhances perception of cooling)
③ Convective vapor transfer: hot water evaporates, vapor mixes with the air and rises
④ Radiant heating: hot surfaces (hot water, walls, and walkway)
⑤ Radiant cooling: cold stream and small cascade of cold water
⑥ Heat transfer by conduction (direct touch): hot pools and channel containing hot spring water under walkway (warming)
⑦ Heat transfer by conduction (direct touch): cold cascade and cold pool (cooling)

E Hot spring pool "Ana Maria" @ ±35°C (95°F)

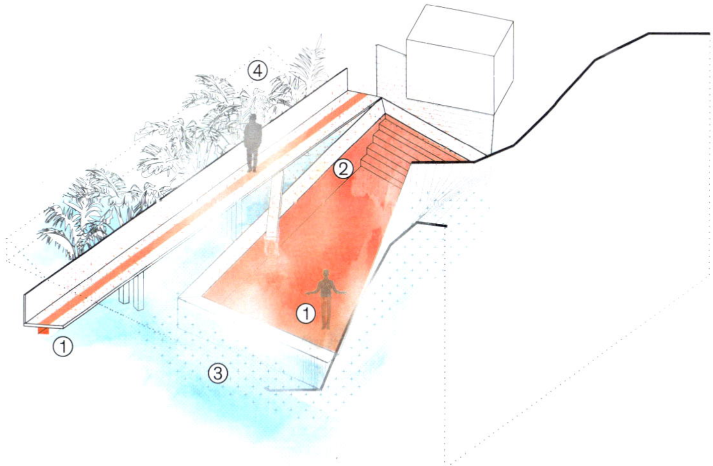

Thermodynamic performance:

1) Heat transfer by conduction (direct touch): hot pools and wooden channel containing hot spring water under walkway
2) Radiant heating: hot surfaces (hot water, walls, and walkway)
3) Radiant cooling: cold stream
4) Convective vapor transfer: hot water evaporates, vapor mixes with the air and rises

F Cold shower @ ±4°C (39.2°F)

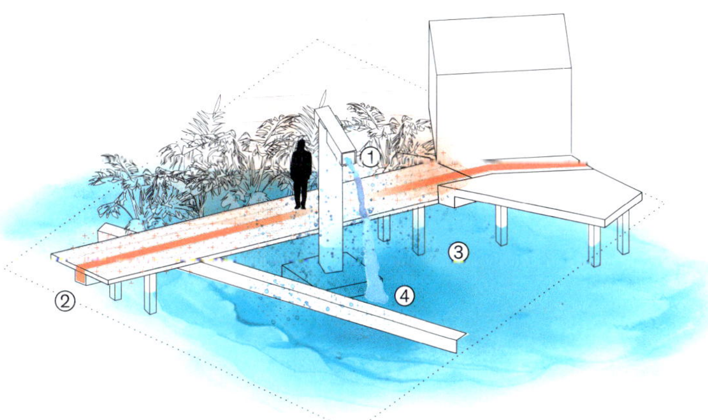

Thermodynamic performance:

1) Heat transfer by conduction (direct touch): cold shower (cooling)
2) Heat transfer by conduction (direct touch): hot pools and channel containing hot spring water under walkway (warming)
3) Radiant cooling: cold stream and cold shower
4) Evaporative cooling / adiabatic evaporation: cold shower (water sound enhances perception of cooling)

SB: The ravine becomes a space of containment—a space that captures and curates exchanges in nature, and its meteorological conditions, as if it's breathing. Your design is tactical and responsive to these processes, including designing with gravity as a natural "engine" to collect and distribute water throughout the complex without consuming electricity. When did the microclimate become important to you?

GS: Microclimates have always been important to me. And I've always had more or less the same goals. One of these goals is to avoid the use of unnecessary means, including energy. Here, the intensification of the microclimate—higher temperatures and humidity—through the heat and steam from the hot pools and the open canals, activated the re-naturalization of the ravine. Because we're in a national park, we couldn't plant anything new, but we activated natural processes by intensifying the effect of the microclimate and by operating with gravity in transporting the water from the hot springs to the various pools.

SB: The vegetation also plays an important role in the creation of a distinct atmosphere—it is lush, strange, luminous, welcoming, and secluded. There is a certain *Totaleindruck,* or "total impression," a term used by the Prussian naturalist Alexander von Humboldt. Can you tell us more about the integration of vegetation in the project?

GS: *Nalcas,* or Chilean rhubarb, is an ancient plant found throughout Chile. We transplanted small *nalcas* to sand beds at the bottom of the ravine, adjacent to the black canal. They need a lot of humidity, and the intense amount of heat and steam from the springs has caused them to grow more actively than they normally would. Since the project was completed in 2009, they've gotten very, very big.

SB: Can you tell me more about the your design motivations and decisions, inspirations or references?

GS: During the project development, I went to Greece and visited Naxos. In the middle of a barren landscape, standing among a chaotic group of stone walls built by shepherds to open up space for sheep to graze, I saw these perfectly circular marble walls, and I realized that they were the Geometric tombs I had been looking for. They were made by people of the Geometric culture 3,000 years ago, to remember and honor their ancestors with a hint of human beauty in the midst of nature. These structures have a purpose beyond utility. They are works of art—they have an ability to transcend the events of daily life. I was also influenced by the geometric forms and colors of the Mapuche textiles and sculptures. These forms reveal a particular interpretation of nature—the careful selection and arrangement of information into something abstract and distinct. I was looking for a sense of order to apply to the structures in the project so that they would feel neither "natural" nor "chaotic."

SB: I sense a deliberate choreography of the project's components. What rules or principles did you establish to guide the design process and to create the conditions you imagined?

GS: I set the rule that the pools should have three sides: two new walls set at an angle against the third wall, the ravine rock. This would put people in close contact with the walls of the ravine; it would also intensify the growth of vegetation along the ravine walls exposed to the heat and evaporation. The water always pours slowly from one side into the creek to keep the pools clean and to generate more steam in the center of the ravine. There is also a mirroring effect—when people are not in the pools, the water surface reflects the sky, the rocks, the vegetation. They are duplicated in the space. This effect was very important for me. But, sometimes we broke our own rules. For instance, we changed the creek course—we dispersed the water on the ravine bed to produce more noise—a lot of noise. This noise increased the presence of the running water through the ravine, in contrast to the still water of the pools. This also produced an increased sense of privacy as it tones down the noise made by the users of the other pools.

SB: How do you control the different temperatures of the pools?

GS: Once the pools are cleaned, we fill them again with the hot water, which is 80 degrees Celsius. Then, we have to wait for five to six hours until it reaches between 41 and 39 degrees Celsius. The body is incredibly sensitive to temperature changes of only one degree Celsius. There is also a very cold pool, 4 degrees Celsius. Once the temperature of the hot pools reaches 41 degrees Celsius, the staff closes the access point but leaves it dripping at a certain speed in order to keep the temperatures stable.

SB: That's a very heuristic technique of controlling the various pools' temperatures. It seems people are trained to think with their hands.

GS: Yes, it takes two to three days for each staff member to become acquainted with the process. I was recently asked to comment on a new book. The book was impressive—the quality of the paper, the

G Hot spring pool “Los Leones” @ ±30°C (86°F)

→ p. 344

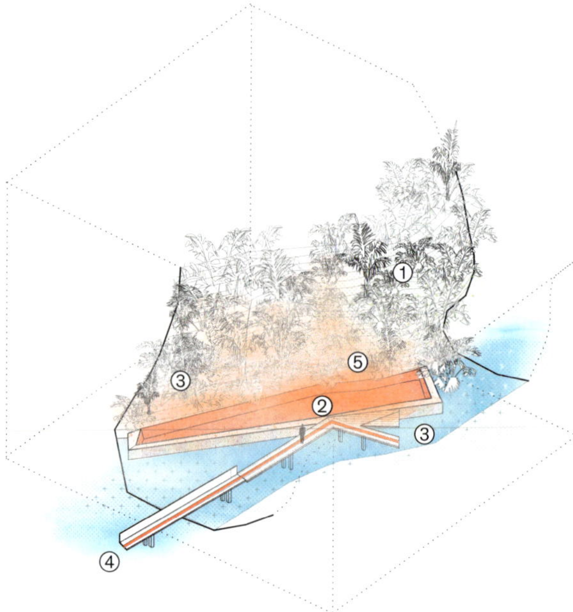

Thermodynamic performance:

① Evaporative cooling / isothermal evaporation: thick mass of vegetation
② Radiant heating: hot surfaces (hot water, walls, and walkway)
③ Radiant cooling: cold stream and shaded canyon
④ Heat transfer by conduction (direct touch): hot pools and channel containing hot spring water under walkway
⑤ Convective vapor transfer: hot water evaporates, vapor mixes with the air and rises

H Entry walkway

Thermodynamic performance:

① Evaporative cooling / isothermal evaporation: thick mass of vegetation
② Evaporative cooling / adiabatic evaporation: cold stream splashing (water sound enhances perception of cooling)
③ Solar radiation (exposed)
④ Radiant cooling: cold stream
⑤ Heat transfer by conduction (direct touch): channel containing hot spring water under walkway

❶ Resting plaza

Thermodynamic performance:

- "Heat trap": exposed to sunlight and wind-protected reduces convective heat transfer to the air
- Low albedo: dark surface (dark red and black) stores heat from sun radiation (not reflective material)
- Heat transfer by conduction (direct touch): warm plaza and seating surfaces
- Solar radiation (exposed)
- Radiant heating: fireplace (inside restaurant)
- Free convection: hot air near heated ground rises, accelerated by adiabatic evaporation on cold stream running below plaza surface
- Evaporative cooling / isothermal evaporation: thick mass of vegetation
- Evaporative cooling / adiabatic evaporation: cold stream splashing (water sound enhances perception of cooling)

images—but there were no ideas, only statistics and data: how many rivers in Chile, length, direction, etc. That's what I was trying to say about pre-Columbian cultures. There was never an image—in a figural sense—the resulting selection always had an interiority. By interiority, I mean something that you have thought about deeply. It means that you understand life, with your life. And it's expressed through reflection and working, not figures.

SB: Earlier you talked about the "poetic position." Is incompleteness or evocation part of this?

GS: I think evocation is one side of poetry. But more important than full articulation are the things left unsaid. I designed my first hotel in San Pedro de Atacama, a region with very witty people. The hotel was based on a series of plots separated by walls. I was coming from the city, and I had my own ideas about plots. And, when I visited the site, I asked the owner if he had a tape measure. He told me: "Oh, the meter will be very imprecise." At first, I laughed, and then I realized that it was as if I was trying to buy an eighty-centimeter long dog. No, first you need to determine the characteristics you're looking for; you don't give dimensions that belong to other realities. He was trying to explain that they had beautiful trees, water to irrigate the land, two small houses to keep the tools—he was telling me to see his reality.

SB: I believe the poetic position leads us to the more inclusive concept of "Aesthetics" as initially proposed by the German philosopher Alexander Gottlieb Baumgarten. He transcended the antagonism between rationalism and sensuous cognition by proposing a concept of beauty founded on the moment of revelation to oneself and/or about oneself, and of continual interpretation. It implies the dynamic act of unearthing and finding oneself. In this act, one experiences beauty.

GS: That's a beautiful idea. God has to be invisible, because beauty, in a real sense, is very aggressive. If you see God, you may die. Even beauty, in a much more modest way, cannot be revealed immediately.

SB: Do you think beauty is threatening because it touches us?

GS: In the Sacred Valley, the Incas designed terraces to cultivate flowers to show splendor. And, when the Spanish arrived, they kept the water infrastructure but destroyed the flowers, because their splendor was threatening.

SB: This makes me think about pleasure—about structures that are designed to simultaneously delight and nurture society. I believe this idea of societal delight offers an integrative way of understanding well-being or, conversely, understanding how a larger whole can be harmed.

GS: Yes—delight goes beyond mere utility. Utility, by itself, may destroy what makes us human.

An earlier version of this interview was published in *Harvard Design Magazine* No. 40 (Spring/Summer 2015): 32–39.

Aerial view of the Geometric Hot Springs

Hot spring pool “Flotante”

pring pool "Los Leones" and wooden walkway with changing pavilions

Restaurant

ging pavilions and cold shower

Hot spring pool "Los Leones"

Hot spring pool "Flotante"

spring pool "Ana Maria"

The gorge and the walkway

Hot spring pool "Texaco"

Hot spring pool "Ultimo Rojas"

Accompanying project:

SEA RANCH, c. 1963–1966

Lawrence Halprin: Landscape architect
Moore Lyndon Turnbull Whitaker and Joseph Esherick & Associates: Associated architects
Sonoma County, California, United States

- A Condominium I residential complex
- B Common meadow
- C Sheltered walkway and cypress hedgerows
- D "Hedgerow houses" with sloping roofs
- E Houses with sloping roofs adjacent to landform for wind deflection
- F Moonraker Recreation Center
- G Wind deflecting fences

Through the disciplinary integration of landscape architecture and architecture, Lawrence Halprin and Associates worked with associated architects Moore, Lyndon, Turnbull, Whitaker and Joseph Esherick & Associates to both increase comfort and foster moments of entanglement with the climatic identity of a site that is cold and damp, with gusty and chilly winds and abrupt masses of fog that come in from the sea. Elaborating on this duality of exposure and retreat, the team established design principles in dialogue with nature by drawing upon the potential for wind-sheered topographic formations, fences, vegetation, and building envelopes to augment the provision of shelter.

Ⓐ Condominium I residential complex

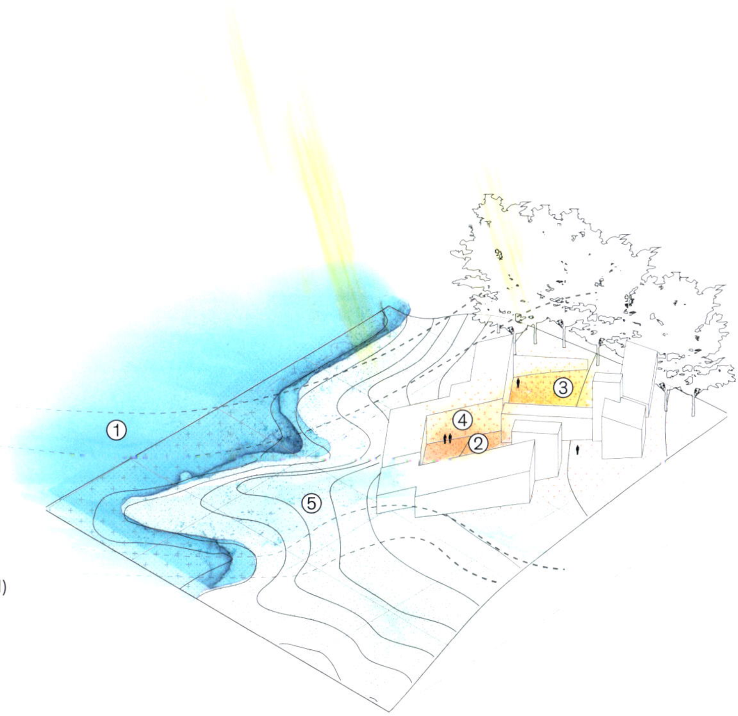

Thermodynamic performance:

①) Forced convection: prevailing winds
②) Wind shelter: courtyards perceived as warmer due to reduced wind deflected by walls
③) Thermal mass / radiant heating: ground and walls store heat during the day and release it at night
④) Low albedo: dark material stores heat from sun radiation (not reflective material)
⑤) Convective vapor transport: sea mist carried by wind

B Common meadow

Thermodynamic performance:

① Forced convection: prevailing winds
② Wind shelter: zones perceived as warmer due to reduced wind deflected by tree hedgerows
③ Solar radiation (exposed)
④ Solar radiation (reduced)
⑤ Convective vapor transport: sea mist carried by wind

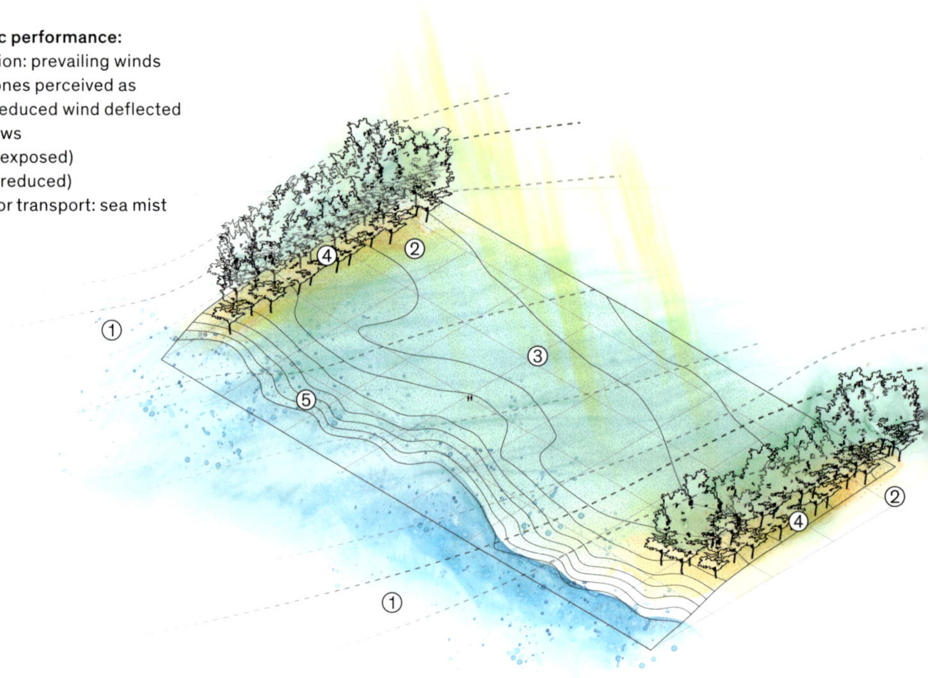

C Sheltered walkway and cypress hedgerows

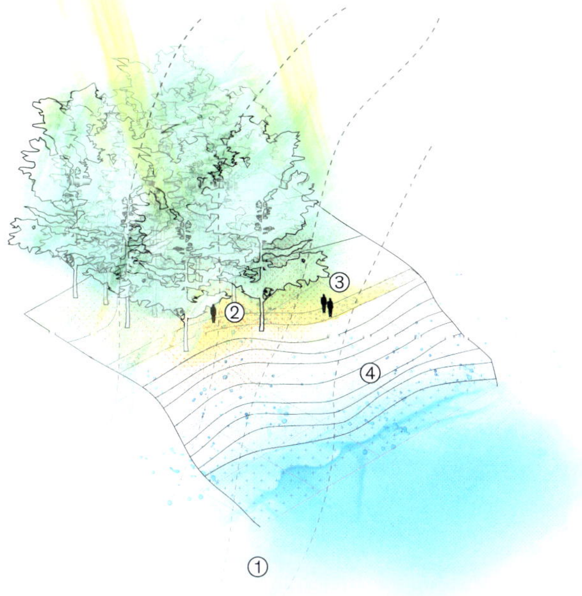

Thermodynamic performance:

1) Forced convection: prevailing winds
2) Wind shelter: pockets perceived as warmer due to reduced wind deflected by tree hedgerows
3) Solar radiation (exposed)
4) Convective vapor transport: sea mist carried by wind

D "Hedgerow houses" with sloping roofs

Thermodynamic performance:

1) Forced convection: prevailing winds
2) Wind shelter: pockets perceived as warmer due to reduced wind deflected by tree hedgerows
3) Solar radiation (exposed): terraces to the west
4) Convective vapor transport: sea mist carried by wind

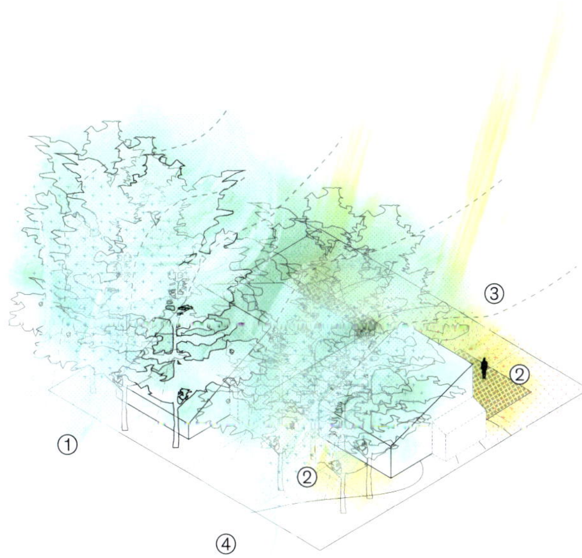

E Houses with sloping roofs adjacent to landform for wind deflection

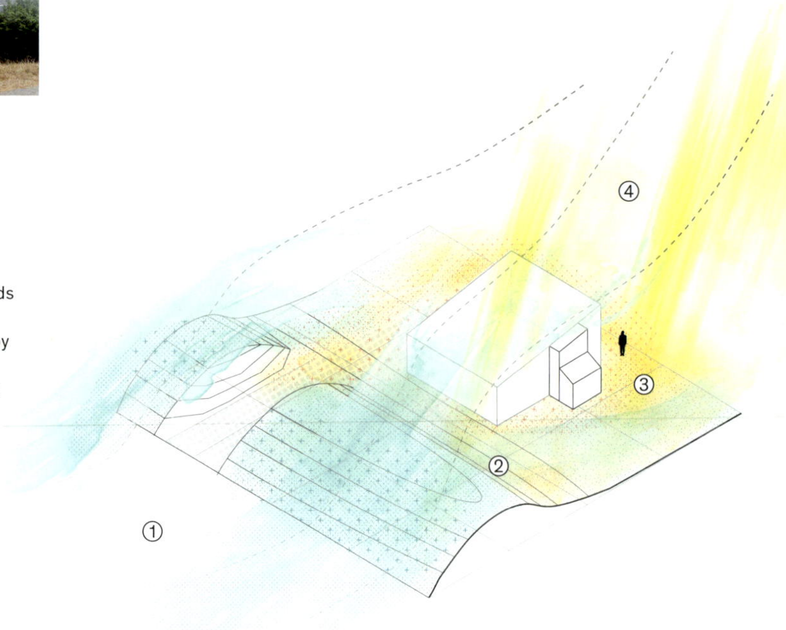

Thermodynamic performance:

① Forced convection: prevailing winds
② Wind shelter: pockets perceived as warmer due to wind deflected by landform
③ Solar radiation (exposed): western terraces sheltered against wind
④ Convective vapor transport: sea mist carried by wind

F Moonraker Recreation Center

→ p. 345

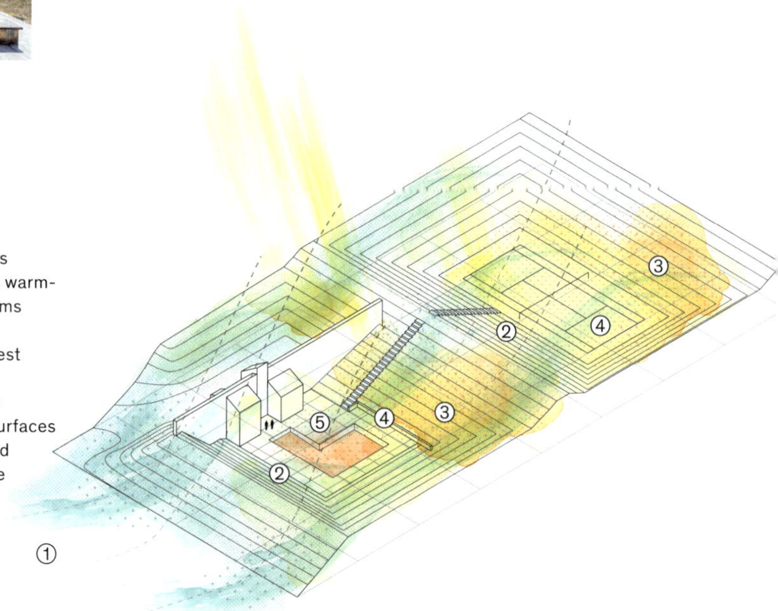

Thermodynamic performance:

① Forced convection: prevailing winds
② Wind shelter: pockets perceived as warmer due to wind deflected by landforms
③ Thermal mass / radiant heating: exposed slopes to the south and west collect heat from solar energy
④ Heat transfer by conduction (direct touch): warm ground and seating surfaces
⑤ “Heat trap”: exposed to sunlight and wind-protected reduces convective heat transfer to the air

G Wind-deflecting fences

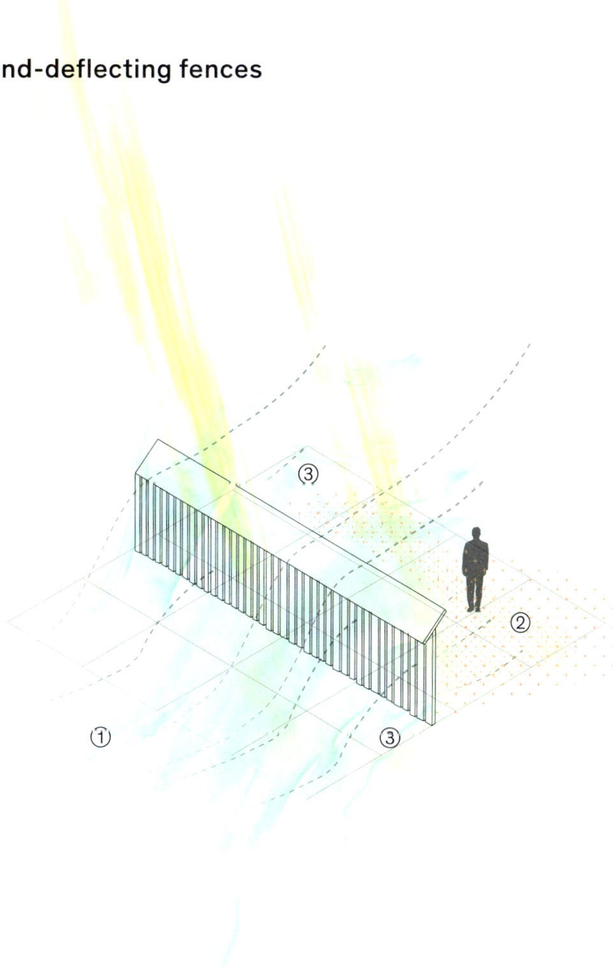

Thermodynamic performance:

1) Forced convection: prevailing winds
2) Wind shelter: pockets perceived as warmer due to wind deflected by lattice fence
3) Solar radiation (exposed)

Aerial view of Sea Ranch with cloud cover

Aerial view of Sea Ranch with approaching clouds

Coastal edge at Sea Ranch

View from Condominium I

n below common meadow

Sea Ranch Lodge

ominium I

Sea Ranch's Condominium I, inside Condo #9 (apartment from the architect Charles Moore)

es Moore apartment, Condominium I

Aerial view of Condominium I

Moonraker Recreation Center

Ohlson Recreation Center

bara Stauffacher, Moonraker Recreation Center supergraphics

Walk-in cabins on the hillside of Redwood forest

ess hedgerow

Common meadows

Aerial view

INFRARED IMAGES

The following set of images pairs a black and white photograph from each of the projects discussed in the book with a corresponding infrared image. In providing a thermal signature of a particular space at a particular time, an infrared image offers more immediate results than measurements made with traditional thermometers. It reveals temperature gradients and values through a spectrum of colors that range from bright yellow (hotter) to dark blue (colder). More precisely, it indexes surface temperatures by measuring infrared light waves, or radiation, emitted by the objects in the photographs, including the human occupants.

Whereas black and white photographs are capable of capturing the spatial configurations, scales, textures, and qualities of light and materiality of a particular project, infrared images reveal an essential aspect of a project's constructed domains—the invisible but sensed qualities that nurture its users. They provide visual evidence of the core principle that the thermal quality of an environment depends on the interactions among various variables associated with the materials in a constructed space. The thermophysical properties of a space's organic or inorganic materials—their density, thermal conductivity, thermal mass, emissivity, and albedo—interact with other variables, such as the scale of a space, its solar orientation, wind patterns, rates of porosity and transpiration, and its exposure to localized air flow and humidity. The energy exchanges among these variables and properties, known as thermodynamic interactions, are complex as they occur over time. Certain of these interactions are diagrammed in the microclimatic watercolor drawings included in each chapter. Building on this diagrammatic analysis, the infrared images enable one to imagine the thermal environment of a space that is capable of leading ultimately to physiological distress or delight.

These infrared images have been selected from a wider collection of thermal registrations taken during visits to the projects in a traveling schedule organized around particular seasonal cycles and meteorological conditions. These particular moments, and their corresponding thermal registrations, embody the spatial argument set forth in the propositions contained in the book. For example, in the infrared image of Rousham Garden, the cooling effects of the water rill, basin, and tree canopy along the pathway are made visible, augmented by the reflection on the surface of the water of both the overcast sky and the dense canopy. It also reveals the intense cooling deriving from the “little Building” tucked into the topography, which is visible on the left side of the image. Despite being light-filled and exposed to solar radiation, the clearing is a relatively cold space thanks to its multiple cooling surfaces.

At the Terrace of the Hundred Fountains of the Villa d’Este, in contrast, water and the thermal mass of the fountain ameliorate the thermal loads that result from the pathway’s direct exposure to sunlight and the radiation emitted from its blazing ground temperature. Here, the visitors seek thermal relief in the shaded areas next to the cold fountain, where their warm bodies gradually cool due to the release of energy to the colder surrounding surfaces. This process is enhanced by the breezes that evaporate the minuscule water droplets on the skin through transpiration part of the thermoregulation mechanism of homeostasis. This exchange of energy with the temperatures of the surrounding surfaces and air flow generates a sensation of cooling during Tivoli’s scorching summer days.

ROUSHAM GARDEN, 1738–1741

→ p. 38

Clearing in the Watery Walk with "Large Octogon Basson" and "little Building"
June 11, 2016 @ 2:40 pm

Geo-Location: Oxfordshire, England
Latitude: 51°55'2.32"N
Longitude: 1°18'24.43"W'

Atmospheric Temperature: 19°C (66°F)
Relative Humidity: 75%

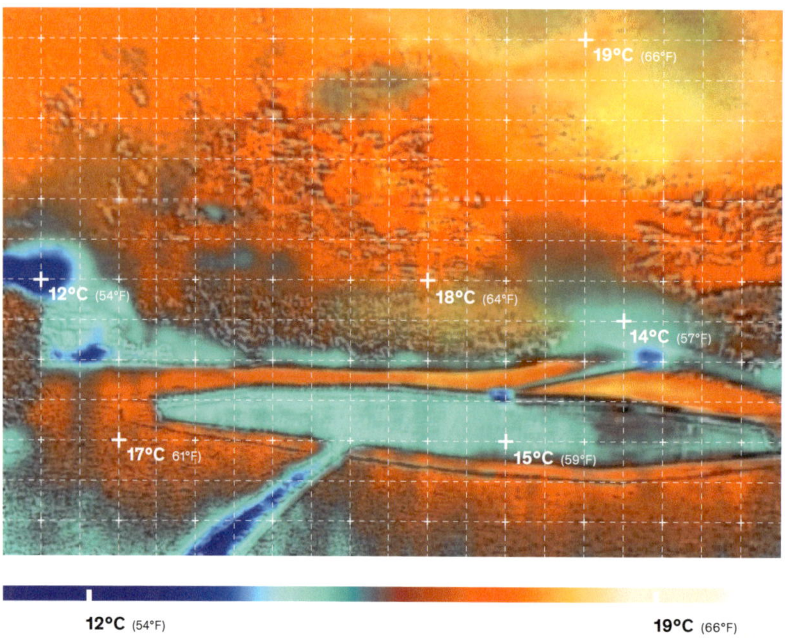

mosphere as Immersive Journey

ILLA D'ESTE, c. 1549

p. 72

errace of the Hundred Fountains
ly 28, 2015 @ 4:30 pm

eo-Location: Tivoli, Italy
atitude: 41°57'47.13"N
ongitude: 12°47'47.07"E

mospheric Temperature: 32°C (90°F)
elative Humidity: 47%

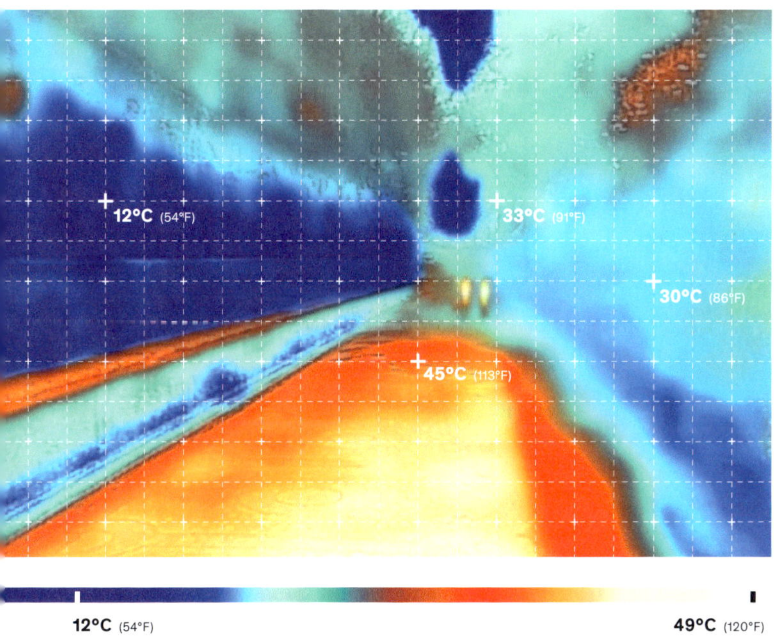

CHANDIGARH, 1951–1966

← p. 96

Capitol Complex, Assembly Building
March 14, 2017 @ 3:50 pm

Geo-Location: Chandigarh, India
Latitude: 30°45'36.80"N
Longitude: 76°48'10.15"E

Atmospheric Temperature: 22°C (71°F)
Relative Humidity: 43%

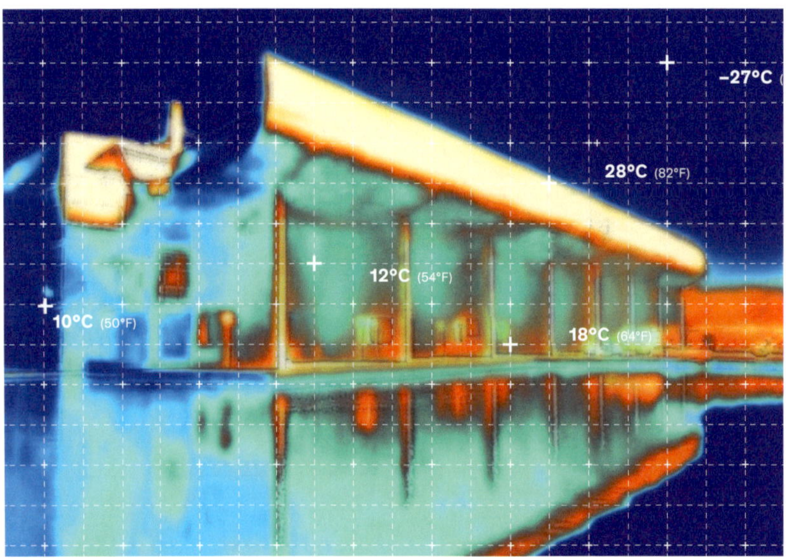

-27°C (-17°F) **28°C** (82°F)

tmosphere as Thermal Thresold

)RTEGA HOUSE AND GARDEN, 1943

· p. 152

terior courtyard
ebruary 16, 2016 @ 4:45pm

eo-Location: Mexico City, Mexico
atitude: 19°24'38.74"N
ongitude: 99°11'33.46"W

tmospheric Temperature: 23°C (73°F)
elative Humidity: 20%

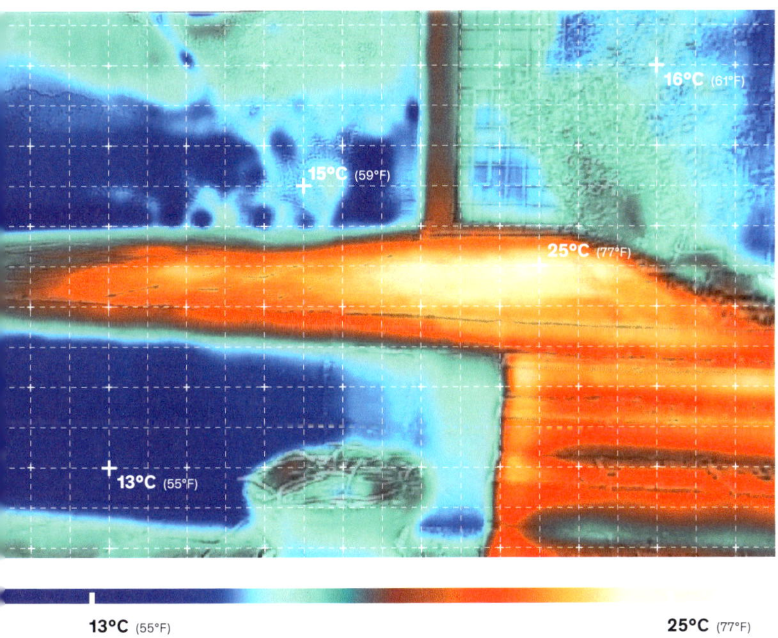

PALEY PARK, 1967

← p. 172

View from park gate to fountain wall
June 21st 2020 @ 11:50 am

Geo-Location
Latitude: 40°45'36.90"N
Longitude: 73°58'30.41"W

Atmospheric Temperature: 25°C (77°F)
Relative Humidity: 85%

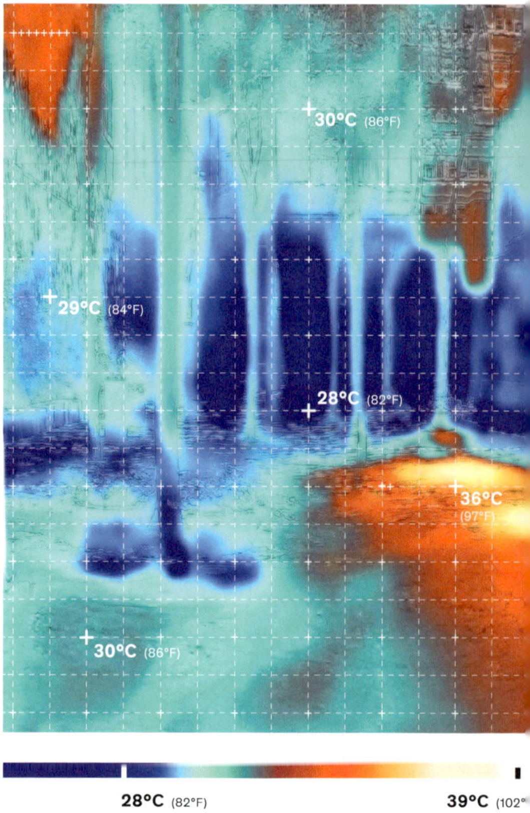

Note: These photos were taken in June 2020 during the Coronavirus (COVID-19) outbreak. Because the park was closed for public use, the fountain shut down, and the movable chairs removed, the full thermodynamic performance of the design is only partially evident.

3AMBOO GARDEN, 1986–1989

p. 190

athway through thick bamboo canopy (sunken level)
ine 24, 2017 @ 1:50 pm

eo-Location: Paris, France
atitude: 48°53'32.83"N
ongitude: 2°23'30.61"E

tmospheric Temperature: 25°C (77°F)
elative Humidity: 50%

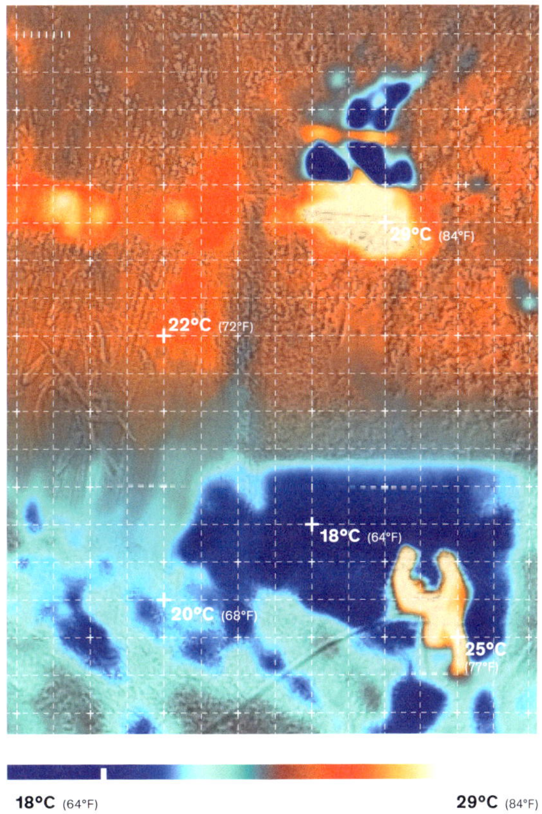

SESC POMPÉIA COMMUNITY CENTER, 1977–1986

← p. 214

Gathering center and reflecting pool ("River São Francisco")
January 2, 2015 @ 5:40 pm

Geo-Location: São Paulo, Brazil
Latitude: 23°31'32.07"S
Longitude: 46°41'0.47"W

Atmospheric Temperature: 33°C (91°F)
Relative Humidity: 50%

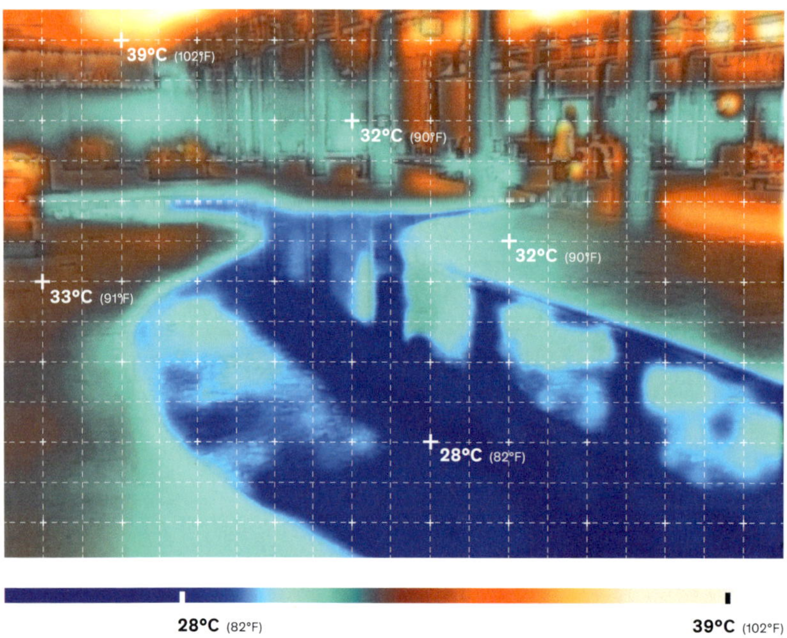

JNIVERSITY CITY OF CARACAS, 1944–1969

p. 254

overed walkway sequence, Engineering Department
nuary 9, 2015 @ 8:40 pm

eo-Location: Caracas, Venezuela
atitude: 10°29'26.09"N
ongitude: 66°53'21.88"W

mospheric Temperature: 27°C (81°F)
elative Humidity: 78%

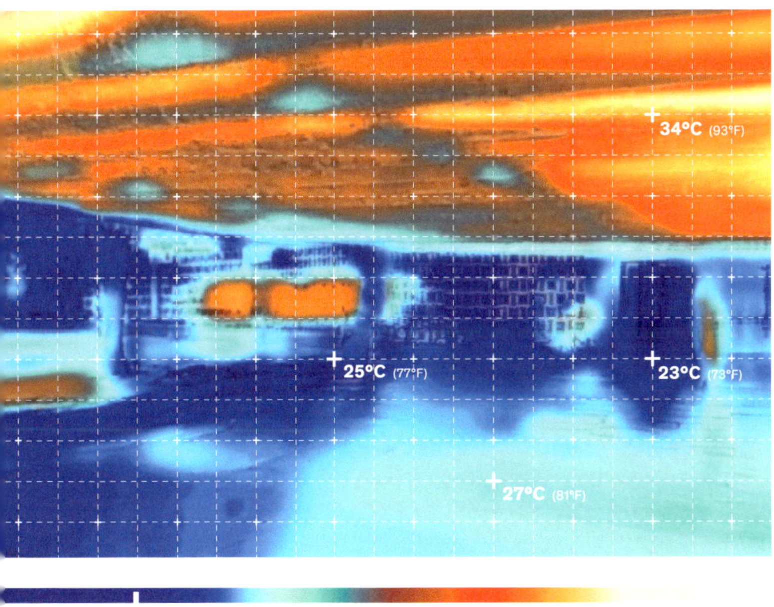

GEOMETRIC HOT SPRINGS, 2009

← p. 274

Hot Spring Pool "Primero"
January 5, 2015 @ 5:20 pm

Geo-Location: Pucón, Chile
Latitude: 39°30'3.02"S
Longitude: 71°52'25.40"W

Atmospheric Temperature: 15°C (59°F)
Relative Humidity: 80%

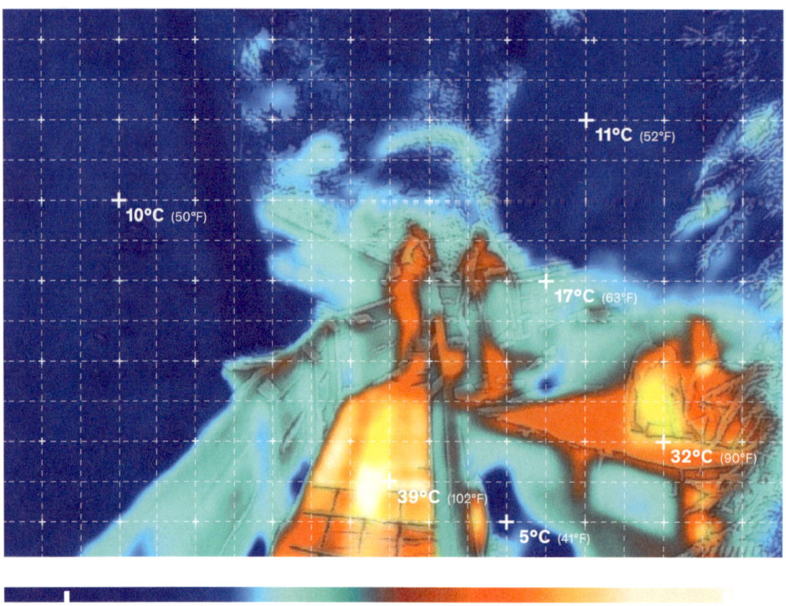

mosphere as Thermal Contrast

EA RANCH, c. 1963–1966

p. 304

oonraker Recreation Center
ay 21, 2015 @ 6:15 pm

eo-Location: Sonoma, California, USA
atitude: 38°41'17.57"N
ongitude: 123°25'38.37"W

mospheric Temperature: 13°C (55°F)
elative Humidity: 63%

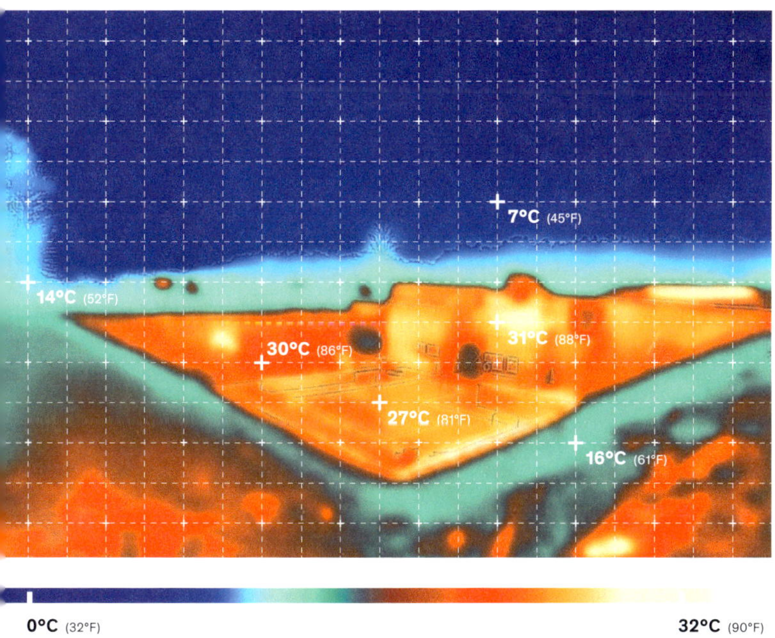

Afterword

EFFECT/AFFECT

James Corner

Given the urgent challenges of rapid urbanization, climate change and environmental resources, much has been said over the past twenty years or so about the "efficacy" of design, or the capacity for design projects to do work, to do things, to possess various performance metrics and influences that produce effects on the world. These effects are typically productive and aimed at improving the human condition, and they result from the specificity of the design work itself. The precise physical qualities of the work are what shape and engender myriad sets of effect.

Design efficacy can speak to a wide range of good things, including environmental improvement (for example thermal cooling and warming, bio-diversification, carbon sequestration, zero-energy draw, and stormwater management), new social opportunities (interactivity, connectivity, access, mobility, health, and well-being), unlocked economic gains (in the form of increased tax bases, development opportunities, jobs, and new investments), and broader cultural effects (behavioral, transactional, moral, and political). As such, design adds value; it comprises more than aesthetic identity and novel form and points instead to constructed actions that effect change. Think of the iPhone, for example: a beautifully designed invention that has completely transformed how people live and interact around the entire world. The design focus is upon how it works, how it performs its work, and how it effectively and efficiently produces multiple sets of opportunity and change. Its formal, physical, and material attributes are all in the service of making it work better.

Much of this extremely intelligent, thoughtful, and original book is devoted to the efficacy of designed places: buildings, landscapes, public spaces, and physical environments. The diagrams throughout speak to how spatial configuration and material specificity can create a host of primarily atmospheric effects, such as cooling, warming, dampening, drying, sheltering, exposing, scenting, darkening, lightening, storing, releasing, dissipating, venting, and other climatic results. Siting, orientation, and configuration can leverage the existing environmental forces in a given location (optimizing prevailing winds, solar angles, water flows, and seasonal variations) to produce any number of productive effects. Similarly, the selection of materials and details can help to modulate temperature, radiation, light, shade, water, and other factors. Halprin's Sea Ranch and Le Corbusier's Chandigarh are excellent examples of this kind of place-sensitive architecture that is highly specific to site and locale and inventively designed to optimize the physical environment as a creative and functioning organism: living, breathing, working, exchanging energy, and propagating new sets of effects.

While this book contains a good deal of information, research and references for those interested in the efficacy of design, particularly with regard to humane and responsible environmental considerations, the real power and originality of Benedito's thesis lies in its concomitant focus upon *affect*—upon the physiological and emotional import of bodily experience. Here the focus is upon the designed environment as a space where any number of energy exchanges, facilitated through design, *effect* measurable environmental changes that in turn *affect* bodily response and emotion. Both the specific physical and atmospheric conditions literally radiate signals that the experiencing body absorbs and responds to physically. The signals come in the form of physical and haptic presences—tangible phenomena that simultaneously awaken, arouse, and inform the sensory body. By extension, bodily experience and emotional response stir the imagination, creating lingering memories, impressions, associations, conjectures, and new possibilities. Body, mind, and environment become one: bound together, entangled and osmotic.

Much has been written and developed with regard to the affective reception of physical space and material settings. As described well in this book, there has been a general affinity in architecture to think in terms of objects—their solidity, materiality, and physical form—and the experience generated therein. And yet this book points to other phenomena of experience—the immersive, all-enveloping "aerosphere" of air, atmosphere, weather, and light. This is the non-visible world of humidity, temperature, aroma, breeze, and ephemerality—conditions that cause the body to shiver or sweat, to turn toward or turn away, to pause or linger, to feel at ease or uncomfortable.

Social anthropologist Tim Ingold explains this co-relational phenomenon in terms of a human as an organism that "feels" its way through the world that "is itself in motion." He writes:

> There could be no terrestrial life were it not for the processes of respiration, by which living organisms bind air with rainwater and nutrients drawn from the soil, in the presence of sunlight, in forging their own growth and movement. Crucially, these processes continually disrupt any interface between earth and sky. Thus to inhabit the open is not to be stranded on the outer surface of the earth but to be caught up in the substantial flows and aerial fluxes of what I call the *weather-world*.[1]

In this regard, Benedito's rich description of the experience of Rousham is fascinating in its dissection of movement and interaction through "a variety of meteorological intensities" or designed settings with specific atmospheres that increase the physiological and emotional awareness of sensation. This, in turn, invigorates the imagination and expands the scope of interpretation. Benedito beautifully describes this kind of experience as "touching the soul of a place," a fully haptic sense of place with subsequent representations in poetry, painting, music, and other media. Her focus is less on scenes and objects and more upon the episodic, ambulatory journey of immersive experiences through alternating atmospheres—from light into shade, from radiant warmth to damp cold, from sun to rain, from immense scale to microscopic detail, from the aroma of molds to scent of roses, and any other number of thresholds and contrasts that produce deep, lingering emotional experiences.

Benedito's rich description of Rousham, Paley Park, and other places depicted in this book, remind us that while the tendency of design is to improve the physical efficacy of a work—its metrics, systems, environmental performance, and other effects—the more imaginative dimensions of world-making, of aesthetic reception, experience, and desire can appear secondary. In all the seriousness of creating complex environments for living, it is all too easy to neglect the lighter, more profound, but also more difficult aspects of beauty, pleasure, and delight. Artful, poetic, and well-crafted design is fundamental not only to the efficacy of the work but also to its capacity to affect human physiology, feeling, and emotion—to provide surprise and delight, novelty and enchantment. As with the strolls and alternating intensities at Rousham, artful design imaginatively curates experiences, encounters, interactions, and extraordinary qualities specific to place and time, providing great pleasure and connection. This feeling of one's way around a world that is itself alive and in flux is Benedito's affective weather world—both designed and natural at the same time.

"Affect" in normal usage is a verb, an action: the weather affects people. But it can also be used as a noun, as in a feeling or emotion. It is commonly used in psychiatry to describe an experience that is simultaneously perception, performance, and thought. Benedito alternates between both verb and noun, as the key focus is always upon affective influence and reception. It reminds me very much of the work of artist Olafur Eliasson, who has created an impressive and varied body of work that seeks to both affect people (or influence them through novel experience and temporal engagement) and also to perhaps leave them with a memorable affect (or a different and new feeling that is perceptible, preformed, and thought). Among his many themes and tropes, Eliasson has a specific series of projects inspired and informed by weather and climate, including works with ice, heat, rain, wind, light, and reflection. Here, atmosphere is the focus of attention, the main effect. Here too, I can't help but think of Diller + Scofidio's wonderful Blur building, a complete de-materialization into a cloud of mist, the production of architecture as pure ephemeral atmosphere

I mention both of these in closing, because Benedito's notion of atmospheric affect is less self-conscious, less obvious, less focal; it is less about atmosphere as foreground as it is about atmosphere as an invisible medium, palpably haptic, and alive, but inevitably *background.* Indeed, she notes several times just how subtle and sometimes unnoticed the affect of a particular environment might be. Its sensual properties might be relatively inconspicuous and might not take shape in the mind until long after, as a kind of memory impression, perhaps profoundly so.

In this vein, one of the things that distinguishes the experience of buildings, landscapes, and places from that of art objects, is that they are typically apprehended by people in general states of distraction. Unlike when contemplating a painting or a sculpture, people in architectural and landscape settings are not really paying deep attention to details and how they feel; they are instead busy doing things, even if just strolling, chatting, or sitting, reading. The sensual experience of atmosphere and place may well be impressed in body and mind through that duration, but its actual recall and deeper affect is often felt later, in retrospect.

This subtle but deep phenomenon of recollection is captured beautifully in this phrase from a poem by the Irish poet Seamus Heaney, in which he writes:

Strange how things in the offing, once they're sensed,
Convert to things foreknown;
And how what's come upon is manifest
Only in light of what has been gone through.
Seventh Heaven may be
The whole truth of a sixth sense come to pass.

At any rate, when light breaks over me
The way it did on the road beyond Coleraine
Where wind got saltier, the sky more hurried
And silver lamé shivered on the Bann
Out in mid-channel between the painted poles,
That day I'll be in step with what escaped me.[2]

Similarly, it may well be that the reader's experience of this book takes time, with its nuances and atmospheres always "in the offing." There is so much beauty and intelligence in these pages that it takes time to digest and absorb. Perhaps, after reading this book, and when next visiting a building, garden, or landscape, the reader might then be a little more self-aware of the effects and affects the work offers, especially as shaped and informed by the ephemerality of air and atmosphere. As Benedito reminds us, the void is never empty; the void is packed full, breathing and stirring, exchanging energy and signaling a uniquely distinctive aura and ambience that one may sense but never actually see.

1 Tim Ingold, "Earth and Sky," in *Being Alive—Essays on Movement, Knowledge and Description* (London: Routledge, 2011), 96.

2 Seamus Heaney, "Squarings," xlviii, in *Seeing Things* (New York: Farrar Straus Giroux, 1991), 102.

Acknowledgments

The production of any publication entails numerous interactions with inspiring individuals and places. Like a journey, this book expresses the ambition to tell a larger story about the formation of the spaces that we live in. I owe a heartfelt thanks to many individuals who have encouraged, taught, and helped me in discovering and constructing these spaces. My appreciation also extends to the many institutions that provided me with valuable assistance in taking the path to research, test, and develop the main concept of this book—to make the design of space, in its capacity to sustain humankind's emotional and physical well-being, an act of infusing it with qualitative, often invisible, attributes related to microclimatic performances. I owe a great debt to the Harvard Graduate School of Design (GSD), and especially to Mohsen Mostafavi, Anita Berrizbeitia, and Charles Waldheim for supporting my teaching and research. The generous support of the Graham Foundation for Advanced Studies in the Fine Arts helped in financing this publication. A fellowship at the MacDowell Colony in 2014 allowed me to revise and refine the manuscript structure.

Throughout my education and the development of my sensibility as a designer, I have been blessed by the guidance of extraordinary mentors. Among these, I would like to foreground the foundational teachings of the architects Fernando Távora, Raúl Hestnes Ferreira, and Gonçalo Byrne. At the scale of the city and the public realm, I am indebted to James Corner for sharing his brilliant spirit and knowledge during my years at James Corner Field Operations and to Marilyn Jordan Taylor for her continuing inspiration.

There are several students at the Harvard GSD to whom I am grateful for their contributions to the research for this book, in particular Michael Keller, Ann Salerno, and Carson Fisk-Vittori. Special thanks to Gabriela S. Rodrígues-Berríos for her assistance in developing the watercolor drawings and to Larissa Belcic for her contribution to the overall site drawings.

For the many remarks on the topics addressed in this book, I am indebted to my Harvard colleagues K. Michael Hays, Kiel Moe, Salmon Craig, Jane Hutton, and Jill Desimini. I am particularly fortunate to have collaborated with and learned from Nadir Abdessemed, engineer at TRANSSOLAR, who helped me unpack the thermodynamic phenomena in each project.

I am grateful to Anita Berrizbeitia, Ed Eigen, Sonja Dümpelmann, Michael Jakob, and Antoine Picon for their peer review and insightful feedback in response to early drafts of these essays, and to John Dixon Hunt for sharing his extensive knowledge about William Kent's garden at Rousham and its literary analogues. I must single out Caroline Constant for her insightful remarks and ready availability for reading and responding to the work at every stage.

Julia Shivers's guidance and enthusiasm with editing were paramount to keep me "buoyant" toward the completion of the manuscript. I want to acknowledge those involved in the book production at Lars Müller publishers, in particular Lars for his commitment in making this a beautiful book, to Maya Ruegg for her continuous patience with the delays in manuscript submissions, and to Esther Butterworth for her assistance in key aspects of its production.

One of the joys of developing this book was the travel involved to experience direct contact with each featured project. In conducting on-site research, I had the pleasure of experiencing the culture and climate of each locale in India, the USA, France, Italy, Brazil, Venezuela, Chile, Mexico, and England. More than a tourist, I became a traveler who spoke with the people who used the designed spaces and observed their experiences in sensing these atmospheres: fundamental premises for the formation of nurturing and memorable built environments. During my visits to the various projects, many individuals welcomed me, offering inspiring conversations and guidance. In Caracas, I am grateful for the discussions with Professor Silvia Hernández de Lasala, Professor Aguedita Coss Lanz, and Professor Franco Micucci from the University City of Caracas, and I thank architects Elisa Silva and Ines Casanovas for their helpful assistance during this trip. In Mexico City, architect Luis de Villafranca guided me on a tour through the Gardens of El Pedregal. At Sea Ranch, Lisa Dundee, architect and Executive Director of the Sea Ranch's Department of Design, Compliance, and Environmental Management, offered a brief history of the project development. In Chandigarh, Professor Rajnish Wattas and architects Sarbjit Singh Bahga and Hardial Singh Johl kindly offered their perspective on the landscape of the city. I also acknowledge the irreplaceable support of the Fondation Le Corbusier in Paris. Finally, I am indebted to Iwan Baan, who very generously agreed to join me on this long journey to seek spaces where life, simply, occurs.

Finally, I express my deepest gratitude to my family, particularly to my son Bartholomeu Häusler and my mother Aida Benedito. Their patience, kindness, and companionship throughout the development of this book gave me all the invaluable energy, love, and inspiration that one needs for challenging enterprises. This book is for them.

WORLD MAP OF CLIMATIC ZONES AND TYPES

Indicating project locations, according to the Köppen–Geiger Climate Classification[1]

1 Marcus Kottek et al., "World Map of the Köppen-Geiger Climate Classification Updated," *Meteorologische Zeitschrift* 15, no. 3 (2006): 259–63, here 261.

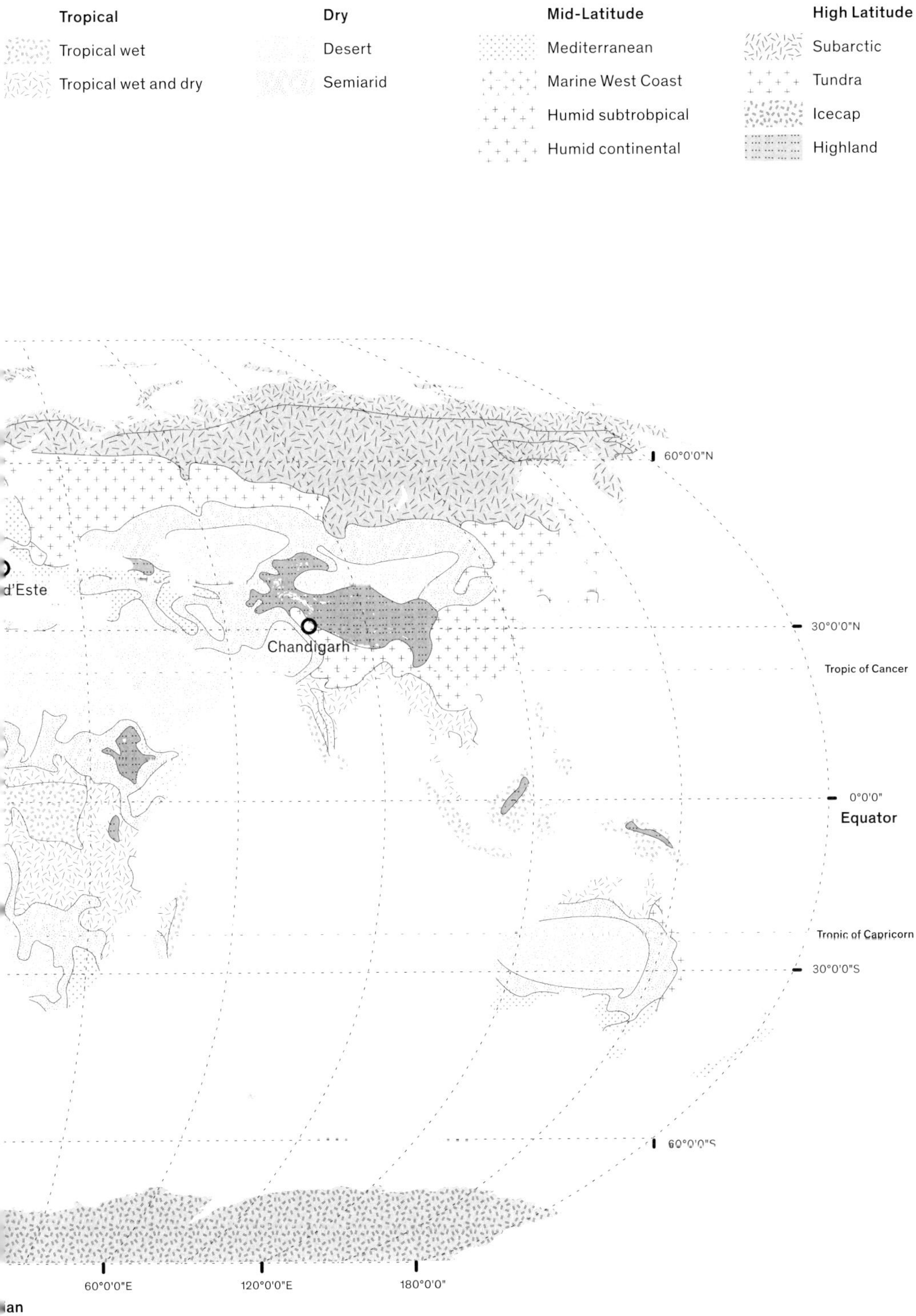
Tropical
Tropical wet
Tropical wet and dry
Dry
Desert
Semiarid
Mid-Latitude
Mediterranean
Marine West Coast
Humid subtrobpical
Humid continental
High Latitude
Subarctic
Tundra
Icecap
Highland
60°0'0"N
d'Este
Chandigarh
30°0'0"N
Tropic of Cancer
0°0'0"
Equator
Tropic of Capricorn
30°0'0"S
60°0'0"S
60°0'0"E
120°0'0"E
180°0'0"
an

Thermodynamic Glossary

Albedo: a measure of how much of the sun's radiation hitting a surface is reflected back to the atmosphere or other surfaces without being absorbed. In sunlight, darker surfaces absorb more solar radiation and reflect less (low albedo). Conversely, brighter surfaces absorb less radiation and reflect more (high albedo). Examples of low albedo materials are asphalt or gray concrete. Examples of high albedo materials are snow or sand.

"Cold trap": a sunken and shaded area in the topography that uses the geothermal properties of the earth (thermal mass) for cooling. When a cold surface absorbs energy from a warmer surface, such as a human skin, it creates the sensation of "cooling." This is also known as radiant cooling. In cold traps, the cold air (denser than warm air) sinks and is typically trapped at the bottom of this zone.

"Heat trap": the result of heat collected and released off surfaces of a sunken area that are exposed to solar radiation. When a heated surface radiates energy toward a colder surface, such as human skin, it creates the sensation of "warming." This is also known as radiant heating. A further increase in the sensation of heat results from reduction in the wind, when the evapotranspiration rates on the skin are also reduced.

"Convective" furniture: seating with a perforated surface material such as cloth, wicker, or rope. The perforation minimizes surface contact with the bare skin and maximizes the skin's evapotranspiration rates in contact with air circulation, thus increasing the sensation of cooling.

Convective vapor transfer: the rising of air vapor that results from the evaporation of water (phase change from liquid to gaseous). At a given temperature, humid air contains more energy than drier air; it is less dense (and lighter) and therefore rises.

Emissivity: the capability of a material to radiate infrared heat. Low emissivity (Low-E) materials do not have that capability and will emit less heat than materials with a "normal" emissivity. Instead these materials reflect radiation from adjacent surfaces.

Effusivity: the capacity of a material to exchange thermal energy with its surroundings in its ability to absorb heat. Thermal effusivity explains, for example, why metals (high effusivity) "feel" colder to the touch than other bodies at the same temperature, since the heat transfer from the skin to the metal is very fast. It also explains why a fabric such as wool (low effusivity) seems warm, since the heat transfer from/to the skin is very slow.

Evaporative cooling: reduction of the perceived air temperature resulting from the evaporation of a liquid into vapor. The phase-changing process in which energy is absorbed from the surrounding air creates a sensation of cooling, referred to as adiabatic evaporation. An example is the water spray from a fountain. On the other hand, isothermal evaporation is a phase-changing process as result of energy input, such as solar radiation. In that change of state, the air temperature remains constant as the evaporation increases, thus compensating for the energy input and providing a relative sense of cooling.

Forced convection: air movement that is observed at a local scale, irrespective of its cause at a larger scale. An example is the prevailing winds and resulting cross ventilation observed in a particular area.

Free convection: air movement resulting from naturally occurring differences in density on a certain observed local scale. The density differences are typically the consequence of thermal effects of atmospheres at different temperatures and/or levels of humidity. Examples include the chimney effect, localized air buoyancy, and katabatic/anabatic flows.

Free convection / anabatic flow or anabatic wind: a low density convective upward air movement occurring from air-volumes adjacent to surfaces heated by solar radiation. It occurs usually during the day, as the earth, with its lower thermal inertia, warms faster than bodies of water, with their higher thermal inertia. The air above heated surfaces rises and is replaced by cold air (at lower elevations this can result from a colder surface—for instance, a body of water). Fishermen returning from the sea and athletes on gliders use these winds.

Free convection / katabatic flow or katabatic wind: a high-density convective downward air movement occurring from air-volumes adjacent to surfaces cooled by the night sky. As the surface of the earth cools down faster than its bodies of water, the denser cold air flows downward along the cooler earth surfaces. These winds are used to ventilate cities and by fisherman departing from their harbors for the sea during the early morning hours.

Free convection / chimney effect: the effect resulting from air buoyancy inside an enclosed volume due to different air temperatures, the associated density differences, and the resulting pressure differences. As warm air rises and is released from an enclosed volume, negative pressure on the lower levels encourages uprising movement of the heavier cold air near the ground.

Free convection / air buoyancy: natural air movement driven by the differences in air pressure and density (relative to heat and/or temperature). Less dense (hot) air will rise and denser (colder) air will sink. The tendency to achieve equilibrium promotes a continual airflow between these two behaviors.

Heat transfer by conduction: the exchange of energy between objects or surfaces by direct contact (touch). When a hotter surface and/or volume transfers energy to a colder surface, such as the human skin, there is a corresponding sensation of heating.

Radiant cooling: the thermal effect generated when cold surfaces (shaded, colder geothermal mass, etc.) absorb heat by radiation from warmer surfaces, including the human skin. This absorption creates the sensation of cooling without direct physical contact. The capacity of a material surface to take part in this radiative interaction is related to its emissivity.

Radiant heating: the thermal effect generated when hot surfaces and/or volumes (such as a fireplace or warm wall) release heat by radiation to colder surfaces, including the human skin. This release creates the sensation of warmth without direct physical contact. The capacity of a surface to take part in this radiative interaction is related to its emissivity.

Reflective walls: walls clad with reflective material able to bounce light back to an interior or exterior space. An example would be glazed tiles.

Thermal mass: the capacity of a material to store thermal energy, commonly known as the material's heat capacity. Examples of materials with high thermal mass are high-density materials such as water, concrete, brick, rammed earth, stone, and metal. Thermal mass can be used concurrently with thermal inertia.

Thermal inertia: the tendency of a material to absorb or release energy relative to its surroundings during a certain period of time. Materials with high thermal inertia, such as bodies of water or rocks, take a longer time to absorb or release energy than materials with low thermal inertia, such as soil or sand.

Contributors

Silvia Benedito is a registered architect and urban designer. Originally from Portugal, where she received her education in architecture, Benedito focuses her design and research efforts on the quality of the constructed environment in its capacity to foster communal well-being and ecological resilience. In her work, Benedito advocates for a vigorous disciplinary intersection of architecture and landscape architecture at the different scales of the territory—from the residential compound to the neighborhood, from the city to the countryside. In such a disciplinary intersection, Benedito's work foregrounds the micro- and macro-climates as design matter through cultural, emotional, and technical domains. Benedito is associate professor of landscape architecture at the Graduate School of Design (GSD), Harvard University, and co-founder of the design practice OFICINAA, based in Germany. At the GSD, she teaches research seminars and design studios exploring the built environment and spatial qualities able to ameliorate climatic loads. Benedito has also been a guest professor in the Fakultät für Architektur at the Technische Universität München and in the Institute of Architecture and Landscape at the Technische Universität Graz. Her design practice has received numerous awards and recognitions, including her submission for the Young Architects Program at the Museum of Modern Art in New York City. She received a Master of Architecture in Urban Design at the GSD, with a concentration in landscape architecture, and she was a senior associate at James Corner Field Operations in New York City. Benedito is the recipient of various prizes and fellowships from recognized institutions. Among those are the Graham Foundation for Advanced Studies in the Fine Arts, the MacDowell Colony for the Arts, the Luso-American Development Foundation, the Foundation for Science and Technology, the Calouste Gulbenkian Foundation, and the Fernando Távora Prize from the Portuguese League of Architects. She was co-editor, with Javier García-Germán, of the award-winning book *Thermodynamic Interactions: An Exploration into Physiological, Material, and Territorial Atmospheres* (ACTAR, 2017).

Dutch photographer **Iwan Baan** is known primarily for images that narrate the human interactions that occur within architecture. Born in 1975, Baan grew up outside Amsterdam, studied at the Royal Academy of Art in The Hague, and worked in publishing and documentary photography in New York City and Europe. After his studies in photography Baan followed his interest in documentary photography before narrowing his focus to record the various ways in which individuals, communities, and societies create and interact with their built environments. With his combined passion for documentary photography and space, Baan's photographs reveal our innate ability to appropriate available objects and materials in order to find a place that we can call our own. In his work on informal communities, for example, vernacular architecture and placemaking serve as examples of human ingenuity. These include a series of images of the Torre David in Caracas, which won Baan the Golden Lion for Best Installation at the Venice Architecture Biennale of 2012. With no formal training in architecture, his perspective mirrors the questions and perspectives of the everyday individuals who give meaning and context to the architecture and spaces that surround us, and this artistic approach has made architecture more broadly accessible. As the inaugural recipient of the Julius Shulman award for photography, Baan is called upon by architects such as Rem Koolhaas, Herzog & de Meuron, Zaha Hadid, Diller Scofidio & Renfro, Toyo Ito, SANAA, and Morphosis to give their work a sense of place and environmental narrative. Alongside his architecture commissions, Baan has collaborated on several successful book projects, such as *Brasilia & Chandigarh—Living with Modernity* (2010), *Insular Insight: Where Art and Architecture Conspire with Nature* (2011), and *Torre David: Informal Vertical Communities* (2013). Baan's work also appears in the pages of architecture, design, and lifestyle publications such as *The Wall Street Journal, The New York Times, Architectural Record, Domus, Abitare,* and *Architectural Digest.* In addition to receiving the American Institute of Architects' Stephen A. Kliment Oculus Award, Iwan Baan was named one of the one hundred most influential people in the contemporary architecture world by *Il Magazine dell'Architettura* on the occasion of its one hundredth issue in December 2011.

Christophe Girot is Professor of Landscape Architecture and Dean of the Department of Architecture at the ETH in Zurich. He received a dual Master in Architecture and Landscape Architecture degree from UC Berkeley in 1986 and 1988. From 1989 to 1999 Girot was Chair of Design at the Versailles School of Landscape Architecture. His teaching and research interests span new topological methods in landscape design, landscape perception, and analysis through new media, and contemporary theory and history of landscape architecture. At the ETH he founded the Institute of Landscape Architecture with professor Günther Vogt in 2005, co-founded the Landscape Visualization and Modeling Laboratory with Professor Adrienne Grêt-Regamey in 2010, and founded the Institute of Landscape and Urban Studies in 2019. Together with Professor Günther Vogt and Teresa Gali Izard, he is currently launching a Master of Science in Landscape Architecture program at the ETH. Girot's professional practice focuses on large-scale landscape projects, using advanced 3D topological techniques that contribute to the design of sustainable landscape environments, such as the 3.5 million cubic meter Alptransit Deposit in Sigirino, Ticino, or the Third Rhône River Correction in the Canton of Valais. Since 2010 he has been co-principal investigator at the ETH Future Cities Laboratory in Singapore and Zurich, where he worked on the Ciliwung River Park in Jakarta and urban heat island amelioration plantations in Singapore. He is also co-PI on the ETH NCCR Digital Fabrication platform, where he is developing research in landscape robotics. In his recent books, *The Course of Landscape Architecture* and *Thinking the Contemporary Landscape* (both 2016), Girot seeks to establish both past and current trends in landscape history and theory.

James Corner, RLA, FASLA, is founder and CEO of James Corner Field Operations. He has devoted the past thirty years to advancing the field of landscape architecture and urbanism through his leadership on complex urban projects around the word as well as through teaching, public speaking, and writing. Corner received a BA (First Hons) from Manchester Metropolitan University, an MLA/UDes from the University of Pennsylvania School of Design, an Honorary Doctorate in Architecture and Engineering (Dr.-Ing.e.h.) from the Technical University of Munich, and a Doctor of Design (honoris causa) from Manchester Metropolitan University. He is Emeritus Professor of Landscape Architecture and Urbanism at the University of Pennsylvania School of Design, where he served on the faculty from 1989 and as Professor and Chairman (2000–2013). He sits on the Board of the Urban Design Forum and the Government Advisory Board of Shenzhen. Corner's public realm design projects include New York's highly acclaimed High Line, London's South Park at Queen Elizabeth Olympic Park, Santa Monica's Tongva Park, Chicago's Navy Pier, Cleveland's Public Square, Seattle's Central Waterfront; San Francisco's Presidio Tunneltop, Hong Kong's Salisbury Gardens and Avenue of the Stars, Doha's new Arts and Cultural District, and Shenzhen's Masterplan for the City of Qianhai. His work has been recognized with the Cooper Hewitt National Design Award, the American Academy of Arts and Letters Award in Architecture, the Daimler-Chrysler Design Excellence Award, and the AA&D Black Pencil Award. It has been published broadly and exhibited at the New York Museum of Modern Art, the Cooper-Hewitt Design Museum, the National Building Museum, the Royal Academy of Art in London, and the Venice Biennale. Corner is author of *The High Line: Foreseen/Unforeseen* (2015), *The Landscape Imagination* (2014), *Recovering Landscape* (1999), and *Taking Measures across the American Landscape* (1996). He was named by *TIME* as one of "Ten Most Influential Designers" and by Fast Company as one of the "Top 50 Innovators." He sits on the Board of the Urban Design Forum and the Government Advisory Board of Shenzhen.

Atmosphere Anatomies
On Design, Weather, and Sensation

Author: Silvia Benedito
Photography: Iwan Baan
Foreword: Christophe Girot
Afterword: James Corner
Copyediting: Julia Shivers
Proofreading: Kristie Kachler
Design: Integral Lars Müller/Lars Müller and Esther Butterworth
Production: Martina Mullis
Lithography: prints professional, Berlin, Germany
Printing and binding: DZA Druckerei zu Altenburg, Germany
Paper: Profibulk 1.3, 135 gsm

Lars Müller Publishers is supported by the Swiss Federal Office of Culture with a structural contribution for the years 2016–2020.

Lars Müller Publishers
Zurich, Switzerland
www.lars-mueller-publishers.com

ISBN 978-3-03778-612-3

Distributed in North America by ARTBOOK | D.A.P.
www.artbook.com

Printed in Germany